LEAVE EVERYTHING

Memoirs Of A Faith
Journey Across America

JOSHUA CARVALHO

ENDORSEMENTS

"We are here in Berkeley praying for a new Jesus Movement for 40 days. Just read the first chapter of Joshua's book. I was moved to tears and totally engrossed in the story of a true evangelist. You know, The Great Evangelist is arising again. Joshua's whole life and story is a forerunner of a Jesus Movement that will fill stadiums. Read the book, be stirred, and go preach the gospel!"

-Lou Engle, Founder
The Call

"Joshua's journey in 'Leave Everything' is a genuine & passionate example of the simple Gospel that should be lived out in every believer's life. I believe God wants to raise his church to be passionate about the Good News of Jesus and live for the Eternal Purpose. This book is a valuable tool to equip every believer so they can do the work of ministry. Let the Holy Spirit inspire you!"

-Eddy Leo, Senior Pastor
Abbalove Ministries, Jakarta, Indonesia

"Joshua Carvalho is one of the new breed of evangelists that God is raising up in America. Josh is fully committed to intimacy with God through intercession and worship. This has produced in him a great faith in God and loving, boldness toward sinners. You will greatly benefit from the stories and insights found in this book."

-Hal Linhardt, Former Director
Forerunner Evangelism at IHOPKC
Director of Kansas City Evangelists Fellowship

"What does it mean to walk as Jesus walked? Or to love as Jesus loved? What does it mean to have radical faith? Josh Carvalho has seriously contemplated these questions and walked in obedience to the answers he received. All those who are bored with their Christian lives need to read this book! Its pages prove that even in our 21st Century modern world, simple acts of love and faith still change it. Captivating stories lead the reader to the threshold between the gospel and lost souls – the sacred ground where God's Kingdom invades human reality. You will be moved, challenged and inspired!"

-Dave Datema, Office of General Directors
Frontier Ventures (formerly the U.S. Center for World Mission)

"Joshua Carvalho is a New Breed Evangelist that God is using to bring His Love into an entire generation. His complete surrender to the Lord and his love for people leap out of the pages of this book. If you want to be stirred for the harvest - I highly recommend this book to you."

-Jonathan Ngai, Founder/Director
Radiance International (24/7 Hollywood House of Prayer)

"Adventure will not fill an empty soul. But the soul filled with God is on Adventure. To know the Only True God is the essence of Eternal Life. This intimacy comes through His Son Jesus, The Savior, The Anointed Prophet, Priest, & King (John 17:3). This account of God's relationship with one soul will encourage you to know Him and to share Him."

-Lloyd Peckham (Uncle Lloyd), Bible Translator
Wycliffe Bible Translators
Professor of Linguistics, Biola University

"Joshua Carvalho's 'Leave Everything' brought joy, challenge and questions to my heart. Joy to see a young man unflinchingly obey God's Word to him to pick up his cross, trust Him, and preach the gospel. Challenged as to what would happen if many more similarly took up their cross to follow Jesus. And questions about how today's church has unknowingly taken its cues about what is and isn't acceptable public behavior from our society instead of from those whose lives we read about in the book of Acts. As a pastor, I have been deeply impacted by the life of my father, Rev. Eddie Lo, who showed me what courage, vision, and leadership look like. His life verse was Acts 20:24: "But none of these things move me, neither count I my life dear unto myself, so that I might finish my course with joy, and the ministry, which I have received of the Lord Jesus, to testify the gospel of the grace of God." This verse rung in my ears over and over again as I read Joshua's book. May it inspire a whole flood of Americans to go and do likewise."

-John Lo, Senior Pastor
Epicentre Church

"Joshua Carvalho is a young man who answers the words of Jesus. He leads a generation who worships The Lord in Spirit and Truth. He doesn't wait for them to come to him instead he answers the command of Jesus to go into the highways and byways and find the lost and dying and lead them to the one who loves and forgives them. Reading his book will impact you to do the same. A wonderful young man who is selfless because Jesus lives in him."

-Judy Ball, Director
Ignite America
Breaker of Dawn Ministries

TABLE OF CONTENTS

FOREWARD

"I've been sent to raise up an army of itinerant preachers who will re-evangelize the western world."

I stopped to listen to the radical story of how this young Brazilian-American had left everything to follow Jesus, preaching the Gospel across the nation and as I listened, my heart began to burn within me. "Joshua, this story belongs to the Church. You need to get this testimony out! Every believer needs to hear this..." - This has become my only echoing demand of him in the years since I first met this dear friend of God.

As a man who has been doing street ministry for well over a decade, I have talked to hundreds and perhaps thousands of the general public. Out of all those who I've talked to on the streets, I estimate only 5-10% of them had a basic understanding of the Gospel of Jesus Christ.

2 Corinthians 5:18 says, "Now all these things are from God, who reconciled us to Himself through Christ and gave us the ministry of reconciliation"

This passage brings two important points; First, the point of evangelism is reconciliation - not condemnation. Second, God has given US the ministry of reconciliation. He hasn't given it to someone else in some other time. The souls of our generation are on our watch, right now... today.

"Whoever will call on the name of the Lord will be saved." How then will they call on Him in whom they have not believed? How will they believe in Him whom they have not heard? And how will they hear without a preacher? How will they preach unless they are sent? Just as it is written, "How beautiful are the feet of those who bring good news of good things!" - Romans 10:13-15

In a world desperately unaware of the message of the Gospel, how can the Church not go? It is a complacent Church that allows the citizens of its cities to remain in ignorance of the Gospel. Whether that complacency comes from unbelief or a lack of love, it is a question everyone must answer before God.

"Take care, brethren, that there not be in any one of you an evil, unbelieving heart that falls away from the living God. 13 But encourage one another day after day, as long as it is still called "Today," so that none of you will be hardened by the deceitfulness of sin. 14 For we have become partakers of Christ, if we hold fast the beginning of our assurance firm until the end, 15 while it is said, "Today if you hear His voice, Do not harden your hearts..."

Are you hearing what He is saying to you now? Everyone reading this book needs to search themselves to see if their hearts are willing to hear the call of God. If you are, I believe you will find Him in these pages and the ministry of reconciliation will be activated in your life.

"And now Lord, ...grant that Your bond-servants may speak Your word with all confidence, 30 while You extend Your hand to heal, and signs and wonders take place through the name of Your holy servant Jesus." 31 When they had prayed, the place where they had gathered together was shaken, and they were all filled with the Holy Spirit and began to speak the word of God with boldness... 33 And with great power the apostles were giving testimony to the resurrection of the Lord Jesus, and abundant grace was upon them all." - Acts 4:29-33

It is rare to find someone today who's life resembles those in the book of Acts. In these pages Joshua and his companions lay a framework for a resurgence in the apostolic lifestyle we read about in the New

Testament. Joshua carries a fire for a fresh missions movement and that fire sparks from each paragraph of this book. The western world needs to be evangelized again and the western Church needs to be awakened from her complacency.

    If evangelism or church planting is part of the mission of your church, this book will prove an ageless support. The straightforward approach to street ministry that Joshua and his companions portray is a model that inspires and ignites passion for the lost while demystifying the fear of approaching people on the streets. If you are anything like me, you will be encouraged by how much God uses these young men and women who decided to pray and go, believing the kingdom of God is truly at hand.

-Jacob Reeve, Founder
Santa Barbara House of Prayer
Isla Vista Church
Retired Pro Bodyboarder

PREFACE

It all began after watching some documentaries about the move of God currently taking place in China: *Beyond the Great Wall* and *The Cross: Jesus in China*. I was blown away by what God was doing in the underground Church in China. The radical love that these people demonstrated for God and their willingness to lose everything, including their dignity and their very lives, left me ashamed of my superficial Christianity. As time went by, I began reading several articles and stories about Chinese martyrs, the torture they go through while in prison, and their fearless itinerant preachers. Some missionaries told me of powerful experiences they had while ministering in China as well as unbelievable stories they had heard from other Chinese Christians they had befriended. Then a friend let me borrow a book that changed my life and completely revolutionized my definition of what it meant to follow Jesus: *The Heavenly Man* by Brother Yun.

As I learned more about the Church in China throughout that year, God continually highlighted to me one of the radical differences between the Chinese Church and the Western Church. The Chinese Church has a foundation of tens of thousands of itinerant preachers who preach the Gospel all across the towns and cities of China, while in the West the most popular forms of evangelism are crusade and friendship evangelism. These itinerant preachers literally give up everything- land, homes, jobs, and families- to go preach the Gospel to all creation, living completely by faith. They have no salary, no home, and very few, if any, possessions. All they have is Jesus, compassion for lost souls, and sometimes a Bible.

After learning about these radical Christians I was ashamed of myself as a Christian and of the American Church as a whole. I began asking myself some serious questions. How could it be that while being raised as a pastor's son in several different denominations and movements, I have never seen nor heard of anyone who lives like this? How could it be that in a largely poor nation, with an impoverished church, where people are imprisoned, tortured, and killed under a Communist government merely for believing in Jesus, the Christians have the boldness to passionately preach the Gospel on the streets and live by faith? Yet in America, a land of freedom and excessive wealth, I have never seen anyone leave their comfortable nest of security to go and preach the Gospel throughout the cities of America living completely by faith.

In the midst of such profound conviction and revelation, I made a covenant with God as I prayed, "Lord, I don't know how and I don't know when, but one day I am going to raise up for You an army of itinerant preachers, here in America and in the Western World." I was fifteen years old. I thought that perhaps when I was thirty or forty years old God would call me to fulfill this mission, but He ended up calling me much sooner than I had planned.

In 2006, at 18 years of age, I completed community college and had everything set to transfer to a Christian university to study theology. However, my parents didn't feel peace about me studying theology right away. They felt that I needed to dedicate myself to practical ministry for six months to a year before studying theology. I was frustrated that my parents weren't letting me get through college as quick as I could, but I submitted to their authority and obeyed their counsel. I began a three-day water fast hoping to discover the next step God wanted me to take.

On the second day of the fast, I clearly heard the voice of the Holy Spirit saying, "Joshua, so you want to raise up an army of itinerant preachers? Well, how do you think you're going to do that? Do you think you could just get a degree in theology and everyone will just follow you? No. You must go first. You must set the example. Go and preach the Gospel throughout America for six months. Take no money with you. Only trust in Me."

Knowing that God had truly spoken to me, I took a deep breath and, full of excitement and wonder, made the decision to leave everything behind and go preach the Gospel throughout America. I called the university I was planning to attend and told them that I would be deferring my enrollment for a year. Many people thought I was being foolish and irresponsible, but I knew that I was simply losing my life in order to find it.

I faced many obstacles that almost stopped me from going on the mission trip, including a car accident that nearly took my life. But in the end, God was faithful to see me through.

In order to prepare myself for the mission trip I went on a forty-day water and juice fast where I stayed isolated in an empty apartment with virtually no human contact. I had a five-gallon water jug and several juice cartons and, once a week or so, my father would come by and restock me with more water and juice. I did not have any extraordinary supernatural encounters or outer-body experiences during those forty days even though I would have loved to encounter God in such a powerful way, but I did get closer to God than I've ever been in my whole life. From the moment I woke up to the time I went to sleep, my only agenda was to seek God. I spent countless hours in prayer, intercession, worship, and the Scriptures. I memorized several chapters of the Bible, wrote many songs, and read the book *From Jerusalem to Irian Jaya*, a book on the history of missions. It was during this fast that God laid out to me the vision of Global Gospel Movement. He showed me that it was not only for the United States, but also for the nations of the world.

Immediately after deciding to obey God and go on this journey, I made a rule with God. Since it was God who was calling me to go on this trip, I would never ask anyone for anything. I would never ask for food, money, transportation, or shelter, and I would never take up an offering or mail out support letters. The only way I would receive anything was if it was freely given to me. I figured that God must be the greatest boss in the world to work for, so if I could trust an earthly boss to pay me at the end of two weeks then I could easily trust God to faithfully provide for me if I diligently worked for Him. After daily experiencing His abundant provision in my life, I can now testify that He was and always will be faithful to provide. For six months, we had three meals a day, every single day. There was never a day where we only had two meals. In fact, we even gained weight; in Atlanta, of course! We only spent four nights sleeping on the street and they were glorious because we had the opportunity to reach out to the homeless and empathize with their suffering. In fact, we wanted to spend more nights on the street in order to reach out more effectively to the homeless, but God always had us meet amazing lovers of Jesus who would joyfully host us in their home free of charge.

Two days before I left Miami, God miraculously provided me with a great partner, Alex Diaz, to accompany me on this journey. I could have never carried out the mission trip without him, and together, we made a dynamic team. We traveled from Miami to San Francisco preaching the Gospel six days a week to countless individuals. It was the most glorious time of my life! Never have I been so close to Jesus and never have I served Him so radically. Words could never express the feeling of trusting in God alone for absolutely everything and waking up each morning with only one aim: to seek God and preach the Gospel all day and night long. Although it was the most incredible time of my life, it was the most difficult season of my life as well. It was not easy to daily deny myself, take up my cross, and follow Jesus, whether I felt like it or not. Through this experience, I discovered that there is nothing greater than to be formed into His likeness, live daily in His presence, and be used by Him to share and demonstrate God's love to people. By the end of our journey, hundreds of souls had prayed to accept Jesus as their Lord and Savior, thousands of people had heard the Gospel, and many Christians were revived with a fresh passion for God and compassion for souls. Hallelujah!!! All glory be to God!

Throughout my journey, the Lord directed me to keep a journal in order to record the stories that took place each day with the hope of one day sharing these stories with others. This book is my best attempt to share these stories with you as descriptively and authentically as I am able.

Joshua Carvalho
Pasadena, CA
February 2014

CHAPTER ONE

MIAMI

Barber Shop

The mall was deserted. You could hear the squeak of each footstep of the twenty or so customers echoing through the vacant facility as they nonchalantly strolled by each store. My close friend, Serge Gustave, had asked me if he could tag along with me for the day. This was his first experience in street evangelism and I was hoping that it would be life changing for him, but now I was not so sure. I didn't know why God had led us here, but I trusted Him.

The first person we approached was an Indian man who appeared to be dying of boredom at his jewelry kiosk. He was leaning over the glass counter trying to stay attentive to the vacant building surrounding him. I don't usually speak to people when they are on the job, but without one potential customer in sight I presumed that this Hindu jeweler would gladly welcome a spiritual conversation. We began an engaging discussion, but within ten minutes his supervisor came by and ordered him to stop speaking with us. The conversation was cordially ended and we continued our quest to find people in this uninhabited shopping center.

We turned the corner to find a Haitian family aimlessly walking around with a baby stroller. We politely approached them and asked them if they had a relationship with God. They confessed that they believed in Jesus, but that they weren't committed to following Him and did not attend a church. I lovingly shared the Gospel with them, challenged them to wholeheartedly follow Christ, and prayed for them. They thanked me for talking and praying with them and went on their way.

Meanwhile, a few minutes into my dialogue with the Haitian family, Serge whispered to me, "I got this." Next thing I knew, he was gone. Once my time with the Haitian family had ended, I looked around for Serge and was impressed to find him passionately preaching the Gospel to two teenage boys seated at a table. They both wore an expression of sincere shock and amazement as Serge boldly proclaimed the Gospel to them. I couldn't hear what Serge was saying, but whatever it was, it was impacting those young people.

*

I looked around to see if there was anyone else I could talk to, but the only people who remained in the mall were the people we had already engaged in conversation.

I prayed, "Lord, I know that you sent me here, so please show me what you want me to do."

As my prayer came to a close, I happened to walk past a barbershop that was packed with men. I could hear the television blaring, men yelling obscenities at each other, and the buzz of clippers cutting through hair. I felt my stomach rush to my throat and my heartbeat accelerate as I heard the Lord tell me to preach the Gospel to everyone in the shop. I couldn't believe God was asking me to do this. I had only open air preached once in my life and I was not ready to walk into a shop with a bunch of huge, intimidating Jamaican men who sounded like they were yelling at each other while having a casual conversation. Also, because I lived in a Jamaican and Haitian neighborhood I knew from experience that Jamaican men were not always the kindest to non-blacks.

In fear and hesitation, I walked away, sat on a nearby bench, and read my Bible. I nervously disobeyed God hoping that, in His eyes, reading the Bible was a holy enough excuse to not preach the Gospel. No matter how hard I tried, however, I was unable to complete one verse. The conviction of the Holy Spirit to preach the Gospel was so strong that it was impossible for me to focus on anything else. Finally, I mustered up the courage to obey God.

I walked into the barbershop with my head up high, a smile on my face, and a confident stride. I boldly approached the nearest barber and introduced myself with a slightly ghetto twang, "Hey, wassup man? My name's Josh and I'm just goin' around today talkin' wit' people about Jesus. Is it cool if I speak to everyone here about God for a few minutes?"

He tilted his head to the side, rudely stared me up and down, allowed an intimidating moment of silence to pass, and skeptically muttered, "Aight."

The television volume was blasting, so I asked him, "Is it alright if I turn down the volume on the TV?"

Again he tilted his head, gave me the same glaring look and said, "Aight."

He grabbed the remote and turned the volume all the way down for me.

I stood confidently at the entrance of the room, gripped the Bible in my right hand, and lifted up my voice so that the fourteen people there could clearly hear me, "Hey, wassup everybody!" The commotion in the room quickly dialed down as all heads turned towards me.

"My name is Joshua," I continued, "And I just felt that God wanted me to speak to you guys for a few minutes." You could hear a pin drop. Shock and respect could simultaneously be seen in the expressions of the men in the room.

Without missing a beat and not letting anyone's reaction distract me, the Gospel message began to freely flow through my lips, "I want to ask all of you a question. Do you know God? Do you have a relationship with Him? Or do you just know about God? You see, you could know all about someone and not know him at all. Take Michael Jordan for example. You could read his biography and know all about his career, but you don't know him because you've never spent personal time with him. You don't know how he acts, how he talks, or what his weaknesses are. It's the same way with God. Many of you know all about God because you've learned about Him in church and you know all the Bible stories, but do you truly know God? I want to challenge you today to not just know about God, but to know God.

To my surprise, I now had the undivided attention and respect of 14 grown men. No one interjected and no one seemed to be offended. They were all engaged in the message. I passionately unpacked the full Gospel message in about ten minutes, elaborating upon the fall of man, the day of judgement, the problem of sin, the coming of the Messiah, Christ's death and resurrection, and his exclusive claim to being the only way to Heaven.

All the men were fixed on the Gospel message as I delivered it, all except one, the oldest barber, Dean. Dean had quite the ego and he interjected with smart alec questions and comments a number of times. I ignored all of his comments and would quickly answer all of his questions. After answering each question I would immediately return to presenting the Gospel, but twice he challenged me with difficult theological questions that were not easy to answer with a few words.

One of the questions was, "What happened to all the people who lived before Jesus came to save the world?" That's a question I didn't want to be asked as a nineteen-year-old in front of a room full of older men who knew their history and had their share of doubts about Christianity. I gave a quick response to each question that he posed, but both times he was not satisfied by my explanation and he challenged me saying, "I don't believe you. Prove it to me!"

Both times I shoved my fears to the side and spoke out in total faith, trusting that God would back me up with an answer even though I wasn't completely sure what the answer was myself.

"Alright! You want me to prove it to you. I'll prove it to you!" As I was boldly making that claim, God immediately reminded me of Scriptures that I had memorized months or years before. Both times, I opened up the Bible to the exact Scripture that had the answer to his question and I proved to him that what I was saying was in the Bible. These questions caused the people to lose a bit of focus on the message, but they turned out to be extremely positive overall. As they watched me answer these tough questions not only with logic, but with Scripture, they realized that I knew what I was talking about and, thus, respected the Gospel message even more.

After answering Dean's objections, I continued preaching the Gospel and, at the end of it all, I asked if anyone wanted to give their life to Christ and genuinely repent of their sins. Three men raised their hands without hesitation. Every man in the shop went silent and the barbers even turned off their clippers as I led the three men in the sinner's prayer. After they finished making their commitment to follow Christ I prayed a general prayer for everyone in the shop. I wrote down the contact information of the three men who had committed their lives to the Lord, so that my church could keep in touch with them. Then I passed out flyers to each person and personally invited them to visit our church.

When I invited the barbers to my church, Randall, who had long dreadlocks and wore a heap of Rastafarian paraphernalia, told me, "We can't go to your church man. We're too busy."

"Too busy? How can you be too busy to go to church," I asked in unbelief.

"We all work in the shop seven days a week," he replied.

I paused for a second, not knowing what to say in response to a man's duty to provide for his family. Then the answer came to me and I boldly looked him straight in the eyes saying, "You have to change your priorities man. That's not right. You can't be putting money in front of God man. God should be your first priority, not your last."

Immediately, Dean called me over to his side of the room and began asking me all kinds of questions about God and the Gospel. We had been talking for about twenty minutes when all of a sudden Randall interrupted us yelling from the other side of the shop, "Hey man! We can't come to your church. We can't. But you could come here and preach to us as much as you want! You could even preach to all our customers!"

"Seriously? That would be awesome!" I was filled with excitement. I couldn't believe my ears.

"Whatever day is best for you, alright," Randall kindly said, "You know what, Wednesdays are perfect. They're right in the middle of the week and they're always slow, so we could take our time and really listen to what you have to say."

"Alright man," I answered, "Wednesdays it is. You got a deal. The only problem is that I'm going to leave Miami in four weeks to continue my mission across America."

Dean suddenly got excited and exclaimed, "We are your mission! You can't leave Miami until you've completed your mission here!"

"Alright man," I replied, thrilled at the challenge. Ironically, God seemed to be speaking to me through the same man who had been speaking against Christ!

By this time, Serge had joined me in the shop and had begun speaking with some of the customers while I enjoyed meeting the rest of the barbers. I was glad that Serge had come with me. We trusted God and He was faithful to guide our steps to a divine appointment.

I returned there four more times and each time I presented the Gospel from a different angle. By the time I left Miami three of the barbers had committed their lives to Christ. The other two, Randall and Dean, were very stubborn, but not far from the Kingdom of God.

The Lord had directed me to begin the mission trip in my hometown of Miami. He told me that I needed to give the first month of this trip as a first fruits offering to my city and my home church. This powerful encounter and amazing opportunity was a confirmation that this truly was God's will.

Spending A Day With Jesus

I noticed Gerald from a distance and felt compelled to meet him. I had come with my brother to preach the Gospel at Miami Dade College, a community college in the heart of downtown Miami. However, after being rejected by a number of students, I decided to walk to Bayside, a lively outdoor mall on Biscayne Boulevard. That's when I spotted Gerald. He was sitting alone on a park bench in the middle of a quiet walkway listening to his walkman. He looked relaxed.

I crossed the street, made my way up the sidewalk, and unassumingly sat down next to him. I greeted him politely saying, "Hello, how are you?" He completely ignored me. I sat there for a while awkwardly waiting for a response. I quickly realized that he probably hadn't heard me because he was listening to the radio so I spoke a little louder the second time.

"Excuse me, sir!" I began. He slightly turned his head to look over at me, "Hi. My name is Josh and I've just been going around today talking with people about Jesus. What's your name sir?" I extended my hand for a handshake, but he didn't return the favor.

"Gerald," he said in his thick New York accent. He was obviously annoyed by me and uninterested in having a conversation, but I gently persisted with a smile on my face.

"Do you have a relationship with God, Gerald?" I asked.

Smirking, he replied, "I don't care about God. He's never helped me. He's never done anythin' for me."

Confused and saddened by his cold-hearted statement, I tried to encourage him by saying, "But God loves you Gerald. He's here with you every day and He wants to help you. He has a purpose for your life."

"Can't you see I'm homeless kid?" he bluntly stated, frustrated that I had not noticed his social status.

I was taken aback. I honestly had not perceived his homelessness. He was wearing a nice hat, a good quality sweater, blue jeans, and was listening to a walkman. Only after he had made his claim did I notice that his shoes, socks, and lower half of his pants were quite ragged and his facial hair was slightly scruffy.

Nevertheless, as I continued listening to Gerald with an open ear and a loving heart, he began expounding upon all the hardships he'd gone through on the streets as proof that God had never cared about him. He shared about the times he had been robbed and beat up by other homeless people, the times he had been arrested by the cops, and how difficult it was to sleep on the street night after night.

"What about the homeless shelters," I asked, "Could they help you?"

"I stay as far away as I can from those places man," he replied with a tone of disgust in his voice, "Every time I go there they either beat me up, want to fight me, or rob me because they are all black and I'm white and because they are all a bunch of crack heads. I don't do drugs. I stay away from that sh--. I don't even beg anymore. I hate begging, so I stopped a long time ago. All I do now is sit on this bench, listen to my walkman, and let myself waste away until I die. I don't want to live anymore, so the quicker I die the better."

After hearing his heart and discerning his pain, I tried a few times to tell him about the hope there was in Jesus, but each time he would abruptly speak over me and continue venting about the problems in his life and in society. As Gerald spoke, God reminded me that I was on a fast and that He desired for me to fulfill Isaiah 58.

Once Gerald finished talking I asked him, "So are you hungry?"

"Yeah," he said.

"I want to take you out to eat," I told him, "C'mon. Let's go over to the food court."

"No, no, no. They don't let me in the food court," he quickly shot back.

"What?" I responded in unbelief, "of course they will. They have to."

"No, they won't," he argued, "They don't allow any homeless people into the food court. And they know me there."

"But you're with me," I persisted, "They can't say anything if you're with me."

"Believe me!" he stubbornly interjected, "I've done it before."

It shocked me that local restaurants would treat someone so unjustly in order to keep their place 'clean' and to make their 'normal' customers feel comfortable.

Finally, I conceded, "Alright. Well, where could we go then?"

"The only place that accepts homeless people in the whole city is the McDonald's and a little Cuban cafe," he explained, "but the cafe's pretty far from here."

"Okay," I agreed, "So let's go to the McDonald's then."

We walked over to the McDonald's and while we were waiting in line another homeless man asked me if I could buy him a small yogurt. Gerald acted hostile towards him because he thought that he was trying to take advantage of me. However, God immediately brought Isaiah 58 to my mind again. So I told him, "Get whatever you want man. A combo, yogurt whatever you want. It's on me."

Gerald turned around and looked at me in disbelief. He couldn't believe that I could be so naive by letting this guy take advantage of me, but I just wanted to demonstrate unmerited and unconditional love. "I know him," Gerald warned me, "He's a crack addict."

"It's okay," I calmly responded, "Don't worry about it."

We sat down to eat together and Gerald was pretty shocked when he realized that I was fasting and I had bought him a meal when I couldn't even eat. So I decided to show him what had inspired me to act this way. I explained why I was fasting and I opened up my Bible to Isaiah 58 and read it with him as he followed along. He didn't seem to care that much about the passage, but he was definitely impressed by my fast.

All of a sudden, he stopped complaining about his life and, for the first time, sincerely listened to what I had to say about Jesus. I could see the countenance on his face change as his heart softened towards me and towards God. He stopped cutting me off. He stopped saying rude remarks about God. He simply looked me in the eyes and listened.

I spoke about the hope there is in God and to the joy of having a relationship with Him. I preached the full Gospel to him and he listened with an open heart, but when I asked him if he wanted to surrender his life to Christ he listed countless excuses to why he could never make such a commitment.

Once he finished his meal and I finished sharing the Gospel with him, we walked out of McDonald's and decided to continue strolling around the block. The Lord once again impressed Isaiah 58 on my heart, so I told Gerald with some fresh excitement, "Hey, let's go to Marshalls! I want to buy you some new clothes."

"No, no, no," he shot back, "there's no use in getting new clothes if I can't take a good shower first. I'm filthy. If I change into new clothes then the clothes will immediately be filthy."

As we continued our walk, I began praying about what I could realistically do to truly help Gerald conquer his hopelessness. Suddenly, the light turned on. I exclaimed with joy, "Well hey! I have an idea! Why don't you come and live with my family and I for a while until you could get a job and get off your feet again?"

He was dumbfounded by my offer, but soon snapped out of his stupor and shamefully stated, "I can't do that. I'm filthy. I would be embarrassed to meet your parents and walk into their house the way that I am."

"No man," I insisted, "we help people on the streets all the time. My parents would love to have you. And once you take a shower you'll be clean and I could buy you some new clothes."

"No kid," he stubbornly persisted, "I can't go to your house."

"Why not?" I begged.

"Cause even though I'm homeless," he humbly responded, "I'm still a man and I still have pride."

I was determined to convince him to accept my offer because I knew that my family would love and help restore him holistically. It broke my heart to see a good man be so beat down by life that his foremost pursuit was to waste away on a park bench and die. Yet no matter how hard I tried to persuade Gerald to allow us to host him, he emphatically insisted that he didn't want our help. With total unbelief, I attempted to process the scene that was unfolding before my eyes. Here was a man who had been utterly broken by life, but who's pride was still big enough to refuse a teenager's offer of genuine assistance. For the first couple hours of our time together he had rambled on and on about all the hardships he had experienced living on the streets and he had bitterly complained against the church, the government, and society as a whole for not effectively helping the homeless, yet when a young man compassionately extended real help to him he refused to receive it because of his pride. This left me perplexed.

So I dropped the subject of helping him. It was interesting because once I gave up on helping him, but continued hanging out with him as a friend Gerald began to open up to me even more. He finally realized that I genuinely cared about him as a person and he wasn't my charity case. With utmost transparency, he disclosed to me his story of how he became homeless. He was born and raised in New York City and his parents meant the world to him. He considered them to be his only true family and friends in life. Tragically, in 2003 both of his parents died in a car crash and, ever since then, Gerald saw no reason for living. He stopped working and paying his bills just out of sheer depression and he ended up on the streets. He'd been homeless for four years when I met him. He was now tired of living and had contemplated suicide several times. He stopped begging for money or food because he would rather eat nothing all day and die sooner.

My heart was moved with compassion for him once I understood that he was not a drug addict or alcoholic, but was simply bound by demons of depression and despair. I knew that if he received

Jesus into his life and lived in a loving community he would be set free and his life would be restored again.

I begged him again to please come to my house and continued to encourage him to give his life to Jesus, but he stubbornly refused to do either. After spending nearly four hours with Gerald I had to go back home, so I prayed for him and drove back home with my brother. Before leaving, I asked him where I could find him if I returned to downtown again. He walked me over to the two spots where he always stayed and I gave him my phone number to call me just in case he changed his mind about staying at my house.

The days went by and Gerald never called. I went back to downtown three or four times and looked for him all over the city, but he was nowhere to be found. I even asked the other homeless men if they had seen him and none of them had.

*

Then Jesus appeared to me through another broken person. His name was Pierre. I was waiting at the bus stop in Aventura Mall after a long, hard day of preaching the Gospel when I began a conversation with the young man standing next to me. He was a tall, twenty-four-year-old Haitian who had handsome features and a well toned muscular build. I struck up a friendly conversation with him and asked him where he was from.

"Well, I'm from New York," he explained, "I lived in Miami for a few years, but right now I just came down from Jacksonville."

"And where do you live in Miami?" I asked.

He said, "I don't know right now. I just came down from Jacksonville today. I have an auntie who lives down here and I'm trying to stay with her, but I can't contact her at all."

I looked at my watch. It was already 11:00 p.m. I knew if I didn't do anything for him he would sleep on the street that night and how could I be so cold-hearted to just leave him on the street right after telling him about Jesus. Jesus said, "And whatever you have done to the least of My brethren you have done it unto Me." I couldn't reject Jesus. He was standing right in front of me, but his name just happened to be Pierre.

"But tonight you have nowhere to stay?" I reaffirmed.

"Nah," he answered as he turned his head away in shame.

"Well," I offered, "let me call my parents and see if it would be okay with them for you to spend the night at our house."

I called my parents and told them about how I met Pierre, who he was, and what his situation was and they readily agreed to let him stay the night. I have such awesome parents! I hung up and happily told Pierre the good news, "You could stay at our house tonight!"

"Thanks man," he replied with some shock and much gratitude.

My parents and brother welcomed Pierre into our home and into our family with open arms. He attended church with us twice a week, went to our cell group weekly, and daily applied for jobs. I even took him to preach the Gospel with me on one occasion. Pierre accepted Jesus, committed to follow him, and even began reading the Bible, but he suffered severely from schizophrenia and we didn't know how to help him except through prayer.

Pierre shared his whole life story with me. As a pre-teen he became a foster child because of issues in his family. No one cared to adopt a child his age, so he got stuck in the institutionalized foster care system in upstate New York until he turned eighteen. During his senior year he was offered a job as a model for an agency in New York City. He couldn't resist the offer, so he dropped out of high school right before graduation and became a model. He was quite successful for a few years. He had several beautiful girlfriends, loads of cash, and was traveling throughout the U.S. However, one day his gay boss told him that if he wanted to keep his job as a model he had to provide him with sexual favors. Pierre refused to engage in homosexual sex, so he quit. Ever since then he had been struggling to survive. He went to Jacksonville for a while, but eventually ended up living on the streets. When I met him, he had just come off the bus hoping to discover a new life in Miami.

*

A few days later, I bumped into a close friend of mine who is homeless, Jimmy. He told me that Gerald had been asking for me and he seemed anxious to see me. I felt bad because I knew we couldn't host him anymore since we were now hosting Pierre. We didn't have room for anyone else and I knew that my parents would probably not feel comfortable helping more than one homeless person at a time. I looked for him for a good while with the hopes of hanging out with him again, but I never found him. I went to downtown again on another day, but to no avail. On occasion, I still pray for Gerald, but only God knows where he is now and how he's doing. I just wish that he had said yes the first time.

*

Meanwhile, we got in contact with Pierre's aunt, but his aunt said that she neither had the means nor the room to host him in her home. She gave him some money to help him out, but that was it. After staying with us for nearly a month and not finding one job he gave up on Miami and decided to return to Jacksonville. I urged him to continue trying, but he would not budge in his decision. So I took him to the Greyhound bus station to bid him farewell. I was worried for him, but something inside of me told me that I would see him again.

Walking In A New Revelation

For several days I had been walking under a self-inflicted burden to win lost souls to Christ. I felt like the responsibility of saving the whole world was weighing heavily upon my shoulders. That morning, however, God showed me why it was wrong for me to live under such a burden. He taught me that I was incapable of saving even one soul, so how could I save the whole world? Only the Holy Spirit can save souls. All that He asked of me was to cast the entire burden for the salvation of the world upon Him, surrender to Him, listen to His voice, and simply obey Him with complete trust and rest in my soul. My only calling was to rejoice knowing that I had been given the honor of participating as a servant in the process of bringing the lost to salvation. Another illusion that I had fallen into was that I had become so personally involved in the salvation of souls that I deceived myself in thinking that I was the one who was saving the lost and when someone didn't commit their life to Christ I viewed it as my own personal failure. God showed me that He does not measure my success in evangelism based on how many people I influence to believe in Him, but rather by how obedient I am to His leading.

This was a life-changing revelation for me and as soon as I understood and accepted it the burden of saving the world was lifted off of my shoulders. I felt as light as a feather and I was filled with a profound peace and overflowing joy. It became a joy for me to preach the Gospel rather than an overwhelming burden. Thus, instead of zealously attempting to witness to as many people as I can with the most radical message that I could proclaim I began to simply listen to the voice of the Holy Spirit as my guide throughout each day and obey everything He asked me to do and say. This shift in mentality changed my world and my mission.

*

I got off the bus at Sawgrass Mills, the largest outlet mall in America. As I walked through the parking lot, He highlighted to me a young man dressed in business attire who was seated on a sidewalk curb. In obedience, I approached him hoping to strike up a conversation, but as I drew closer I noticed that he was talking on his cell phone. I continued walking straight past him and prayed, "Lord, I know that you want me to speak to him, but I'm not going to walk up to him while he is on his cell phone."

I strolled into a secluded area behind the back door of a department store to continue praying for guidance. A few minutes later, the same man drove into the secluded lot, parked directly in front of me, and rolled down his window. He patiently sat in his car as if he was waiting to pick someone up from the mall. I couldn't believe what had just happened. It was as if God was telling me, "Joshua, I want you to talk with this man so much that even though you walked right past *him* I am going to have him drive up to *you* so that you have no excuse." It was surreal. I laughed at God's great sense of humor and I was amazed to see that if He truly wanted me to speak to someone He would make a way.

So I walked up to the car with a smile on my face and introduced myself saying, "Excuse me. My name is Josh and I was just walking by and God told me to come and talk with you if that's alright. What's your name man?"

Jacob was very polite and friendly, so we enjoyed a dialogue with each other for about fifteen minutes. He explained to me that he was a Christian, but in the past few months he had begun to slip away. He hadn't been reading the Bible or going to church because he had allowed work to become his main priority. I challenged and encouraged him to fully return to God, to seek Him with all of his heart, and become committed to a church. He ended the conversation by remarking, "Thank you so much for talking with me man. I really appreciate it. I needed it. That's crazy that God told you to talk with me. He's got my attention now! Yeah...I gotta get back on track."

Jacob and I prayed together and went our separate ways. I was amazed to see God's love for this prodigal son. I could feel God's heart of compassion for Jacob as He led me to reach out to him. His love for him was so great that He even manipulated the situation just so that I could plant a seed in his heart that would potentially lead him back to his Father before he had drifted even farther away.

*

As I entered the mall and strolled down the main aisle I spotted a young man sitting on a bench by himself. I felt the Holy Spirit leading me to speak to him, so I unassumingly sat down next to him. I didn't feel peace to quickly jump into a conversation, so I asked God to give me a personal word for him. I randomly opened up my Bible and it fell on Matthew 22, the parable of the wedding banquet. Immediately, God gave me a clear and powerful word for him. The parable was about the wedding feast of the Lamb, the Father inviting guests, the guests being too busy for God, God rejecting them, and, thus, selecting others.

"Excuse me," I began as I extended my hand out, "my name is Joshua. What is your name?"

He turned to me with a perplexed countenance.

"No hablas Ingles*?" I inquired, realizing that he didn't speak English.

"No," he answered, relieved that I knew Spanish, "I am from Ecuador. We are spending our vacation in Miami, but in a few days I'll be returning to Ecuador."

Thus, I naturally segued into an engaging dialogue with Rogelio in Spanish.

"I was just sitting next to you reading my Bible," I explained, "and God told me to share a word with you that is specifically for your life."

He was amazed to hear that God had a message for him and he had an honest desire to know what God was communicating to him through this stranger. I went right to the point and was very straightforward with him.

"God loves you so much," I compassionately began, "He wants you to come to Him and He has been inviting you to His party, but you are always too busy for Him. If you continue to reject God's invitation because of your busyness then God will reject you and pick someone else to come to His banquet."

Rogelio was blown away and deeply impacted.

"Do you follow God," I inquired, "Do you have a relationship with Him?"

*You don't speak English?

"No, I don't," he sincerely replied, "I don't follow God and I don't have a relationship with Him. I just go to Mass with my family every once in a while."

I beseeched him to give his life to Jesus and to truly follow Him. I described to him what it meant to follow Jesus and how amazing it was to have a relationship with Him. After speaking with him for over thirty minutes, I asked him if he wanted to give his whole life to Jesus and serve Him with all of his heart.

With red, teary eyes he answered, "After what you said, yes, I do."

"Would you like to give your life to Christ right now?" I lovingly asked, "I could pray with you to receive Him into your life right now."

"I would like to," he apologetically began to explain, "But I don't want to make my family wait for me any longer, so I think I have to go." I had been so intensely focused on sharing this message with Rogelio that I hadn't even noticed that his family had been waiting for him to leave for several minutes already. I was slightly embarrassed, yet very grateful that his family had the courtesy to allow us to finish our conversation.

"It was great meeting you Rogelio," I stated as I locked eyes with him one last time, "Before you go to bed tonight I encourage you to dedicate your life Jesus."

"Thank you Joshua," he sincerely responded with an equally intense stare, "I will."

And with that final statement he joined his family as they continued shopping. I stayed on the bench praying and reading my Bible for a while before witnessing to the next person. About twenty minutes later, Rogelio and his family passed directly in front of me on their way out of the mall. I continued reading, but out of the corner of my eye I saw Rogelio staring at me with an unforgettable expression. The look on his face was one of such awe and wonder that it seemed like he was trying to figure out whether I was an angel or a human. He was confounded. I don't know how else to describe it, but I praised God for using me to so deeply impact this young man's life.

*

Once I finally stood up and began meandering through the mall again I said to God, "Lord, I've only spoken to youth so far. Challenge me. I want to speak to grown men."

Immediately, I noticed a man who appeared to be in his 50's happily seated close to the Rainforest Cafe. I went over to him with a big smile and we began a jovial interaction. Juan only spoke Spanish and was from Medellin, Colombia. When I told him that I was Brazilian and I had been to Bogota he told me that he had gone to Rio De Janeiro for Carnaval.

"But you've probably never been to Carnaval," Juan pointed out, "because you're carrying a Bible in your hand."

"You're right," I said in agreement.

Then he unashamedly exclaimed, "Oh! But the beautiful black women of Brazil are the most tremendous women to have sex with. You don't know what you're missing out on!"

I looked him straight in the eyes and said, "I guarantee you that I will have better sex then you've ever had because I will be able to look into my wife's eyes and tell her that I loved her so much that I waited and kept myself my whole life just so that my body and love could be fully hers."

He began laughing hysterically at my zealous statement. "The best sex is in your youth," he proclaimed as if he were giving me a nugget of wise counsel, "and when you get married you will no longer have your youth. But don't worry...even when you're married you could have sex with all the women you want because your wife will never know."

I couldn't believe my ears. I knew that Juan was speaking from experience and, frankly, I was disgusted. If he were some immature teenager I wouldn't have been so surprised, but this was a man in his fifties who was married and had children. Yet he was proudly boasting about his abominable lifestyle and trying to convince me to live the same way. A part of me just wanted to spit in his face in revulsion, but a stronger part of me burned with compassion for this man to encounter the greatest pleasure in all of existence.

"Do you fear God at all?" I honestly asked.

"Of course I do," he confidently shot back with his head up high, "I go to Mass sometimes and I repent for my sins."

"God is not stupid," I strongly replied praying that God would deeply convict this man of his hypocrisy, "He knows that you did not repent from your heart, but merely with your lips and God will not forgive you until you are truly ashamed of your sin. Look, one day you will die and be judged by God for every sin you have ever done. And it won't matter if your wife knew about it or not because God will know about every sin that you have committed. God is calling you to repent. That's why He sent me to speak to you. He wants you to repent of your sin and if you genuinely repent He will forgive you and change you."

Laughing away my rebuke, Juan walked away and wished me a good night.

As he walked away I prayed that our conversation would torture his mind until he was brought to his knees in repentance. Although I was very direct and strong in what I said to this man my heart was burning with compassion for him the entire time. These are the sick who need a doctor, who need Jesus. If Jesus reached out to prostitutes then surely He desires to reach out to Juan as well.

*

I took a break for about ten minutes in order to recharge my spirit with the presence of God. Then I walked over to a nearby T-Mobile kiosk that had no customers. I really needed a phone for my mission trip, especially once I left Miami, so I wanted to see if T-Mobile had a strong plan with nationwide coverage. While I was at it, though, I took advantage of the fact that business was slow to preach the Gospel to the T-Mobile salesman.

The representative had a name tag on, so I opened up the conversation with an inquiry, "Michael, before I ask you about a phone could I ask you another question?"

"Sure," he replied.

"Have you ever read this book?" I inquired placing my Bible on the glass counter.

"Nope," he responded.

"This is the greatest history book in the world," I enthusiastically declared, "Every year it is the number one bestseller worldwide."

"Really? Wow," he answered, his brows furrowing up in surprise.

"Do you know God, Michael?" I asked, "Do you follow him with all your heart?"

"Nope," he said frankly.

For a good while I told him about the Bible, why he needs to read it, and urged him to genuinely seek God.

"Let me tell you about how I came to follow God," I eventually said, "First, I realized that He truly was real and so I decided that if He was real I should follow Him.

"How did you come to know He was real?" he asked, honestly wanting to know how I had come to that conclusion.

I expounded upon several different reasons why I had become convinced that God was real. The answers I gave made a lot of sense to Michael and, as a result, he became very receptive to the Gospel. At the end of our conversation, I asked him if he wanted to give his whole life to Jesus and follow him with all of his heart and he said, "YES!" I asked him if he wanted to pray with me right now to commit his life to Jesus, but he told me that it was too awkward for him to genuinely give his life to God while he was on the job, with people talking all around him, and standing in the middle of a mall. Nevertheless, he promised me that he would make the decision to believe in and follow Jesus. He wasn't a part of any church, so I invited him to my church and cell group and he quickly agreed to come. Then I prayed for him and his friends and wrote down his contact information.

While I was overjoyed by this fruitful encounter with Michael, I was saddened and disappointed by the other two T-Mobile representatives working at the kiosk. They both claimed to be committed members of their local churches and confidently declared to me that they were born-again Christians. However, Michael disclosed to me that never once had either of them talked with him about God, let alone even mentioned the word "God". What was even more disturbing was that one of them was ceaselessly checking out girls as they passed by. He constantly interrupted our conversation solely to make graphic remarks about each girl's body. He knew that I was sharing the Gospel with Michael, but this self-proclaimed "born-again Christian" was unashamed of his vile comments. He was ashamed to talk with Michael about Jesus, but definitely not about his lust.

When Michael noticed how annoyed I was by his co-worker's interruptions about girl's body parts, he tried to console me by saying, "Don't worry about him. He's not even that bad, but that other guy," he stated as he pointed his finger at the other 'born-again Christian', "He's the most sinful person in the whole mall."

What a sad state much of the Church is in today. How could we ever expect the Holy Spirit to transform our nation if we don't even want Him to change us?

Police Threat

The bus ride was nearly two hours long, so I had to leave Sawgrass Mills around 8:30 p.m. get home at a decent time. Pierre, who my family had been hosting for a couple of weeks, had come with me to apply for jobs at the mall.

As we walked onto the bus, I instantly felt the Lord impressing upon me to preach the Gospel to everyone. I first sat down and waited for the bus to fill up with more people. Once the seating was full, I stood to my feet at the front of the bus and boldly began preaching, "How's everybody doing? My name is Joshua and I just wanted to talk to you guys about Jesus."

As soon as the word Jesus came out my mouth the bus driver violently yelled, "Sit down!"

I politely responded in a calm voice, "I will sir, as soon as I finish."

I continued speaking and a few sentences later he exclaimed even more aggressively, "Sit down, NOW!!!"

"Okay. I will," I said, "I'll just speak sitting down." I sat on my seat at an angle, so that I was still facing the people and kept on preaching.

"Haven't you ever heard of separation of church and state?!" the driver snapped.

"Yes, I have," I replied, "but I've also heard of freedom of speech." And I continued speaking.

"This is against separation of church and state!" he self-righteously declared.

I cordially responded, "I believe freedom of speech surpasses separation of church and state, sir." I continued once again.

Then suddenly he angrily shouted, "Shut up, kid!!!"

"I won't sir," I kindly replied.

"No one wants to hear what you're saying!" he flared.

"Really?" I questioned with a bit of skepticism in my voice. I turned around to the passengers and asked them, "Does anyone here not want to hear what I am saying?" No one raised their hand or said a word. "There's no one who doesn't want to hear what I'm saying sir. It looks like you're the only one sir."

This shut him up for quite a while. I continued preaching while the bus driver remained silent in frustration.

Then he threatened with an ominous tone in his voice, "If you don't stop I'll call the police!"

"No problem, sir. Go ahead," I calmly responded.

"Chill out Josh," Pierre urged me in a whispering voice. He wore a mixture of shock and worry on his face, "Sit down. Don't get yourself arrested."

"I'm cool Pierre," I whispered back, "I'm gonna finish." I wasn't afraid of the police or of getting arrested. If anything, I was excited by the idea of finally be persecuted for preaching the Gospel. I had always dreamt of the day when this would become a reality in America and here I was experiencing it. I was exhilarated.

Thus, I continued the message right where I had left off. Normally, I would share the Gospel in less than ten minutes, but the driver's belligerent interruptions kept stalling me from finishing my message. Once he saw that his threats had no effect on me, he took out his cell phone and called the cops. When the people saw that he was really calling the cops a few of them took out their phones and started calling their parents and friends to tell them either that they'd be home late or to please come and pick them up.

You could hear the different phone conversations begin to emerge. "Girrrl, you wouldn't believe what just happened!" one African-American teenager began explaining to his friend on the phone, "Some boy started preachin' about Jesus on the bus and the bus driver called the police to come arrest him. Mmhmm."

Another man called his wife, "Baby, I'm just gonna be home late cause the bus driver wants to arrest a boy on the bus for telling us about Jesus."

Within a few minutes, the driver parked the bus on the side of the road, walked outside, lit a cigarette, and continued talking with the police on the phone. That's when almost everyone began calling their friends and family. No one was mad. It was more like they were throwing their hands in the air and sighing, "Oh great!"

Others were saying, "Man, what's up with that bus driver? What's his problem?"

A few were somewhat irritated with me too. However, most of

them seemed to respect me for having stood up to the driver. They were mainly annoyed by the driver's attitude and that he had stalled the bus.

As I witnessed this chaotic scene I felt somewhat guilty and responsible. I had assumed that the driver would kick me off the bus or have me arrested at the end of the bus route, but I didn't think that he would hold up everyone from reaching their final destination because of me. So I finally stopped preaching, stepped outside of the bus, and spoke with the bus driver: "Sir, please! I'll stop preaching right now and you could leave with all the people. I'll stay right here on the curb until the cops come to arrest me. I promise you that I won't leave until they come, but please, sir, don't hold up the entire bus just because of me. These people need to get home."

He calmly puffed out a cloud of smoke into the air and said, "It doesn't matter now. I'm gonna wait for the police to come whether you keep preaching or not."

Then he yelled in my face as spit and smoke simultaneously flew in the air, "It's because of people like you that what's happening right now in Iraq is taking place!"

His prejudice remark deeply offended me and I was about to sharply rebuke him for his ignorant words, but, with God's help, I held my tongue and walked right back into the bus. I respectfully addressed the people, saying, "I'm very sorry for the hold up. I had no idea that he was going to stop the entire bus just because of me. I sincerely apologize for that. But I just finished talking with the bus driver and he said that he was going to wait for the cops regardless of whether I continued preaching or not. So I'm just going to finish my message and then pray for you all."

I finished the rest of the Gospel message in about five minutes and then I prayed for everyone in the bus, including the bus driver. I thanked them for their time, attention, and respect, and then walked off the bus with Pierre. I decided to patiently wait next to the bus driver for the cops to arrive. "Maybe I could witness to the bus driver," I thought to myself. Eventually, however, the bus driver threw down his cigarette to the floor in anger and yelled, "Forget this!" He walked onto the bus and drove away in a fury. The cops never showed up.

By the time the next bus arrived it was past 10 p.m., so most of the people were sleeping on the bus. Instead of open air preaching I spoke to the girl seated next to me. She came to the brink of giving her life to Jesus, but in the end, she hesitated.

What a night. What an adventure.

Conversation With A Philanthropist

I had a tough day at the Aventura Mall where I was rejected by everyone I spoke to. I had become quite weary and discouraged, but towards the end of the day I had a powerful conversation with a wealthy philanthropist. It was worth suffering through an entire day of rejection merely to meet this man and share the Gospel with him.

As I approached him, I began the conversation by speaking to him in English, assuming he was American from his distinctly Caucasian features. He answered back in flawless English, but when I asked him how he was doing he explained that he was enjoying his vacation in Miami and that he was from Brazil. He had gone to college in the United States, but, otherwise, he was from Brazil.

The man was wide open to discussing the deep philosophical and philanthropical challenges of humanity, so we immediately dove into a fantastic dialogue that lasted for nearly an hour. As I further gained his trust, he began to indirectly disclose to me that he was a multi-millionaire philanthropist who helped thousands of people in a number of ways. He was not pompous about his generosity, but humbly stated facts about his life and works as I inquired further concerning his spiritual life. He nonchalantly shared with me that he donated 90% of his income every year and only lived off of 10%. Now, for a man who was well dressed, shopping without restraint at Aventura Mall, living in Sao Paulo, and on a vacation in Miami, that 10% had to be a hefty sum of money. He named off several organizations he donated to and said that he was paying for the college tuition of four of his nephews. As we conversed, I discerned that he was a man who genuinely loved people to the point that he could feel their pain and weep with them in their suffering. He longed to help the world and was truly a selfless man. I admired him for all of these attributes that were evident in his life and character. He admitted to being a Catholic, but didn't hesitate to clarify that he hasn't attended church in decades, doesn't read the Bible, and thinks that religion is a waste of time and money. He saw religion as something that distracted people from what was truly important in life and sucks out billions of dollars from them in order to do so.

"Religion is the biggest waste of money in the world," he emphatically claimed, "if people used their money in order to genuinely change people's lives then the world would be a much better place." He didn't see religion as something helping the world, but something further corrupting and dividing it.

"In part, I definitely agree with you," I explained to him, "Religion can be a destructive force just as it was when it was used to crucify Jesus...but God is the solution to all things."

"I am bitter and angry towards God for all the evil and suffering in this world," he stated without one ounce of guilt, "I don't understand how God could ignore it all. So many people in this world are suffering and God does nothing about it."

"The vast majority of the world's suffering is caused by people themselves," I respectfully explained, in response to his genuine frustration with God, "Look at Africa for example. Europeans, Americans, and Arabs raped Africa of its natural resources, bound millions of people into slavery, and colonized the continent. Moreover, now the Africans themselves are extremely violent towards one another and are constantly engaged in civil war, coup d' etats, genocides, military dictatorships, and revolutions. Witchcraft, promiscuity, and pollution are out of control and are main reasons for rampant spreads of diseases. I could go on and on about the problems plaguing different parts of the world.

"However, God has indeed intervened through giving us the Bible, sending His prophets to speak to us, raising up modern-day preachers, performing miracles, and, ultimately, in sending Jesus Christ. God created us for a purpose and loves us all. He doesn't want us to live in a world of suffering and pain. He wants to save and transform our lives."

This discussion naturally led me into sharing the glorious message of the Gospel of Jesus with him. I preached the Gospel to him with all of my heart, passionately telling him about God's plan to save and redeem this corrupted and broken world. Few times had I ever so eloquently and fervently preached the Gospel to an individual. He listened intently and respectfully the entire time. Our eyes were locked on each other as I poured out the truths of the Gospel to him.

Once I finished, he responded with complete indifference stating, "All that you have said is very interesting and curious. However, it is frustrating to me that a relationship with God is not mutual, but merely us expressing ourselves to Him with nothing in return." Thus, he saw the Gospel as merely a beautiful story that had no grounding in the daily reality of human beings.

Understanding his struggle to see the Gospel as an agent of transformation and not just as an abstract theory, I took the time to describe what my daily relationship with God looked like and how God had encountered me as a young boy. "A relationship with God is not a one way street," I lovingly elaborated, "It is the most real and satisfying relationship that a human being could ever experience with another person." He was sincerely impressed by what I had to say, especially by my personal encounter with God.

At the end of it all, I asked him, "Do you desire to give your life to God today? Do you desire to give your life to God at all in your lifetime?"

He wasted no time in giving me an answer as he frankly confessed, "I still struggle with believing in the existence of God because of all the suffering I see in the world. If I ever live for God in my lifetime it would be years from now." Then he extended his hand to me as he politely ended our time together by saying, "Thank you for the conversation Joshua. I enjoyed it. You had some very interesting things to say. I'm going to look for my wife now."

This insightful encounter with a multimillionaire philanthropist caused me to glimpse things from God's perspective for a quick moment in time. This man had wholly given himself to help others, yet he was convinced that he helped and loved people more than God ever did. He saw God as the unjust forsaker of all mankind and viewed himself and other people like him as the saviors and hope of all mankind. He sincerely believed that he knew more about saving the world than God did and claimed to be more ethical than God.

This caused me to clearly see the arrogant, self-righteous, and blasphemous nature of unbelief. That day I came to understand why unbelief is truly the greatest sin of all.

Construction Workers

As I walked to the city bus stop each morning to begin my mission for the day, I always enjoyed having an intimate time with the Lord. I would praise Him for how glorious He was and intercede for the souls I was going to encounter that day. It would revive my spirit to feel the warm sun beating down on my face, the wind blowing on my body, to see the palm trees laden with coconuts gently swaying with the spring breeze, and to hear the sound of the canal flowing through our neighborhood as I passed by it. I would take in a deep breath of fresh air to enjoy the smell of wildflowers and fresh grass, and when I saw a beautiful flower I would stop to smell it and pick one out. In fact, I picked so many flowers that I ended up drying them to create a beautiful art piece for my girlfriend, Brooke*.

Besides all of these beautiful sites I would witness as I walked to the bus stop, I daily encountered something even more precious: construction workers in need of Jesus. A new development of tract homes were being built in our neighborhood, so I would always walk

*Brooke and I were courting. We got married in 2008.

past dozens of construction workers, mainly from Central America. Most of the time they would be working hard, but sometimes I would catch them when they are on their break. During these brief intervals of rest, I initiated several fruitful conversations with these men.

The first encounter took place when I caught a group of five workers eating lunch next to each other as they quietly sat on the floor of the house they were constructing. I felt the Lord compelling me to speak to them, but I inwardly resisted the Lord for a moment because I didn't want to be rude by disrupting their break. I was certain that the last thing they wanted on their lunch break was for someone to preach to them. Nevertheless, the Holy Spirit wouldn't leave me alone no matter how much I disagreed with Him. He continued convicting me until I finally obeyed.

I boldly walked up to the group of men and introduced myself. I shook their hands, learned their names, and began speaking to them in Spanish saying, "My name is Joshua. I was walking to the bus stop right now, but I felt God telling me to come over to you guys and speak to you about Him. I want to encourage each one of you to seek God with all of your heart. He is real and He wants you to know Him. Could I ask you guys a question? Do you have a relationship with God?"

There was a dead silence partly because they were all eating, but also because they most likely didn't have relationships with God or simply because they didn't care to answer me.

I encouraged them to seek God and then asked, "If you were to die tonight do you know for sure where you would go?"

"I don't know," most of them responded.

I shared the Gospel with them for about fifteen minutes. They all listened intently and respectfully, but when I asked them if they wanted to give their lives to Jesus they all remained silent.

I pleaded with them to give their lives to Jesus, but again they had no response. I finally prayed over them and then continued on my walk to the bus stop.

This non-spectacular encounter, along with many others like it throughout my journey, sometimes caused me to wonder if my preaching was fruitless when I didn't see an immediate response from the person I witnessed to? As time went by, however, God began replacing my worldly way of thinking with His kingdom's way of thinking. He taught me that what mattered most in His kingdom was not necessarily measurable "results", but doing what one sees the Father doing. God directed me to preach to those men and I obeyed and that's all that matters. Obedience is what God is looking for, not sacrifice. Man looks at numbers, but God looks at surrender and obedience. His word does not return to Him void, so God will be faithful to complete the work He's begun in the lives of those men.

*

About a week later, I passed by a crew of four men who were installing the metal framing inside one of the houses. They had just taken a break, so I walked up to them and asked them for a moment of their time to speak with them about Jesus. They were very open and began listening intently to every word I said.

As I spoke to them, God strongly guided me to ask them some questions.

"What are you living for," I asked them, "What is the purpose of your life?"

They didn't know what to say, so I singled them out one-by-one and looked them in the eyes as I asked, "What do you live for Esteban? There must be something you live for."

"I live for my family," Esteban replied.

"And what about you," I asked the next worker, "What do you live for?"

"I live just to live," he lifelessly muttered.

"And you?" I questioned the next man.

"I don't know," he blankly stated.

"And you?" I asked the last man.

"I just live to make money and to help my family," he stated with a measure of confidence and pride.

As I looked these men in the eyes, I felt the presence of the Holy Spirit descend so strongly in that empty house. His words began flowing out of my mouth as I said, "Each one of us will die one day and on that day we will meet God. And in that moment He will ask you, 'What did you live for? Did you live for Me or did you live for yourself? Did you life for the world, for sin, and for money or did you live for My glory and for righteousness?' On that day what will you say to Him?"

"The Bible says that each one of us will one day stand before the judgment throne of God and on that day all of our works will be stacked up in a huge pile before Him. The Bible says that all of our works will be made up of wood, hay, gold, silver, or precious stones. And on that day God will set fire to all of our works. Whatever is wood and hay will burn to ashes, but whatever is gold, silver, and precious stones will endure. You see, some people live their entire lives building a huge pile of wood and hay. They work hard to build it and they think that they are constructing something amazing, but it means nothing to God and, in the end, it will just be a heap of ashes. We live for fame, money, sex, houses, cars, to have lots of friends, and to be respected by everybody, but, in the end, it's all worthless.

"But if you live for God and to love and help others your works will be of gold, silver, and precious stones. If you live for righteousness, truth, and love you will have much to show, but if you live for yourself and for sin you will have nothing.

"So that's why I'm asking you 'What do you live for?' When you die and go before God what will you have to show for your life? Will you have a mountain of wood and hay or of gold, silver, and precious stones?"

All four of the men stood in awe of what they were hearing. They were stupefied.

One humbly asked, "Is that really in the Bible?"

"Yes, it is," I confirmed.

"Wow," he sighed as he looked to the ground in deep contemplation, nearly moved to tears, "I've never thought of that."

I began imploring them to live their lives for Christ and give their lives to Him.

"I want to," each one of them contritely responded, "but I know I'm not ready. When I commit my life to God I want to truly mean it, but I know that in this moment I'm not ready yet."

I persisted in challenging them to give their lives to Christ because I knew that one of the Devil's main tactics to keep people from giving their lives to Jesus was to convince them that they were not ready. No matter how hard I tried, however, they would not budge. They insisted that they were not ready. I could push, but I couldn't force them to make a decision.

I prayed for each one of them with all of my heart and wrote down their phone numbers to invite them to my parents cell group. Then I walked off to continue my day in evangelism.

I had many more encounters with different construction workers and nearly all of them were very open to the Gospel, but very few committed their lives to Christ. However, I know that the seed of the Gospel was planted in each one of their hearts and some of those seeds will grow to one-day bear fruit.

Door-to-Door Experiences

For three days, I went door-to-door to over one hundred homes in my neighborhood, talking to people about Jesus and inviting them to my parent's and my cell group. It was a much more fruitful endeavor then I had imagined it would be. I sincerely enjoyed going door-to-door and all my fears about this type of evangelism were proven to be false. I was surprised to find that most of the people were friendly and respectful upon meeting me on their doorstep. I had a number of great conversations and God powerfully touched several people's lives through engaging in this often-despised form of evangelism. Also, I made quite a few friends since all the people I witnessed to lived in my neighborhood. There were a few door-to-door encounters that I'll never forget where the people we met were powerfully encountered by the Holy Spirit right on their doorstep.

One of the most powerful encounters was with a young man named Charles. He was about seventeen-years-old and was home alone doing nothing when I knocked on his door. I introduced myself, got to know him a little bit, and then passionately preached the Gospel to him. Initially, Charles thought that he was a good person who would most likely make it to Heaven since he had never killed anyone. However, as he heard the Gospel message he came to realize that he was utterly lost and in need of a Savior. Towards the end of our conversation I asked him if he wanted to commit his life to Jesus and he genuinely responded saying, "Yeah. What do I gotta do?"

This is the modern way of saying, "What must I do to be saved?" I led him in the sinner's prayer, prayed over him, acquired his contact information, and invited him to my cell group. I was elated at his desire to commit his life to Christ. I almost couldn't believe it. Here was a young man giving his life to Jesus at the doorstep of his home just because some random Christian decided to get out of their own house, knock on their neighbor's door, and talk to him about Jesus. It was really that simple. I used to be terrified of doing door-to-door evangelism, but after this experience with Charles I knew that my fears and skepticism about this form of evangelism were false.

*

In another instance, my mother came along with me to evangelize in our neighborhood. It was so much easier to evangelize with her because two is always better than one, she was so sweet that virtually no one was rude to her, and she had a different way of talking with people than I did. She would focus on getting to know people and inviting them to the cell group in order for them to encounter God at the cell group. I, on the other hand, would try to preach the Gospel, have them encounter God, and pray over them all on their doorstep. Our different styles of evangelism complemented each other and made the mother-son witnessing experience more memorable and exciting.

As my mother and I went door-to-door, we met a kind gentleman named Derek. Upon meeting us at his doorstep, he immediately invited us into his home and offered us drinks. He had a beautiful home with high ceilings, elegant furniture, and, above all, a grand piano. We gawked at the piano, especially since my mother is a pianist, but when we asked him if he would play us a song he told us that it belonged to his roommate who was a dean of an arts school.

My mother enthusiastically shared the Gospel with Derek as he listened with a wide-open heart. Towards the end of the conversation, we asked him if he had a need we could pray for. He somberly dropped his head and allowed his entire composure to become overcome with grief. He attempted to hold back his tears as his body quietly quivered. Finally, he shared with us that his nephew had been diagnosed with muscular dystrophy and the doctors had only given him a few months to live.

My mother was able to empathize with his pain since she had been born with a life threatening illness as an infant. She compassionately shared her testimony with Derek of how God healed her of an incurable disease when she was five-years-old. Derek was dumbfounded by my mother's story of healing. His heart was encouraged with faith and a tinge of hope appeared in his eyes. We laid hands on Derek and compassionately prayed for his nephew, believing that God was definitely going to heal him. As we prayed, Derek began sobbing and when he lifted his head up at the end of the prayer his eyes were red with tears. He asked us to please return whenever we could and genuinely thanked us for our prayers.

*

Another remarkable experience I had while going door-to-door in my neighborhood was when I went along with my close friend, Michael Vergara. After we finished meeting everyone who lived on 11th Court, we turned the corner to meet our neighbors who lived on 10th Place. We knocked on the first door and a tall, African-American person swung it wide open almost hitting us as we instinctively stepped back.

The person had skinny dreadlocks, white tiger pants, a gaudy scarf, and glittery make-up on his/her eyes. He/she had a high-pitched voice, feminine mannerisms, but the build of a tall, thin black man. He/she was extremely friendly and immediately invited us into his/her house, which he/she later on told us was a miracle because he/she never lets strangers into his/her house. He/she had highly fashionable decor all throughout his/her house, which gave me the impression that he/she was a designer of some kind. After a while, I concluded that the person was a woman. I was at peace with that assessment until she told us that her name was Jerry. Later on, she referred to herself as a "he". Finally, a friend of hers called her "man" and referred to some of her things as "his". Thus, about thirty minutes into our conversation I decided that Jerry was a man. I turned out be right the second time. Jerry is a man*.

Jerry introduced us to his two professionally groomed dogs, a few of his friends, and some family members who lived in the house with him. He led us up to the loft on the second floor where we sat together on a set of comfortable sofas. Without a moment's hesitation, he candidly blurted out, "C'mon, tell me about Jesus. Give me some of the Word. The Lord knows I need it right now." He wasn't patronizing us in any way. He was just being honest.

Michael began sharing first by reading some Scriptures that God had put on his heart at that very moment. He challenged Jerry to wholeheartedly give his life to Jesus and repent of his sins because Jesus had nothing but love for him and only wanted to see his life restored.

*This is not meant to be humorous or derogatory. I only want to honestly tell the story as I experienced it. I am sorry if this story offends you.

I tagged along with what Michael was saying and eventually segued into the Gospel message.

As we spoke to Jerry, we could see in his eyes a sincere yearning to return to Christ and be forgiven of his sins, yet a deeply rooted sense of failure and hopelessness seemed to cloud his motivation to change. Throughout our conversation, he elaborated on his desire to change and return to Christ, but would eventually admit that it was unrealistic because he was so deeply bound by his vices. It seemed like he had once tried to follow Jesus, but had given up. Nevertheless, Jerry was extremely convicted, amazed, and touched by everything Michael and I shared with him and he genuinely did want to change.

He eventually confessed to us that he came from a devout family of Christians and he was the black sheep of the family. In fact, his uncle was the senior pastor of a fairly large church in Fort Lauderdale and most of his relatives were heavily involved in ministry. I was certain that his family must have been persistently interceding for his salvation and I felt so honored to be used as one of God's instruments to answer their prayers. Our conversation with Jerry lasted for well over an hour.

I felt led by the Lord to share Hebrews 10:26-31 with him and to urge him to stop living in hypocrisy. He felt so convicted by the scripture that he asked for me to write it down so that he could meditate on it after we left. He then began confessing all of the vices that were binding him. He candidly admitted that sexual promiscuity was his main addiction and he needed God to set him free from it. He told us over and over again that God had divinely sent us to him to confront him about his sin and help him be set free. He was so grateful for our visit and our strong words of love and rebuke.

When we prayed over Jerry he claimed to have felt a great deal of freedom and peace and he enthusiastically invited us to daily visit and pray for him. We encouraged him to commit to his uncle's church, distance himself from his worldly friends, and read the Word of God. He committed to us that he would faithfully carry out those three objectives.

I visited Jerry's house several times after that, but only twice was I successful in finding him at home. I also talked to him three or four times as he drove by my house in his car. Each time, we would catch up on life and he would update me on how he was doing with the Lord. The couple of visits I made to his house were fruitful. I spoke to him and prayed over him for large amounts of time on each visit. By God's grace, Jerry ended up becoming committed to his uncles' church once again and every time I talked with him his walk with God was improving. He confessed that he was still struggling with some of his vices here and there, but that he was slowly overcoming them. Our prayer was that he be thoroughly discipled, counseled, and set free at his church.

South Beach

As we drove into the heart of South Beach we were bombarded with blaring music, piercing lights, and an overwhelming sense of darkness and depravity. The city seemed to be hopelessly lost, yet we were filled with joy and faith because we knew that this night light was going to invade the darkness and lost souls would be saved. Rice rockets and luxurious cars surrounded us as we moved through the bumper-to-bumper traffic at a snails pace. Bling-bling was everywhere and everyone walking the streets seemed like they were out to be the toughest, sexiest, wildest person they could be. Our hearts broke for them. Why were they here? What were they looking for? How could they delight in such darkness and hopelessness? It seemed that most of the people had come to experience joy, love, friendship, and satisfaction, but all they would actually come to find was a cheap, artificial version of all these needs their souls were longing for. South Beach was the perfect place for us to bring the light of the Gospel because it answered all of their questions and satisfied all of their desires in a real way.

We parked on Collins Avenue with the beautiful, serene beach on our right and a wild, raging party scene on our left. Brooke, Michael, and I prayerfully walked by the upscale restaurants and through the crowds of richly clad men and women. The place was teeming with people, but we wanted God to direct us to the ones He wanted us to speak to that night.

We continued walking and eventually Brooke and Michael began saying, "What are we waiting for? Let's talk to somebody." They were waiting on me to initiate a conversation with a group of people, but as I walked through the crowds I had become overwhelmed by the darkness of the place and I had been gripped with the fear of man. No matter how hard I tried I couldn't get myself to initiate a conversation with someone.

So finally, Brooke, in her frustration with me, just walked up to two tall, well-built black men standing by a light post, puffing on their cigars and drinking beer.

As soon as we mentioned the name "Jesus", one of the men shouted, "Oh no! I'm in trouble!"

I laughed and said, "God caught you red-handed!"

They seemed to not be able to bear the guilt of having us preach to them while they sinned, so they desperately walked away from us trying to flee the conviction of the Holy Spirit.

Immediately, I turned around and began talking with a middle-aged white American couple. As soon as we mentioned Jesus the woman stepped back, but the man curiously spoke with Michael and I. The moment I asked him if he had a relationship with God, a man who was a few feet away from him exclaimed, "I don't want to hear about this! Don't talk to me about God!"

I responded, "Sir, we aren't talking with you. We're talking with him."

The man snapped back, "He's my cousin. He doesn't want to hear you. He's just being polite. Leave him alone!"

I could see the struggle going on in the man's spirit because he wanted to be respectful and was a bit curious to talk with us, but he didn't want to disrespect his cousin. He muttered a few words to us quickly, but then a group of about six people joined them and one of the men who appeared to be in his 40's loudly joked, "I am God! I'm my own God! Ha, Ha, Ha!"

So the man we were speaking with looked at us apologetically, turned around, and walked away with his friends.

Brooke was deep into a conversation with another person, so Michael and I continued walking to talk with some more people. Michael noticed an elderly man seated on a bench, so he walked over to him and began conversing with him.

As I glanced over at the beach, I saw a sight that nearly moved me to tears. A man directly across from me was dressed in a mini skirt, bikini top, pink shoes, wearing lots of makeup, and had a feminine haircut. His hairy chest, belly and legs were all exposed and some girls were flirting with him and taking pictures with him. My heart broke when I saw this man. I could see that he was just a wounded boy who was desperately crying out for someone to genuinely love him.

I walked up to the man with a genuine desire to demonstrate God's love for him and to open his eyes to the Hope of salvation. Surprisingly, Edward had no hostility towards me when I asked him if he knew Jesus. Instead, he was very friendly, wide-open to hearing the Gospel, and gladly walked away from the party scene to have a one-on-one conversation with me on a park bench. Michael and Brooke soon after joined us. He kindly listened to us as we shared the Gospel with him and he even remarked that he loved God and Jesus.

A few minutes later, a group of about seven Arab, tough-looking guys in their twenties ganged up around us and began demanding that Edward pay them back the forty bucks that he had stolen from them. I was shocked by these young men's behavior because they appeared to be preppy, well-educated people who were most likely college graduates or students. Edward told them that he didn't have forty bucks and he had never stolen anything from them. One of the men began yelling and threatening him saying that if he didn't pay the money back in five seconds they would beat him up. The man aggressively took off his shirt and was getting ready to swing at Edward when I stood up in front of him and said, "Hey! What are you doing? Leave him alone! Do you think this is worth forty bucks? You wanna go to jail just because of forty bucks?"

I had no idea what effect that statement made on the band of young Arabs, but the man who was threatening Edward put his shirt back on and yelled, "If I see you again I'll put a bullet in your head!"

Another guy said, "Next time we see you, you better have the forty bucks!"

I took the opportunity to witness to the mob by boldly confronting them and saying, "Hey! Could I ask you guys a question?"

They all froze for a second and looked at me with a scowling, confused expression on their faces.

"We've been telling people about God tonight," I began, "And I want to ask you, if you were to die tonight where would you go?"

They all walked away and shouted with disgust such outbursts as, "I don't care about God," "I don't believe in God," and "Ahh!"

As soon as the men left, Edward asked me to please walk him all the way to the bus stop, so that he could leave Miami-Dade County safely. He feared for his life. He told me that it was not the first time that those guys had messed with him, but it was the first time that they had threatened to beat him up and even kill him. He said that they knew he lived in Hialeah, so he wanted to move all the way up to West Palm Beach tonight. It was a long walk to the bus stop, but it was great because I got to talk to him the entire way.

As I lovingly preached the Gospel to him, I realized that he had a genuine hunger for God. I also saw that he was full of pain, loneliness, and emptiness. He asked me why God had allowed his mother to die and he told me that he had no family except for an aunt. He made a living by being tipped for dancing in front of bars, clubs, and businesses. He claimed to have made several friends through his work, but I could see that he was deeply lonely inside. He had no family, probably no real friends, was constantly being harassed and made fun of, and everyone looked at him and treated him like a freak. From spending time with him,

I realized that all he was looking for was love and healing. I implored him to find a good church to be a part of, but inside of me I wept for him because I knew that the vast majority of churches would never accept him because he was a 'freak'.

His bus arrived before I was able to offer him the opportunity to give his life to Jesus, but I knew that God done his work and that Edward would never forget us. I was thankful that I was still able to pray for him before he hopped onto the bus. He was overwhelmingly grateful to us for having stood firmly alongside him and for saving him from the hostile mob of men. He was convinced that if it weren't for us he would've been dead right now or in the hospital. Before getting on the bus, Edward looked me in the eyes and said to me, "Now I know that God really loves me because He sent you guys to save my life."

*

After Edward got on the bus, I found Michael and Brooke and joined them in witnessing to more people. Michael was talking with two teenagers and Brooke was talking with a really old homeless man who I later on discovered was nicknamed "Bad Santa". He actually looked like a skinny version of Santa and he had a large bottle of liquor in his hand. He had a white beard that was straight, thin, and about a foot long in length. He wore a dirty skully on his head and his face was so red that it looked like he had been tanning all day long.

While Brooke talked to Bad Santa, I struck up a conversation with a homeless man named Roger who was sitting on a bench next to Brooke. He was also drinking a large bottle of liquor and staring off into space. He was fairly drunk by the time I met him, but as we talked his responses showed that he was following and comprehending everything I was saying. He claimed to be a member of the Catholic church and to have struggles same-sex attraction.

I preached the Gospel to him as he attentively listened. I was astonished at how much he understood and how open he was to the

Gospel even though I candidly explained to him that homosexual sex was a sin. The moment I stated that Jesus died on the cross in order to pay the penalty for his sin he began weeping profusely. I asked him if he wanted to believe in Jesus and repent of his sins and, with tears streaming down his face, he exclaimed, "Yes! Yes! Oh yes I do!" So we prayed together and he gave his life to the Lord.

Feeling that he hadn't understood what repentance meant, I explained it to him further and asked if he truly wanted to repent of drinking, smoking, illicit sex, cursing, etc. "Yes!" He declared. I reiterated to him that if he truly wanted to follow Jesus he would have to end his homosexual lifestyle. He responded, "Yes! I know it's wrong! I don't want to do it anymore!" He wept openly for about five or six minutes, from the time I had mentioned Jesus death on the cross all the way up to the end of our conversation.

Now, he was drunk. I honestly did not know if he had truly committed his life to the Lord, if he would ever remember our conversation, or if he understood the decision he had just made. Only God knew. However, I had faith that God truly did touch and save him. Also, Brooke mentioned that his face looked totally different after I had spoken with him from when she had first seen him.

A Day With Punks

Aventura is a small, upper-class city that is filled with Jewish people, retired snowbirds from New York and Canada, and wealthy immigrants from Latin America and Europe. The Aventura Mall is the third largest mall in America and is the most posh shopping center I have ever visited. Thus, it attracts residents and tourists from all of South Florida and is a prime location for evangelism.

The mall is only a fifteen-minute drive from my house, so it is a common place for me to go witnessing. So today I decided to evangelize at the Aventura Mall, but the first few people I spoke with were all Christians. One man was even an evangelist and he preached to me for about half-an-hour. I was growing weary of talking to Christians, so I prayed, "Lord, lead me to the people You want me to speak to today. Lead me to those who truly need You."

Suddenly, I saw an old friend of mine from high school. He was a Wiccan and a full-blown punk with a two-foot, multi-colored mohawk. He was standing in a circle with about five other punk friends as they joked around with each other. I greeted him, chitchatted with him for a bit, and then he introduced me to his circle of friends. He excitedly told me that he had just gotten engaged as he proudly held up his fiancés hand showing off the ring he had bought for her. They had only been dating for a few months and at the age of eighteen they were deciding to get married. They had no idea what they were getting into. My heart broke for them and I wanted to talk to him about the weight of his decision, but they randomly decided to walk off by themselves.

So I was left standing around with a crew of punks that I had just met. It was a somewhat awkward situation since we didn't know each other and the only guy I knew from the group had left, but I felt the Lord guiding me to hang out with them. They all went inside the mall and sat inside the food court, so I tagged along and they didn't seem to mind at all. I smiled at the irony of a bunch of punks choosing the mall as a hangout spot.

Sitting at the table, they all seemed to be bored out of their minds as they monotonously rambled off pointless statements or stared off into space. I sat next to Trevor, who was hopelessly staring into nothingness. He had on a black vest full of sinister patches, a few piercings, and an ungelled mohawk, but none of those things intimidated me.

I decided to strike up a friendly conversation with Trevor and slowly lead it into Christ.

"So Trevor, how you doin' man?" I calmly asked.

"I'm super pissed off!" he vented, "My ex-girlfriend is with another guy now and I'm so pissed off at her! Every time I see her I just get so angry. I don't know what to do with myself. I've already had several anxiety attacks because of it."

"Man, I'm sorry to hear that," I compassionately responded, "How long ago did you guys break up?"

"Just a few weeks ago," he resentfully stated, "and now she's all in love with this guy. Ahhh! It get's me so mad!"

"That sucks man," I sympathized, "What do you do to relieve all your stress?"

"I don't know what to do anymore," he frustratingly responded flopping his hands into the air as if giving up.

"You know Trevor," I began, "when I'm stressed out I just pray man. I just pour out my heart to God and tell Him what I'm going through and all the pain and stress just leaves. And then He fills me with peace. It's awesome man. Do you believe in God Trevor?"

"Nah," he quietly responded, "I'm an atheist. There's nothing you could tell me that could convince me that there's a God."

This led into a deep conversation about God and Christianity that lasted well over an hour. We covered several topics including atheism, agnosticism, Judaism, the person of Jesus, Trevor's life story, my testimony, and, of course, the Gospel.

Trevor explained to me that he was Jewish and had attended synagogue for most of his life. He had even visited some churches, but was always weirded out by them. However, his father was an atheist and during the past few years Trevor had become a convinced atheist as well.

I shared with Trevor why I personally believed in God, how God had powerfully transformed my life, and what my relationship with God was like. Surprisingly, he was very attentive and seemed to be impressed by all that I was sharing. As soon as I finished speaking, however, he immediately brought up several arguments he had against Christianity and the person of Jesus. We tackled each argument, one at a time, until all of them had been totally dismantled.

Once all of his walls had been taken down, I was finally able to share the Gospel with him. For the first time in his life, Trevor was openly hearing and comprehending the Gospel message. It was beautiful. Towards the end of our conversation he made a remark that impacted and encouraged me so much.

"You know," he began, "this is the first peaceful conversation I have ever had in my life about God. Yeah," he chuckled as he reminisced, "Usually I just yell at the person and cuss them out 'till they leave. Sometimes I just throw something at them. I absolutely hate talking with people about God, but for some reason I've been nice to you and I've listened to everything you said."

"Praise God!" I responded, "Well Trevor, I want to encourage you to live for God man and to give your life to Him. He loves you so much and all you have to do is put your faith in Him, believe in what He did for you on the cross, and repent of your sins. Do you want to give your life to Jesus Trevor?"

All of a sudden, that gentle spirit he had carried for a time morphed back into the little rebel he was trying so hard to be.

"Honestly man," he frankly replied, "everything you said was really nice, but even if I saw Jesus crucifixion and miracles right in front of my eyes I would still not believe. I hate being told what to do. That's why I'm a punk with a mohawk. That's why I believe in anarchy. I love to sin and I don't want to change. I'm an atheist Josh. I'm not just gonna start believing in God."

I was saddened by his heartless response after we had enjoyed such a rich conversation. He appeared to have been genuinely impacted by the Gospel, but some kind of demonic force seemed to have been influencing him to reject Jesus. I prayed over him and then he decided to leave.

When Trevor left, I moved over a couple of seats to talk with the last two remaining punk kids at the table. Their names were Danny and Eva. I struck up a conversation with them in a friendly way just like I had with Trevor, but they had already overheard me speaking with Trevor, so it was a lot quicker and easier to transition the conversation to Jesus. Danny casually told me that he was gay and that he has a boyfriend that he's been with for a while now. Eva had been crying for a long time when I was talking with Trevor, but I didn't know why. She shared with me that it was because her boyfriend had left her and was now engaged with another girl. Luckily, she hadn't been present when I had greeted my friend because he was the ex-boyfriend that she was referring to who was now engaged to another girl.

I eventually asked them, "So do you have a relationship with God?"

"No, not at all," they both humbly responded.

"Do you guys believe in God?" I continued.

"Yeah, we do," they replied, "We just don't follow Him, or pray, or go to church or nothing like that."

"I've been to church before, "Danny proceeded, "But they don't really like me to be there cause I'm just different than they are."

"And what do you guys think about Jesus?" I asked.

"Honestly," they simultaneously responded, "We don't really know anything about Jesus. Yeah...umm...we're pretty ignorant about Him."

"Well, is it okay if I share with you guys why I believe in Jesus?" I politely inquired.

"Of course. Of course," they kindly answered with an air of anticipation in their tone of voice. They're eyes were poised on me and they sincerely wanted to hear why I personally believed in and followed Jesus. I could tell that their curiosity was aroused to hear how I could be so passionately devoted to Someone they hardly believed in.

So with this open door into their hearts and minds I wholeheartedly explained the Gospel to them. At the end of it all I asked them, "Do you see why Jesus is the only way to Heaven and why we must believe in Him?"

They both responded as if a light bulb had turned on in their brains, "Yeah, I understand. I never had someone sit down and explain to me everything about Jesus and your analogies really helped me understand it better. The way you put it all together makes total sense."

"So do you guys want to give your lives to Jesus?" I asked full of faith and excitement.

"You know what...I think we will," they thoughtfully responded, still trying to fully grasp the Gospel story I had just explained to them, "But I honestly don't think we're ready yet."

I understood their desire to be genuine in their decision and I respected that, but I still urged them to give their lives to Jesus. They thanked me for the talk and I finished our time together by praying over them.

Trevor returned to the table as soon as we had finished our conversation and he bombarded me with questions about the Bible, such as the virgin birth and the end of the world. He didn't barrage me with questions as an arrogant skeptic this time, but rather as a student yearning to learn more about a whole new concept that he had never been aware of before.

We all went to the bus stop together and there I spoke with two other punk kids for about thirty minutes. I got everyone's phone number from the punk clique I had witnessed to and I went on my way back home on the city bus. I had hung out with the punk kids for about four hours and they all asked me when we could hang out again. I wasn't sure when we would hang out again, but I sure was looking forward to it.

CONVERSATIONS WITH MEN

I jumped out of bed excited to conquer the day. I quickly got dressed, ran down the spiral staircase, and happily ate my granola cereal for breakfast. As I ate breakfast I read from *Operation World*, which is one of the most amazing books in the world. It contains a rich amount of detailed information about all the countries in the world, including tiny islands. The authors thoroughly explain all the answers to prayer and all the challenges for prayer in each nation. The book is organized in such a fashion that by the end of the year a person will have read about and prayed for every single nation in the world. Therefore, every morning while I was eating breakfast I would read about the nation of the day and during my prayer time I would intercede before God on behalf of that nation. On this particular day I had read about the Dominican Republic and lifted up that nation before God in my time of prayer and all throughout the day this nation lay heavily upon my heart.

Again, I enjoyed a peaceful walk through my neighborhood as I made my way over to the bus stop. However, once I boarded the bus and sat down I couldn't muster up the courage to stand up and preach as I usually did. Little did I know that God had other plans. I sat there struggling within myself about whether I should get up and preach or not. Finally, I felt peace to just relax and not worry about it. So I pulled out my book and peacefully read.

Suddenly, the man next to me asked me in Spanish, "Where did you buy those pants? I really like them."

Caught by surprise I stumbled over my words, "I don't.... don't really remember sir. I'm sorry. But I'm sure that you could find pants like these at the Aventura Mall."

"Okay. Thank you very much. I really like their material," he graciously replied.

This insignificant, little question opened the door for me to speak with Raul, a very wealthy businessman from Santo Domingo, Dominican Republic. He was light skinned, but slightly tanned and was obviously of direct Spanish descent. I could not perceive any Native or Afro mix in his genes as most Dominicans have. He had a slender, fit figure, hair neatly combed to side, and the perfect, well-trimmed mustache one would picture on a stereotypical Spaniard. He had on well-pressed khaki pants with a polo shirt, new sneakers, and a leather belt. Without saying a word, I already knew that this man was well to do, but when he opened his mouth I knew that this man was definitely a part of the upper class of the DR. His speech was impeccable. Every word he spoke was well pronounced, highly intelligent, but above all, formal and respectful. This man had class. And yet, little ol' me was being given the opportunity to share the Gospel with this man. Had I open air preached I am certain he would have never said a word to me because he would have been offended and thought I had no class. But God had put unrest in my heart to not open air preach, had given me peace to read my book, and for some strange reason this man happened to take interest in my four-year-old pair of pants that I randomly decided to put on that morning. God is so much fun. He works in the most mysterious and, sometimes, humorous ways.

So I began a simple dialogue in Spanish with Raul. He explained to me that he was on vacation in Miami and just wanted to do some shopping. We talked a little bit about the Dominican Republic and when I told him that my family was Brazilian we talked about Brazil. I was getting a little frustrated because I couldn't seem to turn the conversation around to Jesus. I could already tell from our casual conversation that if I were to bluntly bring up Jesus in our dialogue he would immediately close up and shun me. I felt stuck. Suddenly, the Holy Spirit reminded me that I had just read about and prayed for the Dominican Republic earlier that morning.

"You know what's funny?" I began, "Just this morning I read about the Dominican Republic and I spent much time praying for your country. Isn't that funny?"

Raul was intrigued by the fact that a young man my age would spend time reading about and praying for his small country. This immediately caught his attention. I began to explain to him how I prayed for all the nations of the world by using *Operation World* and that today was the day for the Dominican Republic.

Boldly, I continued, "And you know what Raul. I believe God had me pray about your nation because He knew that today I would meet you."

"I must admit," he stated with reservation, "that is interesting."

"Do you have a relationship with God Raul?" I politely inquired.

This opened us up into a whole new conversation that lasted at least thirty minutes. We began talking about the meaning of life and the reasons why God created us. I enthusiastically shared with him some bits of my testimony, yet I could tell that although he was enjoying the conversation he still had a sliver of skepticism in the back of his mind. Finally, I explained the whole Gospel to him and the entire time he respectfully conversed with me and listened.

At last, he began to be honest with me and explain his thoughts and emotions. He shared with me that he was raised his whole childhood as a Catholic. He also had a very good friend who was a strong Christian, and another close friend who was a pastor. Both of these friends of his have talked to him constantly about Christ, but for some reason, even though he was brought up as a Catholic and has strong Christian friends who preach to him he just cannot get himself to believe in God, Jesus, the Gospel, or the Bible. He respected it all and, at times, wished he could believe it, but for some reason he could not get himself to sincerely believe in any aspect of Christianity. His way of thinking was atheistic and he couldn't free himself from that atheistic box even though, sometimes, he wished that he could.

I passionately challenged him to believe in God and give His life to Jesus. I elaborated on several of the reasons why I believed in God, but nothing seemed to change his mind. "What holds you back from believing?" I asked him.

"I don't know. I really don't know," he candidly replied, "Honestly, I don't have any reasons for why I don't believe in God. I just simply cannot get myself to sincerely believe in Him."

"If you seek Him you will find Him, Raul," I pleaded with him, "Just take a step of faith and seek Him and you will see that He is real."

"I don't know," he said, "Maybe when I get older I'll believe."

I couldn't believe my ears. I had heard many teenagers and young adults say such a statement, but never would I have thought that I would hear a 71-year-old man saying such a ridiculous statement. Part of me wanted to burst out in laughter and the other part of me wanted to weep over Raul because he was so blind. I prayed for Raul and we parted ways.

*

Eventually, I arrived at the Aventura Mall and, immediately, God drew me to a Colombian man from Bogota. He was in Miami on vacation and when I approached him he was very polite and friendly. He was completely open towards God, so I began zealously speaking to him about Jesus. His eyes were glued on me and he was attentive to every word I uttered. He seemed to be deeply impacted by what I was telling him. He shared with me that He was a strong Catholic who daily prayed to the Virgin Guadalupe and Virgin Carmen. Thus, I kindly and gently explained to him why Christians believe praying and/or worshipping the virgins and saints is idolatry. He wasn't at all offended, so I asked him if he agreed with what I had said concerning idolatry. He replied that it made sense and that he had never put much thought into it before, especially from the angle I had explained it from. He promised to consider everything I had said and to seek God more. Although he didn't want to make a commitment to follow Christ right then and there, he was truly impacted and sincerely thanked me for our conversation and the prayer I prayed over him.

As I continued walking around the mall, I found a heavy-set, elderly man named Francisco who seemed to be vegging on a bench by himself. He wore thick, square glasses, was dressed in sweatpants and a white shirt, and had a brown skin complexion. He was definitely over six-feet-tall and had a huge potbelly that rested on his thighs. I casually sat next to him on the bench and began a friendly conversation with him. He was extremely friendly and happily conversed with me about several different topics. Eventually, I asked him about his faith and he began to explain his religious background and share parts of his life story.

Francisco was from Cuba and had been a Catholic his entire life. He genuinely loved God with all of his heart, read the Bible, and would spend time in prayer on a regular basis. He expounded on the point that he loved Christians and had many close Pentecostal friends who would take him to their churches quite frequently. He thoroughly enjoyed the worship and preaching at Pentecostal churches, but he also loved the solitude and reverence he experienced in the Catholic Church. After talking with him for a good while I was convinced that he was a true believer and that God was sovereignly moving in his life.

He then began telling me all about Cuba and how it was before Fidel Castro took over. I felt like a little boy having his grandfather sit down with him and tell him old war stories as this man shared with me his fun and horrific experiences with a communist government. He said that before Fidel took over Cuba in 1958 it was the most prosperous country in all of Latin America and now it was one of the poorest Latin American countries. Now, when people go to the government-controlled supermarkets where everyone is supposed to receive free food that is distributed equally amongst all citizens there is practically no food to distribute. Public transportation is completely incompetent to where you have to wait hours in line in order to catch a bus. There are only two television channels, which are both run by the government and there is only one hour of old cartoons that play each day from 5 p.m. to 6 p.m. Religion is illegal and many churches have been demolished. In fact, both Christmas and Easter are illegal holidays to celebrate in Cuba.

However, all of a sudden, he changed from being in a somber attitude to a joyous mood and began urging me to become a missionary to Cuba. I was blown away! Here I am challenging this man to serve God with more devotion and now he's the one challenging me to be a missionary to his communist nation. God is hilarious!

He began explaining to me with excitement, "I still visit my country every year or two and in the past few years something extraordinary has been happening in Cuba! Everywhere I go all the churches are overflowing with people and new churches are being planted everywhere. There are people standing outside the doors, peering in through the windows, and inside the buildings there isn't one foot of space because they are so packed with people.

"Before, whenever I came to Cuba I would bring them many different presents, but now everyone just asks me to bring more Bibles.

That's all they want now! So I fill my suitcases with Bibles every time I go to Cuba. You should go there as a missionary right now. Now is the greatest time to be a missionary to Cuba. I mean, you probably will be persecuted by the government, but the people are so open and hungry for God!"

*

I took a small break after speaking with my newfound friend and strolled around the mall asking the Lord to guide me to the next person He wanted me to speak to. As I walked through the central plaza of the mall I spotted a black man sitting by himself on a bench. I felt compelled to approach him, so I politely introduced myself to him saying, "Excuse me sir. How are you doing? My name is Joshua and I've just been going around today encouraging people to follow Jesus."

"No, no, no, no, no," he rudely snapped, "I don't want to talk about Jesus. Don't talk to me."

God burned within me to persist with this man and not give up so easily on him, so I pleaded with him, "But sir, do you know God? Do you follow Him with all of your heart?"

Suddenly, he let his guard down and confessed, "I believe in Jesus man. I am a Baptist, but I have not been to church in a long time. Go ahead man. You could sit down."

I sat down on the bench next to him and attempted to share the Gospel with him, but he would barely permit to me to say a word. Instead, he just poured his heart out to me and shared all the burdens and hardships he had been experiencing in his life. For over an hour, this middle-aged Haitian man completely humbled and exposed himself to a nineteen-year-old, Latino boy. This was nothing short of a miracle. Since I was familiar with Haitian culture, I knew that grown men never sought counsel from teenagers and they were not always so friendly towards people of other ethnicities. I felt humbled and honored to have been the one to listen to this man's pain and struggles and to be able to comfort him with prayer and encouragement.

With much pain in his eyes and frustration in his voice, he explained to me that his wife had died due to cocaine. He did not know that she had been using cocaine and by the time that he discovered it she had already become addicted. Eventually, she overdosed on the drug and died. His wife's family was furious with him and blamed him for killing their relative, so they took his children away from him and prohibited him from seeing them. Moreover, his own family, including his very own mother and brothers, hated him, envied his money, and were convinced that his wife's death was his fault.

For the past few years, he had been in a committed relationship with another Haitian woman. She claimed to be a Christian and she attended church regularly with him. However, he just recently broke up with this woman because he found out that she had secretly been using cocaine as well.

Now, he was completely alone. He had no family, no children, and no friends. He was broken. This was the exact moment that God had me walk into his life. God used me simply to be a friend that he could dump his problems on and, for that, I was grateful.

I tried to speak sometimes with the hope of encouraging him and pointing him to Jesus, but he would always speak over me. So I only spoke when he would rest from talking. I prayed for him with great compassion and he seemed to be comforted at the end of it all. He thanked me for speaking with him and we went our separate ways.

CHAPTER TWO

ORLANDO

Preparation And Anticipation

My heart was exploding with excitement. At last, I would be fully immersed in a life of faith and trust in God. For the first time in my life I would have to rely completely on God for my daily bread, shelter, direction, safety, and survival. No parents would be providing for my constant needs and I would have no job promising me a steady income. I would have no guaranteed home to lay my head, no safe neighborhood I could depend on, and no back up plans. This was the life I had always dreamt of living for God, but never had had the opportunity to explore. My anticipation and excitement were soaring higher than the clouds. Of course, I knew that I might have some days of homelessness and hunger, but that would be no sacrifice compared to the joy of bringing the Gospel to the lost. I knew that God would provide, but if Paul had to go through such hardships then I was ready to go through them as well.

The mission trip had begun one month before in Miami, but the element of living by faith had still not come into play. The Lord had told me to offer up the first month of my trip as a first fruits offering to my home church and hometown. I am glad I obeyed.

As I witnessed in Miami, I realized that I was not yet spiritually and mentally prepared to be witnessing all day, every day. Although I had many powerful encounters witnessing to people I often felt weak, confused, and very alone. I soon realized that God's caring hand had allowed me to stay in Miami as a time of training and spiritual formation. No one had trained me to carry out this mission and I had no leader or team with me. My only teacher and team was the Holy Spirit. He had to teach me how to obediently and passionately preach the Gospel for eight hours a day, six days a week. It was much easier for me to be trained in my hometown with the support of my family, friends, and church then for me to have been trained in a new place with no one to fall back on.

Furthermore, during my time witnessing in Miami I still had not found a partner who was willing to go with me across the country. I had several different friends preach the Gospel with me for a day or two, but I noticed how significantly more difficult it was for me to evangelize with confidence on the days I was alone. Jesus sent out his disciples two-by-two and I had been praying for a partner to come with for several months, but none of my friends could come. Either they were still in school, had a fixed job, their parents wouldn't let them go, or they simply didn't feel ready to embark on such a radical journey.

However, two days before I left for Orlando I met a young man who would eventually become my companion for this expedition. I was scheduled to leave for Orlando on a Monday morning, but on the Saturday before I left for my trip my brother put together a house concert and art show in our home. All the artists and performers who were coming to our party were friends of ours from church, work, school, and our neighborhood who happened to write songs, play in a band, or create art. So we invited them to our home to perform their music and display their art. We had at least a dozen performers play, just as many artists submit their work, and well over one hundred people attend. All of the performers and all but one of the artists were Christian and everything that was played and shown was original.

So in the midst of this incredible party I met my soon-to-be revolutionary compadre, Alex Diaz. About thirty minutes before the concert began one of the main bands had come to setup their equipment for the show. They were accompanied by a handful of groupies who quickly began perusing the artwork displayed throughout the house. I was in my room making some final touches on a couple of art pieces when one of them walked right in.

He was a tiny little guy standing at about 5' 2" with a scruffy beard and a sly smile. Yet he simultaneously had the look of a tough-as-nails, punk anarchist who could cuss you out without a moment's notice. He had some pretty stylin' dreads that were over a foot long and had colorful beads around them, but it was obvious that he had done them himself because they weren't the neatest. He wore the typical black, punk jeans that were extra tight, spotted with colorful patches, and a few chains hanging out from the pockets. He was also wearing an extra small punk band t-shirt, some metal rings, several different colored bracelets, and a cool necklace.

I welcomed him in and struck up a friendly conversation with him. We sat down on a padded bench in the room and started to get to know each other. My immediate assumption was that he was a vegan, anarchist punk who was either an atheist or agnostic. I was excited to share the Gospel with him, so I thought that telling him about my upcoming trip across America would be a cool way to introduce Jesus into the conversation. I was shocked, however, by Alex's response.

"So," I began, "on Monday I'm gonna leave for six months to preach the Gospel across America. I'm not taking any money or any car. I'm just gonna go."

Out of nowhere, Alex bolted straight up in his seat bursting with excitement as if he were a little kid who had just been told that he was going to Disneyworld. His eyes brightened up as he exclaimed, "Dude!!! Could I go with you man!!!? Could I go? That's been my dream for so long...to just walk across the country with no money preaching the Gospel every day. You don't understand. I've been wanting to do this for forever man!"

Startled by the revelation that the guy I thought was an atheist punk who desperately needed Jesus was actually a radical Christian, I conservatively responded to his child-like exuberance by asking, "What about your parents?"

"My mom will totally let me," he declared with such confidence, "she doesn't care at all. I don't even need to ask her. I just tell her where I'm going and she always just says 'okay'. If I tell her I'm going across America for six months to preach the Gospel she'll be totally fine with it. It's no problem man. She's used to me doing crazy things and being away for extended periods of time."

"Okay. Cool man," I responded with astonishment at his mom's willingness to let him do whatever he wanted. Still with a bit of unbelief that this guy was actually serious about joining me I asked, "What about school or work?"

"I'm done with high school," Alex answered, "and I've been working at Waldenbooks, but I could just quit. It's no problem. I was going to go to community college next semester, but I could just wait until after the mission trip to go."

So many thoughts were rushing through my head as I heard Alex making all these statements. On the one hand, I was overjoyed that for the first time in nearly a year of fruitlessly asking dozens of my friends to come with me, I had finally met someone who had no excuses and was ready to just do it. I had been praying for months for God to provide me with a partner and Alex would be a direct answer to my prayers only two days before leaving for Orlando. It sounded too good to be true.

On the other hand, I had just met this guy and I had no clue who he really was, if he had serious issues, and if he was sent from God to be my partner or sent from the devil to destroy this mission trip. I didn't want to be naïve and invite someone who wasn't living in holiness and had serious issues in their life that could jeopardize this entire mission. I was full of mixed emotions.

Too many people were walking in and out of my room by now to view the artwork, so we moved downstairs into the den to have a little more privacy as we prayed and talked more seriously about the trip. So Alex and I talked for about an hour as the bands began playing their music in the living room. He shared his testimony with me and I shared my testimony with him. He told me about his walk with the Lord since he had been saved merely two years before. Then we discussed the logistics of the trip. Alex explained that although his mom would definitely allow him to go and he could easily quit his job, he had already made a commitment to go to Shane Claiborne's house in Camden, New Jersey for ten days. He simply wanted to meet Shane, hang out at their community house, do ministry with them, and learn from them.

"That's perfect," I concluded with peace in my heart, "So I'll leave on Monday by myself and you could go to New Jersey. And during those 10 days or so we'll seriously pray about whether or not it's God's will for us to do this trip together. If we both feel peace in our spirit for you to come then you could join me, but if either of us does not feel peace I'll just continue on my own."

Excitement filled the air as I understood that this could be the partner I had been praying for God to provide for so many months, and as Alex realized that he was possibly about to embark on the most epic journey of his life. It was surreal how much peace and joy I felt within a few minutes of meeting my new friend and hearing his passion to preach the Gospel and follow Jesus alongside me.

Overwhelmed by the glory of God's sovereignty in orchestrating our meeting exactly two days before my journey began, we prayed together. We soon joined the house concert since Alex's friend's band was about to play and I was going to be performing later on as well.

During the show, I introduced Alex to my parents, my brother, and to Brooke. They all liked him very much and committed to pray along with us for God to confirm if it was His will for Alex to join me on my trip.

*

Alex later shared with me his side of the story of our first encounter. Here's his account of what happened:

I met Josh at a house party that he threw to raise money for Invisible Children to help them build a school for kids in Uganda. A friend of mine named Henry, who played in an amazing band called Mod'lone, invited me to the party and told me that he would like me to meet Josh. I was really excited to go, but unfortunately I had to work on that day, so I wasn't going to be able to attend the party.

Oddly enough, however, on the day of the party my manager called me to say, "Alex, don't come in today. We got someone to cover your shift."

I thought to myself, "But I didn't ask anyone to cover my shift." Immediately, I realized it was God intervening, so that I could go to the concert. As I walked out the door I jumped for joy praising God and hoping that no one had noticed that I was talking to myself.

When I arrived at the party, Mod'lone began setting up the stage to get ready for their performance. Meanwhile, I waited in Josh's room staring at all the art on his walls. Josh walked in and we began chatting. He told me about his vision of preaching the Gospel across America and I immediately asked him if I could join him on his mission trip.

He explained, "Well, I have been praying for a partner and I'm leaving in two days."

So I thought to myself, "Wow, just in time!!! God's plan must be unraveling as we speak." I quickly told him, "I don't care. I'd like to go anyway."

We prayed about it and immediately felt a close spiritual connection. What can I say? It was spiritual love at first sight. So I quit my job, postponed college, and decided to travel across America preaching the gospel everywhere and anywhere with no money, food, or home.

*

So after our first encounter, Alex and I bade each other farewell and I left for Orlando on Monday all by myself. My parents were a bit worried, but I was confident that I would do just fine on my own. That day was a Saturday. On Monday, I was to be launched out on my journey.

The Craziest Night Of My Life

I woke up with my heart beating a million miles per hour. At last, the day had arrived. I confidently grabbed my backpack that I had packed the night before and wore it with an air of adventure.

"There's nothing to hold me back now," I thought to myself, "This is what I was made for. This is going to be so awesome!"

I ate breakfast with my parents as my mother tried to look excited for me even though she was holding back countless tears of worry and fear. My father was calm and reassuring of my mission. Regardless of their composure at the kitchen table, both of them were proud of their son for choosing to follow Jesus in such a radical way even though they did not know what the future had in store for me.

We finally got into the car and made our way over to the Greyhound bus station. My parents walked me out to the line of people that was rapidly diminishing as the passengers entered the bus. They stood by my side the entire time in the line. When it finally came my turn to store my bag under the bus and step on board my parents each gave me a huge hug as tears welled up in their eyes. They quickly prayed over me and blessed me on this journey God was calling me to.

I took out my wallet and handed my dad my credit and debit card.

"I won't be needing these," I told them.

As I looked into my dad's eyes I could see him silently saying, "Are you sure son? You might need these in case of an emergency."

Balling her eyes out, my mom quickly fumbled through her wallet, pulled out forty dollars, and cried, "Here Joshua! Here! Please take this! This is all I have with me. I wish I had more, but this is all I have in my wallet right now."

"Mom," I gently responded, "you know the rule, that I have to go out with no money."

"Please Joshua!" she begged.

"Okay mom. I'm sorry. Thank you so much." Thus, out of honor for my mother I gratefully received the forty dollars and began my journey of faith with some money in my pocket.

I finally got situated in my seat and bade farewell to Miami. The journey had finally begun.

On the greyhound bus I fearfully kept silent from 11:40 am to 3:30 pm. It was one of the greatest struggles I had ever experienced in being obedient to God when He commanded me to preach. Yet I realized it was all part of His plan because at each stop the bus would fill up with more people without anyone getting off board. By the time we reached Fort Pierce the bus had become almost entirely full. My heart seemed to be growing bigger and bigger as time went by to the point that it literally felt like something in my chest was going to explode. It was an overwhelming, yet painless sensation. Finally, I stood up and began preaching the Gospel to everyone on the bus. Honestly, I was barely conscious of what I was saying and I knew that God was the one who was speaking through me. I had nearly finished sharing the Gospel message when the assistant bus driver ran up to me, looked me straight in the eyes, and, with a firm, yet quiet voice, repeatedly told me to stop and sit down. I eventually obeyed the driver out of respect and intimidation. I abruptly ended my message with an encouragement for everyone to seek God. Then I said a quick "God bless you all" and sat down. I continued quietly praying for everyone on the bus for a good amount of time.

There were probably more than eighty people on that bus. Many individuals, Christian and non-Christian, walked up to me once we got off of the bus and thanked me for having had the boldness to preach the

Gospel. One woman told me to be encouraged by the fact that the bus driver shut me down because Jesus said that we would be persecuted for preaching the Gospel. A young man who was not a believer complimented me for being such a captivating speaker.

Those small words of encouragement were a breath of fresh air for a soul who already felt like a coward for bowing down to the fear of man on the first day of his journey outside of Miami.

Once I arrived in downtown Orlando I preached the Gospel from 4 p.m. to 10:30 p.m. The LYNX bus station was constantly packed with all kinds of people, so I spent the whole day talking with people there.

Finally, as the day came to a close, I was faced with one of the harshest realities of my life: that night I was going to sleep on the streets of downtown Orlando. I had always wondered what it would be like to be homeless and I had always felt confident that I had what it took to rough it out all alone on the concrete, but I had no idea what I was getting into. It's one thing to know a lot of information about something; it's another thing to experience it. I had served in soup kitchens quite a bit, befriended several homeless people, and even taken some people into my parent's home, but I had never been the homeless man myself.

I had all the faith in the world that God was going to provide a place for me on the first night, but I was also mentally prepared to sleep on the street for as long as I had to if that's what God wanted me to go through. I knew that if I had to sleep on the street it was not because God was being unfaithful to provide me, but because He wanted to teach me something and mold my character to be more like Him.

So even as I spoke to the very last woman who was around at the bus station at 10:30 p.m., I was believing that God would move on her heart to host me in her home. However, once the last person left and I was all alone in dark downtown Orlando I was not disheartened and I did not feel that God had let me down. In fact, I knew that it was all part of God's plan. He desired for me to grow through this tough experience.

Thus, with a sense of raw excitement and a bit of worry about the unknown, I prayed and accepted the fact that I was going to sleep on the street that night. I called my parents and asked them to pray for me. They were extremely worried, but at the same time were at peace because they knew I was in God's hands.

I gathered together my few possessions, stood up, and began walking. As the cold wind began to blow through the city streets I suddenly realized that I had forgotten to bring a jacket! Ahhh! I wanted to kick myself. How could I be so stupid? Out of everything that I could have forgotten to bring on this trip it had to be a jacket. I remembered that I had packed one long sleeve shirt and a beanie, so I quickly put them on and was thankful for the small amount of warmth they gave to my body.

I walked around the streets of downtown Orlando for a while looking for a grass area to sleep on. As I walked past a chain-linked fence with a thin green screen wrapped around it, a tear in the screen allowed me to spot an abandoned dirt lot with tons of overgrown weeds and a couple of trees. Feeling a sense of victory from my discovery I hopped over the fence and found a soft spot to sleep on. The dirt was comfortable enough to make it feel like I was sleeping on an odd kind of mattress, the green screen on the fence hid me from any people who were passing by, the high weeds gave me a sense of privacy, and the small tree hanging over me gave me a sense of tranquility. However, my initial optimism soon was darkened by the reality of my wretched experience of trying to sleep on the streets of Orlando.

The night wouldn't have been so miserable if it weren't for the cold. Florida is usually a warm place, even in the winter. However, whenever there is a strong blizzard or snowstorm in the Northeast region of the country the wind currents continue down all the way to Miami. These cold fronts could sometimes be under 40 or 30 degrees Fahrenheit. Since I was completely disconnected from the media I had no idea that a cold front was hitting Florida on my first night sleeping on the streets of Orlando. Later on, I learned that this night had been the coldest night of the year thus far.

The blistering cold wind of the incoming cold front consistently blew with a fair amount of intensity throughout the night. The temperature was so cold that I couldn't feel my hands, nose, or any other part of my body that was exposed to the air. Furthermore, I felt like I barely had any clothes on because even the clothes I was wearing were being easily penetrated by the freezing wind. My body violently shivered throughout the night and the cold made it almost impossible to sleep.

If the cold wasn't bad enough, the spot I had chosen to sleep in made it even worse. I ignorantly chose a place that was directly in between the interstate and the railroad tracks. The interstate wasn't so bad, but the trains were unbearable. Every 45 minutes or so a train would pass by, the ground would tremble, and the train would sound its horn so loud that I had to plug my ears in order to protect my eardrums from exploding. Many times, I was just beginning to sleep when suddenly the train would come by and wake me up again.

Then there were the creatures of the night. For starters, I could feel small bugs and ants crawling on my body, even inside of my shirt and pants. At first, I was annoyed by their presence, but as they began biting me a quick warmth would rush to the surface of my shivering skin. Never in my life had I imagined that I would appreciate bug bites, but that night I did.

To top it all off, at about two in the morning, when I was finally starting to fall asleep, I suddenly felt a rat crawl on my left arm and then onto my chest. I frantically jumped up to my feet and began kicking around the tall weeds like a maniac. Anyone who would have seen me at that moment probably would have thought that I had gone mad. This caused me to become completely paranoid. I feared that I would have to be fighting rats all night long and I honestly felt like I was starting to lose my mind. Yet God, in His mercy, instantly brought to my mind the memory of Mary Slessor saying that at any given time she would have six or seven rats crawling around her small mud hut in Nigeria. I'm sure she experienced rats crawling on her many times throughout her lifetime as a missionary. So if she could live with it, so could I. Bring it on! Let the rats crawl on me. If it's for the sake of the Gospel, I will still sleep in peace. That realization gave me total peace and my fear of rats immediately disappeared.

A greater fear than that of rats was the fear of humans. I had conversed with many homeless people in Miami when I was ministering there and several of them had mentioned that they would often get mugged in their sleep by other homeless people. Also, some cops were hostile towards the homeless and, later on, I found out that in the city of Orlando it was illegal to sleep on the street. Anyone who was caught sleeping on the street would automatically be put in jail for 72 hours.

Many times while I was sleeping, I could clearly hear footsteps coming in my direction and it always sounded like the person was walking right up to me. This would often cause me to wake up to see who was coming for me. Fortunately, I was always relieved to see the person's feet walking by on the other side of the screen-wrapped fence.

What was most horrible, however, was the thought of no relief. The truth is that when someone is cold it's not so bad because they know that soon enough they'll be inside their house, a building, a heated car, or supplied with a good jacket. However, that night I had no comfort because there was no place to go and nothing more to put on. This reality of having no comfort tortured my mind. Perhaps this was a taste of what Hell was like.

I feared that I might not be able to sleep at all, but around 3:30 a.m. I switched from sleeping on my back to sleeping in the fetal position. This enabled me to finally sleep a little because it gave me more body warmth. Two hours later, I woke up from the painful numbness in my leg and arm and I turned to sleep on my other side. I was able to go back to sleep and woke up at 6:50 a.m. as the sun quietly rose over me.

At that moment, I appreciated the warmth of the sun more than ever even though it was still cold outside. As I walked to the bus station, my body wouldn't stop quivering, my lips were swollen from the bug bites, and even my head was twitching. Now I understood how a homeless person could lose his sanity after living on the streets for too long. Now I saw how homelessness could take someone to the point of desperation where they would lose all self-dignity and just begin begging people for money in order to survive. I was never able to grasp it before, but now I could empathize with them a bit.

Only once I found myself in the warmth of a building, sitting down, and eating a honey bun from the snack machine did I feel normal again. I prayed that the following night God would provide me with a place to lay my head.

A Homeless Man

Discouragement overwhelmed me. I had been feeling more like a homeless man than a Christian on a mission for God. The more I talked with people the more I realized that hospitality towards strangers, no matter how godly the stranger may be, was simply not a part of American culture, even amongst American Christians. This saddened me. Also, I've been feeling like God hasn't been providing for me because no one has given me a place to stay, I'm running out of money fast, and no one is giving me money. I haven't asked anyone for anything and I don't plan to.

Nevertheless, that morning I met Salvador Rodriguez, a small-statured Mexican man who worked as a cook in a local restaurant and who had never attended school for one day of his life. He recently committed his life to Christ and was now one of the most joyful, spirit-filled believers I had ever met. I was astounded when he told me that he had been illiterate his entire life, but now, miraculously, he was reading the Bible. He was still unable to read any other book, but when he would read the Bible he had one hundred percent comprehension of what he was reading! As a result of the transformation God had done in his life, he just couldn't stop talking about Jesus.

I was overjoyed to have met him because I had been asking God to guide me to a solid church for me to partner with during my time in Orlando and since he was the most passionate believer I had met thus far I assumed that his church must be a great church as well. So when I asked him about his church he gleefully pulled out a business card with his church's information and invited me to attend.

As I spoke with this loving brother, my mind rushed back to the harsh reality of my current living situation. Then I remembered my mom's testimony of how she went to a church to ask for help when my parents first came to America as missionaries. Assuming that this memory was brought to my mind by the Lord, I broke a rule. I asked him if he knew of anyone in his church who would let me spend the night at their house. He said he didn't know of anyone, but he told me to go ahead and call the pastor's number on the church's card to ask for assistance.

After this quick encounter, I felt led by the Lord to witness at the financial district in downtown Orlando. That was the last place I wanted to witness at after spending my first night on the street as a homeless person. I could feel the stares of the business people as I walked past them. Everyone was dressed in formal business attire and were either working on their laptops or chatting on their smart phone. As they sipped their coffee, chatted on the phone, or conversed with their business partner they would horridly turn their heads to glance at the kid walking by with a huge backpack on, a Bible in his hand, and a disheveled look from a long night spent on the street.

All kinds of feelings of inferiority and intimidation invaded my heart and mind. I felt so filthy speaking to such sophisticated professionals and it seemed like they felt the same way towards me. I was only able to harness the courage to actually approach four different business people and all of them rejected me as soon as I mentioned the name of Jesus.

God had put in my heart a burning compassion to reach out to White Americans, but, in my experience, they always seemed to be the most hard-hearted, stiff-necked people to talk to. Asians were often a mixed bag of responses. Sometimes they were extremely open and sometimes they would be very rude. So whenever I would become discouraged from speaking with White Americans, I would just start talking with Blacks, Latinos, and the homeless because they were almost always open to hearing the Gospel. Even if they didn't want to give their lives to Jesus, they respected God enough to listen to the Gospel and not rudely reject someone who was preaching about Jesus.

So I soon left the financial district and found a Mexican construction worker peacefully leaning against a wall. I quickly shared the Gospel with him and he practically got saved on the spot. He sincerely wanted to give his life to the Lord, but when he looked at his watch he realized that his lunch break was over and he was late in getting back to work.

I then strolled over to Eola Lake where I found a woman intensely weeping. I wanted to be sensitive to her privacy, but I strongly felt the Lord leading me to comfort her with some prayer. So when she had finished weeping I gently approached her and asked if she needed prayer. She said she needed lots of it. I asked her for her name so that I could pray for her and she yelled, "That's the first thing you should pray for me about. I don't even know who I am anymore!" She swirled around and quickly walked away. I prayed for her intensely, especially because I sensed that she was suicidal.

After praying for several minutes, I met Steven, a bitter, astute homeless White American man. We talked for a long time even though he tried to shoo me away at first. We talked a lot about homelessness in Orlando and about God. He didn't believe in God, but I could see that the statements I made about the reality of God made him think twice about his atheistic worldview.

Then came the turning point of the day. This entire time I had been feeling deeply discouraged because I felt more like a homeless guy than a man on a mission from God. No matter who I talked to, as soon as they realized that I had no place to lay my head they would immediately lose respect for me and ignore any message I had for them about Christ. I was treated as if I was subhuman even though I had only been on the street for one night at this point.

However, when I met Joe, Sam, and Bob, three Southern hicks from different parts of the South, that all changed. It turned out that they were homeless as well even though they looked quite normal to me. After talking about Jesus with them for a little bit they asked me for some gas money because their car had run out of gas. Their car really had run out of gas, but I told them that I myself was homeless at the time and was short on cash.

They were shocked that such a young kid like me would be homeless. In response, they immediately switched their demeanor to that of a caring friend. All of a sudden, I was one of them and they wanted to help me out as much as they could. They asked me where I slept last night and informed me about the areas of the city where I shouldn't sleep. They warned me about the cops and the drug-infested homeless shelters. They gave me survival tips for the streets of Orlando, told me a brief history about homelessness in Orlando, and even shared with me the current court cases that an ACLU lawyer was fighting for on behalf of the homeless population there.

It was amazing! For the first time in my life I felt accepted and included in the homeless community. I had volunteered countless hours serving and witnessing to the homeless in the past, but I knew that I was always viewed as an outsider who couldn't understand what they were going through. Now, however, I was one of them.

Eventually, the conversation steered back to the Gospel and they began making some remarks that blew me away. Joe began saying the following while Sam and Bob both nodded their heads in agreement as they repeatedly said "yep":

> "You know, so many preachers ride up in their fancy cars to our homeless shelters every day and preach a nice sermon. Then they go back to their nice house and beautiful wife and have a good night sleep. But you...you're different. You're one of us. I respect you because you don't know where you're gonna sleep tonight and you don't know where you're gonna get your next meal just like us. You're able to feel what we feel. I respect that.

So I'll listen to you kid. I don't listen to those fancy preachers, but I'll listen to you. Go ahead kid. Preach. We're listening. "

Suddenly, I felt so honored to be called homeless and to be considered subhuman by 'normal' people. I resolved that if God wanted me to be homeless and only talk with the homeless throughout this entire trip then so be it.

I preached my heart out to those men and prayed over them. They didn't give their lives to the Lord, but they listened with open hearts and thanked me for sharing the Gospel with them.

I preached to six more men today who appeared to be normal, but were actually all homeless and they all listened to me more and respected me because I was homeless as well. What a joy to become homeless in order to reach the homeless!

After talking with so many homeless people in Orlando I learned that their living situation was a little different than that of homeless people in most cities I had ministered in. In Orlando, the majority of the homeless population lived in the woods. Since it was illegal to sleep on the streets and the downtown area of Orlando was not too big the homeless people would take the bus to the outskirts of the city and live in tents in the forests surrounding the city. I caught on pretty quickly to this trend, so that's what I decided to begin doing.

My plan was to visit Salvador's church that night with the hope that they were having a Tuesday night service and then after the service I would either be provided with a place to stay or find an open field nearby where I could crash for the night. So I arrived at the LYNX central bus station around six o'clock and asked around to see what bus drove down Goldenrod Road.

While I waited for the bus I preached to Jeremiah and his girlfriend. Jeremiah had given his life to God a little more than two years before and had been on fire for God in the beginning. He claimed that he would preach on the streets, have daily devotionals, and had a strong walk with God. However, seven months ago he completely backslid into the world. Sex, drugs, and several other sinful habits were now a part of his daily life, yet as I spoke he was so impacted that he started smiling and saying, "I feel the Holy Spirit right now just like I did in the past." He promised me with sincerity in his eyes that he would go back to church with his girlfriend this Sunday. I prayed over them, they sincerely thanked me, and then my bus arrived.

When I stepped onto that bus I was so full of joy from the revelation God had given me earlier in the day that as everyone sat in their seats I stood up in the front of the bus and boldly preached my heart out. I had absolutely no fear or hesitation because the joy of the Lord was my strength. The presence of the Holy Spirit filled that bus and several people were genuinely listening as I spoke. I finished the Gospel message in about ten minutes and then I prayed over everyone in the bus.

Once I took my seat, an Indian man came onto the bus and we engaged in conversation for the next forty minutes. We first talked about India and Brazil and then I explained the Gospel to him. He listened very attentively as I shared the good news with him. Then the very moment I finished the message we arrived at his stop and he had to get off the bus. I love God's perfect timing!

After about an hour's bus ride, I found Salvador's church and got off the bus. The church was located on a tiny strip mall with three or four shops and a parking lot that fit maybe six or seven cars. Above the door was a small sign that read "Tabernaculo de Vida". There were a couple of cars parked in front of the church, so I was hoping that they were at least holding a Bible study.

As I walked up to the building, I met a very kind woman who was getting out of her car. I asked her if there was any church service going on that night. She told me that they were just having band rehearsal to prepare for tomorrow night's service.

I explained to her who I was and the nature of my mission trip and asked her if she knew of anyone who would be willing to host me. She politely replied that there wasn't anyone who would be able to host me and she gave me $20 in hopes that it would help me get a motel room for the night. Unfortunately, the money wasn't enough for a motel, but I still received it with much gratitude and saved it for food expenses.

I found a hole-in-the-wall Mexican restaurant where I ate an authentic Mexican burrito with Mexican rice and beans. It was the best burrito I had ever eaten since I had moved to Florida from California as a teenager.

Afterwards, I walked around for a bit and found an expansive open field. The front of it was made up of dirt and grass, but as I walked further and further into the field the grass became nearly three feet high and past the tall grass was a full-fledged forest. "Perfect," I thought to myself, "I won't have to worry about cops seeing me there and it'll be comfortable sleeping on the grass."

I was right. It was perfect. The cold front had ended and the warm nights had returned. Thus, humidity became my blanket, the tall grass the walls of my room, the padded ground my mattress, and the stars of the sky my ceiling. I slept like a baby in the peace and tranquility of nature's home.

My First Home

After a long day of preaching the Gospel, I joyfully visited the small, but quaint Tabernaculo de Vida congregation for their Wednesday night service. Never in my life had I felt so glad to participate in a church service. All day long I had been wrestling with demons and meeting countless people who were so desperately far from God. I often felt like it was me versus the world and I was alone in this never-ending battle for human souls. I would sometimes think, "This is the most epic battle in all of history, but why are there so few soldiers fighting against the powers of darkness?" In reality, I knew that millions of Christians in the world were fighting the good fight, but sometimes when I was out preaching the Gospel all day long by myself that's how I felt.

Thus, the moment I stepped through the church's door I was filled with ecstasy. I was significantly underdressed since all I had on was my backpack, t-shirt, and jeans and it had been three days since I had taken a shower, but I wasn't self conscious one bit. I felt right at home because I knew I was amongst family.

About forty people were in attendance and all the men, including the youth, were dressed in suits and ties. The women had long hair and wore skirts that reached all the way down to their ankles. Some of the women swayed from side-to-side waving their tambourines in the air and shouting "Gloria" while the main usher walked up and down the isles playing a percussion instrument with a lively Latin rhythm.

I immediately jumped right into the party, exuberantly lifting my hands into the air, and raising my voice in unashamed worship to God. In that moment, there was no greater feeling in the world than to praise God together with my brothers and sisters in Christ. It was so comforting to know that after a long day of preaching to a world that seemed to be entirely lost there still were people who truly believed in and followed Jesus. That night I did not pay one bit of attention to denominational differences between this church and my Christian upbringing. I was so overwhelmed with love and joy for God and for my family in Christ that none of our differences mattered.

The woman who I had met the night before and who had welcomed me in again that night told the pastor a little bit about my story, so once the worship ended the pastor called me forward to briefly introduce myself and share about what I was doing here in Orlando. For ten minutes, I shared about my mission trip and experience thus far in Orlando. I challenged the people to zealously preach the Gospel in their city and many of them were impacted by the challenge.

Once the meeting had ended, several of the people approached me and excitedly asked me more questions about the mission trip, but as soon as they realized that I was sleeping on the street they would quickly calm down, awkwardly look down at the floor, and wish me good luck. A couple of the people, including the pastor, gave me some money that added up to about $25, for which I was extremely grateful.

However, a young woman named Lourdes lovingly approached me in tears as she shared with me how deeply she had been impacted by my short message. It had woken her up from her complacency and had opened her eyes to the urgent need to evangelize. Several times she told me, "Joshua, this is your home. If you need anything just know that this is your home." I felt that she was going to be the one through whom God would provide a home for me to stay, but for some unknowable reason, she never offered to host me. I put on my backpack and began walking away from the church and, again, Lourdes ran up to me weeping, "This is your home." I was impacted by her sincere love, but confounded by her actions.

I left the church that night, walked a couple of blocks down the street to the field I had found the night before, and went to sleep once again on the soft grass. It was a bittersweet feeling to be lovingly embraced by my family and then obliviously rejected on the same night. I didn't know what to make of it.

*

As I spent time with the Lord the following morning, He spoke to me to open-air-preach inside of a Burger King that was nearby. In fear, I hesitated to obey His leading for a good while. Once I finally mustered up the courage to obey Him, I boldly walked into the Burger King only to find that there were no longer any customers present. Then I took the bus to downtown Orlando and on the bus ride the Lord told me to open-air-preach on the bus, yet, again, I cowered in fear and did not obey His voice.

Hence, I arrived at the LYNX central bus station that morning tired, defeated, and discouraged. I read my Bible hoping that God would renew my strength as I read His word. While I was reading, God directed me to walk over to a certain paralyzed man in a wheelchair who was sitting on the other side of the station. Although my heart was moved with a measure of compassion for the man and I wanted to be obedient to the Lord, I felt so exhausted and defeated that I simply answered the Lord by saying, "I'm sorry God, but I can't. I'm too tired." So I ignored the leading of the Holy Spirit and continued reading my Bible.

After a few minutes, I lifted my eyes from the pages of the Bible only to be shocked at the sight of the paralyzed man moving in my direction with his eyes fixed on me. He wore an authentic cowboy hat, a white t-shirt, and jeans. He hadn't shaved in a couple of days, but he had a young, good-looking face that appeared even more handsome with the big smile he wore as he extended his hand out to me and introduced himself saying, "Hi. My name's Greg."

"My name's Joshua," I replied as I shook his hand and smiled, "It's nice to meet to you Greg."

"Is that a Bible you're reading?" he immediately asked as he pointed his finger to the Bible in my lap.

"Yeah," I responded, humbled and in awe that God had drawn Greg to me after I had been disobedient to the Lord's drawing to him.

"So are you a Christian?" he asked.

"Yeah man," I replied, trying to sound radical after feeling so ashamed for my disobedience, "I follow Jesus with everything I got."

I briefly told him about my mission trip and what God had called me to do. He was impacted by my mandate and, in response, looked straight into my eyes as he declared, "Yeah, the Lord is calling us to stop being cowards."

No statement could have convicted me more deeply in that moment, especially coming from a paralyzed man who had approached me after I had been too much of a coward to walk up to him. Greg and I became immediate friends and we ended up talking with each other for well over an hour. He eventually asked me where I was staying, so I gave him the honest truth, "I'm staying at a really nice, comfortable field surrounded by lush grass and covered by the starry sky."

He took a moment to think about what he would say next, but within a few seconds, he looked at me and said, "Well, I really don't have much. My place is real small, but you could stay with at my house if you don't mind sleeping on a sleeping bag on the floor of my bedroom."

"It would be amazing to sleep on floor of your room," I replied. I was so overwhelmed with joy and gratitude for God's faithfulness towards me shown through Greg.

As we rode the bus towards Greg's neighborhood, he educated me about the part of town he lived in: the OBT or the Orange Blossom Trail. The OBT was notorious in Orlando for being the main center for gang activity, prostitution, and drug addiction. I was thrilled to discover that I would be living in the OBT because my heart longed to reach out to the neediest areas of the city.

Once we arrived at Greg's apartment complex and entered his small, two-bedroom apartment, I was astounded to find that he was already hosting three homeless men in his apartment! "This man is like Jesus," I thought to myself, "he's paralyzed, lives off of disability paychecks, lives in the most ghetto part of town, has only been saved for one year, has three homeless men living in his home, and now he has welcomed me in too?!"

All I could think of in that moment was not being cared for by a church full of loving, ideal Christian families who had stable jobs and nice homes and now being taken in by a former alcoholic and drug-addict who had become handicap and who had only been saved for a year. Yet here he was, already helping three other homeless men with the little money that he had and now welcoming in a fourth person. God truly uses the weak things of this world to shame the strong. After three days of homelessness and now witnessing Greg's Christ-like love, any trace of spiritual superiority that was left lingering in my heart after beginning this ultra radical journey was completely and utterly destroyed. Now I just wanted to follow Greg as he followed Christ.

When I saw that Greg didn't have much food to eat in his fridge, I decided not to eat at his house during my stay so that I wouldn't be a financial burden to him. Instead, I ate out every day with the money that I had been given and, on occasion, I would bring back some food for everyone in the house. Two of the men lived in the living room while the third man had the second bedroom to himself. I later learned that Greg had been discipling the three men. During the time they had been staying with him, they had all found jobs and were currently helping to pay the rent. Greg let me borrow a blanket, pillow, towel, and even his laptop whenever I needed it. He simply gave and gave and gave, never expecting anything in return.

Greg and I formed a deep friendship during our time as roommates. Every night, he shared with me his personal struggles, stories from his past, and deep theological questions. We usually stayed up talking until around two in the morning.

Greg was raised in an atheist household with a drunkard father and became an alcoholic and drug addict himself as a teenager. One day, his friends were drunk driving their pick-up truck through the windy roads of the Ocala forest at high speeds. The truck eventually flipped over and Greg, who was sitting in the bed of the truck, flew 75 feet across the air, hit a tree, and broke his neck. He immediately became paralyzed from the waist down. Eventually, his wife and children left him and, as a result of his depression thereafter, he became a crack addict for six years. It was through watching the teachings of Dr. Christian and Robin Harfouche on TBN that Greg heard the Gospel and surrendered his life to Jesus. Greg ordered and discipled himself using all of the teachings of the International Miracle Institute. After meeting Greg, all of my complaints about TBN were put to rest.

Although Greg was definitely more of a blessing in my life than I was in his, I had the privilege of being an answer to his prayers as well. Due to Greg's condition, it was difficult for him to leave his home for extended periods of time and, as a new believer, he was still intimidated by the idea of sharing his faith with strangers. He told me that he had recently been asking the Lord to provide him with the courage to preach the Gospel on the streets and he felt like I was God's direct answer to his prayers. My lifestyle inspired and challenged him to preach the Gospel more than ever before and one day Greg decided to go witnessing with me. After a few hours of witnessing together, Greg and I both realized that he was a natural evangelist. What he thought would be extremely difficult proved to be second nature for him and because he was paralyzed no one dared reject him. Everyone we approached listened to Greg with their full attention and some were even moved to tears as he shared the Gospel and his testimony with them.

*

At the end of the week, I visited Tabernaculo de Vida for their Sunday morning service. As soon as I walked into the building, Lourdes ran over to me weeping for joy and gave me a big hug. I was taken aback by how happy she was to see me. I listened intently as she opened her heart up to me.

She explained to me that the night I visited their church I had walked in together with one of the women of the church, so she had automatically assumed that I was being hosted by this woman. This was the same woman who I had met the night of the band practice and who had introduced me to the pastor, so it was perfectly understandable to see how Lourdes would have made that assumption.

Lourdes explained that even as I was putting on my backpack and leaving the church she didn't realize that I was walking off to go sleep on the street, but thought that I was just taking the backpack to the woman's car.

Once she realized that I was sleeping on the street I was already out of sight. She began to panic because she had felt like the Lord had told her to take me into her home, but she had hesitated to ask based on her assumption. Immediately, she got into her car and drove up and down the street looking for me, but she couldn't find me. She said that she even stopped at the field and yelled my name several times, but I never heard her because I was so deep into the field. Lourdes felt so horrible knowing that I was on the street and she had not done anything about it. She said that she felt as if I was her little brother and she had failed in helping me.

For the next two days, she drove up and down the streets looking for me and went to the mall to see if I was evangelizing there, but never found me. So when she saw me come in on Sunday morning, the burden lifted from her shoulders and she was overjoyed to see that I was fine. She stuffed me with all kinds of breads and pastries for breakfast and loved me as if I were her little brother.

"How could someone have such a deep love and worry for someone they don't even know?" I thought to myself. The answer came as soon as I asked the question, "Only by the Holy Spirit." In that moment, I knew that it was through the Holy Spirit moving on people's hearts like Lourdes' that I would be provided for throughout my entire journey.

After the church service, Lourdes and her husband Franchie invited me over to their home for lunch. I joyfully accepted their offer and had a blast hanging out with them and two young men from their church for the rest of the Sabbath day. Our hearts were instantly knit together and it felt like we had been friends for years.

Lourdes told me that meeting me has left a seal upon her heart and she would never be the same again. God has put on her a burden for evangelism through the example I have given. Glory to God!

Lourdes and Franchie sent me back to Greg's house with forty dollars, two loaves of Cuban bread, a large box of freshly baked pastries, and a sleeping bag since all I had to sleep with at Greg's house was a blanket. I was so overwhelmed by their love and hospitality.

They pleaded with me to stay at their home after I was done staying at Greg's house. They were a newlywed couple with a spacious, beautiful home all to themselves. They had a large guest room with a full-sized bed, television, and video games that had yet to be occupied by a guest. Thus, they wanted me to be the first visitor to ever use their guest room.

I returned to Greg's house for a couple of days, but later on that week I went to stay with Lourdes and Franchie for about four or five days. We had a wonderful time together. Lourdes was a professional baker, so every morning she would serve us delicious pastries for breakfast and every night she would make us five-star meals from scratch.

Both Greg and Lourdes allowed me to experience the overwhelming love and reality of the family of God. I discovered that we truly are a family. My friend Aldo put it best when he said, "The connection between brothers and sisters in Christ is deeper than the connection between blood relatives because our spirits connect."

Breakthrough

I was paralyzed with fear. I felt helplessly incapable of performing even the smallest task for God. I couldn't seem to even open my mouth to utter one word. I felt like the greatest failure in the Kingdom of God. "Surely, there is no greater bluff than me," I thought to myself. For years I had dreamt of leaving everything behind and sacrificing my life for the sake of the Gospel. I would boast to my friends that one day God would use me to bring countless souls to Him, but now here I was, a false hero, weeping like a sissy; unable to lift my head up to speak with one human soul about Jesus. I was a wreck. No matter how much I prayed, no matter how much I read my Bible, there was no possible way for me to muster up the courage to share the Gospel with even one individual.

I knew that God was still with me and He loved me, but I had failed Him and everyone who had believed in me with their prayers, words of encouragement, donations, and deep admiration. Back in Miami, there was a whole crew of young people who looked up to me as a role model and who thought of me as one of the most radical people they knew, but not anymore. If anyone were to have seen me in that moment of brokenness they would have pitied me for how pathetically weak I truly was and they would never admire me again or donate one dollar to this cause I felt so deeply called to.

"Ha! And I feel called to raise up an army of itinerant preachers?" I began thinking to myself in disgust as I reflected on my cowardly state, "Yeah right! I can't even kick my own butt to initiate a conversation with a kid right now even if my life depended on it. So how could I have the audacity to say that God has chosen me to lead an army of the most radical preachers America has ever seen? I am a fool. I might as well go home, go to college, get married, get a nine-to-five-job for the rest of my life, and die. I am not worthy to even call myself a preacher." I felt like burying myself away in a corner and just hiding from the world. Shame consumed me.

I tried to encourage myself, yet the scrutinizing thoughts continued, "What is wrong with me? Why am I so, so weak? Do I truly love God or I am just doing this for the sake of adventure and to be able to boast that I preached the Gospel across America to all of my Christian friends?"

I was so confused. Just a couple of days before this I had felt so strong and victorious. God was using me to save souls, people's lives were being impacted, and I felt like God was intimately training me to lead an army of itinerant preachers. But today my strength was sapped and my courage evaporated. I walked through the mall several times, yet I had no physical, mental, emotional, or spiritual strength to initiate a conversation with anyone that I passed by. I felt like the ultimate coward.

I needed to make a decision at that moment. Either I sucked it up and began preaching or I would have to give back the money that Lourdes and Greg had donated to me and go back home.

"Should I keep going or should I call it quits?" I debated with myself, "I know beyond a shadow of a doubt that it was God who called me to do this, but am I strong enough to persevere through it victoriously?"

In that moment, the one thing that I knew for sure was that if I were to quit the trip I would be in direct rebellion against God because He was the One who had commanded me to go. I concluded that if I gave up on the mission I would be running from God's call on my life just like Jonah.

With every bit of resolve that was left in me I said to myself, "I must get up. I must preach. I must obey God because I love Him and because He is worthy."

As all of these dark thoughts were clouding my mind, a crack of light began to appear in my heart of hearts. With faith in my heart I began quoting Scripture, proclaiming God's promises in His Word, and the promises He had spoken over my life. After a good while of declaring His truths, the oppression that was overwhelming me suddenly broke off and I was free from my fear, shame, and sense of failure. I was free from the demonic oppression that was attacking me.

Thus, I stood up, walked confidently into West Oaks Mall, and began to boldly proclaim the Gospel. Joy and peace overflowed from my heart as I walked past the shops and began sharing Christ with anyone who was open to listen.

*

One of the first conversations I had was with a young Indian man named Raja. He was about twenty-years-old and he was sitting on the chair of the kiosk appearing somewhat bored. He was selling some strange Middle Eastern medicinal pillows that were full of herbs and rocks and supposedly alleviated muscle pains; somewhat similar to Icy Hot, except the Middle Eastern version.

As I struck up a conversation with him, he expressed to me how thankful he was towards me for engaging him in friendly dialogue. He explained that in the past eleven days only one person had bought a product from his kiosk and he was miserably bored just sitting and doing nothing all day long. He worked ten hour shifts each day and the day we had met he had already been sitting down, doing absolutely nothing for four hours.

Raja had a very interesting upbringing. His family was Indian and he was born in the United States, but he was raised in India and England and had now been living in the United States for the first time since his birth. Something else was very interesting about Raja: He was a Sikh, as in a follower of Sikhism.

I knew that Sikhism was a religion from India. I had had some personal contact with the religion as a child because there was a small Sikh temple next to our apartment complex in Buena Park, CA and I had once defended a Sikh boy at my elementary school who was being teased by bullies. I was always mystified by Sikhs as I saw them walking to and fro in front of their temple with large daggers hanging on their belts, as they tied up their extremely long hair into a bun in order to put on their turban, and as they bowed down to a gold bed in their ceremonies. Although I knew more about Sikhism than the average American, I still had no idea what Sikh's actually believed. So how was I supposed communicate the Gospel to Raja? I had no clue what he believed or how to effectively reach him with the Gospel. I was lost for words.

In a split second, I felt the Lord lead me to simply ask him about his religion. So I respectfully asked him several questions about Sikhism, confessing my ignorance of the religion. He answered all of my questions very kindly. We talked about Sikhism for about twenty minutes and I was very thankful to be learning about a religion I was utterly unfamiliar with.

Once he had explained Sikhism to me, I asked him if it would be okay for me to explain to him why I believed in Jesus and in Christianity. With great respect, he encouraged me to please tell him everything. He seemed to be very interested in what I had to say, so I confidently shared the Gospel with him. I was amazed to see how open he was to hear and how intently he listened. He didn't debate me about one thing and was not offended by anything I had to say. In fact, something quite astounding took place.

With utmost sincerity and transparency, he confessed to me something that he had never told anyone in his entire life. He told me that he had always believed in Christianity, Sikhism, and much of Islam, but he had never wanted to decide which religion was the absolute truth because he knew that when he did he would have to reject the others as not being true. He realized that all three religions could not possibly be simultaneously true. Only one of them could be true, but because he did not want to offend his family and culture and always wanted to appear to be the 'good guy' to everyone, he had never made a definite decision about what he believed.

I was blown away. This was the first time in my life that I had ever shared the Gospel with a Sikh. I was in awe of his openness to Jesus. Growing up, whenever I saw those men with turbans and daggers hanging on their belts I would tremble with fear and always think of them as being so unreachable. Yet here I was with a Sikh who was so close to the Kingdom of God.

I passionately urged Raja to make a definite decision about what he believed and reiterated that only one of these religions could be absolutely true. If all of them were simultaneously true, then religion and belief in God would be a sham.

He acknowledged that indifference and laziness were serious sins and that he needed to make a concrete decision about what religion was true. He told me that he had already read most of the Sikh scriptures and he had read some parts of the Bible. He confessed that he thoroughly enjoyed reading the Bible because every sentence was full of meaning even if he didn't understand the meaning. He explained that in the Sikh scriptures there are many stories, but there is not much meaning behind them.

I wholeheartedly encouraged him to give his life to Christ right then and there, but he insisted that although he was sincerely interested in following Jesus he needed to learn more about Christianity before making a definite decision.

Thus, I urged him to read *More Than a Carpenter* by Josh McDowell and wrote down the book title and author for him on a scratch piece of paper. He committed to me that he would read it as he jokingly reminded me of how board he was at work. Raja was very glad to receive prayer, so I prayed for him with all of my heart. He was greatly touched by my prayer and appreciative of our profound conversation.

Our hour-and-a-half conversation had finally come to a close, but it was a truly glorious close. I left there knowing that the Holy Spirit would continue working in Raja's heart and that he was going to give his life to Jesus in due time. I unsuccessfully looked through all of the bookstores in the mall trying to find *More Than a Carpenter*. I returned to Raja to tell him that I couldn't find the book, but he again reassured me that he was going to buy it and read it anyway.

*

After walking and praying around the mall for a bit, I found an elderly man sitting on a bench by himself most likely waiting for his wife to finish shopping. I sat next to him and began engaging him in small talk. His name was Dewey, he was 77-years-old, and he was a native of Guyana.

As I transitioned the conversation to Jesus, he proudly declared to me that he had never missed one Sunday church service in his entire life. He had lived in Guyana, Canada, Michigan, and Florida and he had always been a faithful Presbyterian or Lutheran, depending on where he was living at the time.

Although Church attendance usually meant very little to me, since Dewey claimed to have been attending church for over seventy years I gave him the benefit of the doubt that he was a true Christian. I asked him if he knew where he would go when he died and if he believed in Jesus as his Savior and he confidently answered my questions as any devout Christian would.

However, there was an uneasiness in my spirit about this man and I couldn't seem to figure out what it was. So after he repeatedly confirmed to me that he was a true Christian I exclaimed, "Well, praise God! It's always a joy to meet another brother in Christ! I was just asking you all those questions because I'm so worried about the direction that America is heading. So many people, including Christians, are being deceived by the lie that Jesus is not the only way to Heaven, all religions lead to God, and as long as you're a good person who doesn't hurt anybody you will make it to Heaven."

Suddenly, Dewey shot back, "Well, who ever said that Christianity is the only right religion?! All religions are good and we need to respect them all. I won't ever tell a man that my religion is right and his religion is wrong."

I was in total shock when I heard these words. I concluded that if this was his response, then surely, he did not have a clear understanding of the Gospel. Thus, I proceeded with our conversation by breaking down the Gospel for him and explaining why Jesus was the only way to Heaven. As I shared, Dewey came against every point I made and would debate me head on. For each protest he made I asked him to please show me where his arguments where in the Bible, but he simply refused to answer my questions. In return, I clearly showed him the Scriptures that pointed to Jesus as the only Savior, but he didn't want to hear it. He was sharply offended that I would ever make the audacious and intolerant claim that Jesus was the only way to Heaven.

Nevertheless, I eventually asked if I could pray for him and he kindly agreed. As I finished my fervent prayer for Dewey his wife walked out of JC Penney. The instant he saw her leave the store he jumped up out of his seat and walked off without saying a word or giving me one glance.

I stayed sitting on that bench stupefied at what I had just heard. All I could think about was how could this man sit in church Sunday after Sunday for over seventy years in at least two different mainline Christian denominations in Guyana, Canada, Michigan, and Florida and still not understand nor believe in the basic Gospel message? How could this be possible? What on earth was the church preaching?

After such an intense conversation with Dewey, I took a few minutes to pray for him, the church, and myself. I was recharged in the presence of the Holy Spirit and I prepared myself for the next encounter.

*

As I strolled through the food court, I spotted two African-American teenagers sitting at a table joking around with each other. I walked up to them, introduced myself, and sat down at the table with them. Their names were James and Tyrone and as we talked I learned that they were faithful Sunday churchgoers, but I could discern that they were not genuinely born again. I shared the Gospel with them and they listened with open hearts.

As soon as I had finished speaking, they called over their friend Brian who was walking by with his arm wrapped around the waist of a girl named Janet.

"He needs to hear this," they explained with friendly concern, "tell him everything you just told us. You need to hear this man," they told Brian as they looked him in the eyes and pointed their finger straight to his face, "Sit down dude! Go ahead Josh, tell him."

So Brian and Janet quietly sat down and respectfully listened to me share the Gospel message with them. Brian was also a churchgoer and he sincerely feared God. As I explained the Gospel message to Brian, he respectfully completed my sentences and commented on every point I made. Eventually, he looked me straight in the eyes and told me, "I fully understand everything you're saying and I know that with this life I'm livin' if I were to die tonight I would go straight to Hell."

I was amazed at the groups' honesty and openness to the Gospel. Before I could ask them if they wanted to receive Christ, Brian cut me off and asked if they could all accept Jesus into their lives together and repent of their sins.

All three of the guys immediately bowed their heads, but Janet refused to pray stating that she was still not ready to follow Jesus. Brian was shocked that she was trying to postpone her commitment to Christ and he started preaching to her. He told her about the parable of the ten virgins and urged her not to be one of the foolish virgins. She stood her ground, however, and stubbornly resisted committing her life to Christ.

I contained myself from bursting out in laughter as I witnessed this unbelievable scene. "Look at this man," I thought to myself, "He isn't even saved yet and he's already preaching the Gospel. He's going to become a great man of God." I was so encouraged and filled with joy as this all took place.

Finally, I prayed with all of them to receive Christ into their lives, repent of their sins, and surrender their lives to Him. As soon as we finished praying together Brian asked if he could lead a prayer out loud as well. So he prayed his own prayer of surrender and repentance towards God and they all began to smile and rejoice at their decision to follow Jesus.

After an hour and fifteen minutes of spending time with these four awesome teenagers who were all on their way to Hell, three of them were saved and were now on their way to Heaven.

God's Supernatural Provision

After spending three weeks in Orlando preaching the Gospel on my own, I was ready to move on to the next city and I was ready to have a partner join me for the rest of the journey. Although I had prayed for a partner because it was the biblical way that Jesus had sent his disciples, when I had first embarked on this mission I was deeply convinced that I was capable of carrying it out on my own. However, during the three weeks I spent in Orlando I came to the realization of how weak I truly was. I was utterly dependent on God every second of every day, I had to have the daily prayers and encouragement of my brothers and sisters in Christ, and I desperately needed a partner to run alongside me in the daily battle that God had called me to fight. During those three weeks, my parents, my girlfriend, several close friends of mine, and myself had all been praying for God to confirm whether or not Alex Diaz was to be my mission trip partner. By the end of my time in Orlando, all of us were absolutely certain that it was God's will for Alex to join me.

I praised God for allowing Alex to join me because if it weren't for Alex I would never have completed the mission. I now fully understood why Jesus had sent his disciples out two-by-two to preach the Gospel. There was strength in brotherhood and unity and God hates an independent, self-sufficient spirit.

Although I knew that my time in Orlando had come to a close, I was still not sure about which city God wanted me to go to next. I clearly had felt the Lord leading me to go to Atlanta, but I wasn't sure if I should stop in Jacksonville first. I asked God for a sign and later on that same day I received a phone call from my mom in Miami. She told me that our grandma was visiting from Brazil and she wanted to go to Atlanta to visit her cousin. So my mom was wondering if I would like to get a free ride to the next city and she offered to bring Alex along with her. I was blown away by God's sovereignty and joyfully accepted my mom's offer.

So my parents, my brother, my grandma, and Alex all picked me up at Greg's house in Orlando. We prayed and worshipped together with Greg for a short while and then hit the road. We spent about four or five days together in Atlanta, so I decided to treat it like a vacation in the middle of the mission trip. We spent time with family and friends, became acquainted with Atlanta, and visited a few churches.

During this time, we were staying with a close family friend of ours, Nilton Dias. Once he found out about our mission trip he insisted that we stay with him during our time in Atlanta, so we happily accepted his hospitable offer.

Thus, my parents returned to Miami and Alex and I stayed to preach the Gospel in Atlanta. The presence and favor of God was with us everywhere we went and God used us powerfully to touch countless lives. Alex and I fell in love with Atlanta and we naturally bonded as a team.

We worked very well together. I was always full of energy and very outspoken and Alex was always relaxed and very introspective. I would spend several hours in prayer and worship and Alex would spend several hours in the Word, studying other religions, and learning how to witness more effectively to people of other religions.

Moreover, Alex and I had totally different backgrounds and upbringings. I was raised in a family of pastors, missionaries, and revivalists who had faithfully trained me in God's ways since I was a child. I became radical for Christ when I was twelve-years-old and I had lived a life of purity ever since. God had taught and trained in me evangelism and the ways of His Spirit as I almost daily preached the Gospel in public high school, community college, on the streets, in my neighborhood, and at work.

Alex, on the other hand, was raised in a completely unbelieving home, with a dysfunctional family, and as a diehard atheist. He viewed all Christians as complete idiots and he hated Christianity with a passion. He wore a huge, multi-colored mohawk, had thirteen piercings, and a few tattoos and was an anarchist punk, alcoholic, drug addict, and much more. One day, his punk friend, who had recently given his life to Christ, convinced Alex to visit his church. Upon the second or third visit, Jesus supernaturally opened his eyes to understand and believe in the Gospel in a single instant and from that day forward he was radically transformed. He became passionately in love with Jesus and zealous for sharing the Gospel with others.

Hence, we were polar opposites in every way and that's what made us such a great team. At times, I would be witnessing to someone and they would dismiss me by saying, "You don't understand what it's like to party, have sex, and live a wild life man. It's so great. You don't know what you're missing out on man. You're just a goody two-shoes church boy." So I would call Alex over and have him talk with the person instead. In other instances, someone would taunt Alex saying, "Dude, you don't know anything. You've only been saved for two years. I grew up in church. I've read the Bible from cover-to-cover so many times. I know way more than you do." So Alex would call me over and I would talk with that person instead. Thus, we became a great tag-team and God used us daily to save many souls from Hell and usher them into His Kingdom.

CHAPTER THREE
ATLANTA

Atlanta, Here We Come

When we reached Atlanta I was expecting to arrive at a typical white and black southern city with a decent skyline, clean streets, churches on every corner, and beautiful country homes. Well, Atlanta did contain all of those elements, but instead of being a traditional southern city, we discovered a gigantic, world-class urban capital planted directly in the heart of the South. The city was easily twice the size of Miami. The public transportation was outstanding, the parks were gorgeous, the streets were clean, the people were extremely diverse, and the food was the very best. Atlanta is home to Coca-Cola, CNN, the world's largest Aquarium, and the host of the 1996 Summer Olympic Games. The civil rights movement was birthed in Atlanta and it has a powerful memorial center dedicated to Martin Luther King Jr. showing the home he grew up in and the church that he pastored. I could go on and on about the universities, theme parks, stadiums, and other world-class attractions that Atlanta has to offer.

What impressed me the most, however, was how green the city was. Tall, lush trees and beautiful parks were spread evenly throughout the entire city. As we began driving outside of the downtown area, it felt like we were in the midst of a thick southern forest that just happened to have some neighborhoods constructed in the midst of it.

It was in one of these dense forest neighborhoods in the city of Roswell where a wonderful man of God, Nilton Dias, hosted us. Nilton planted the first spirit-filled Brazilian church of Atlanta. So even though he was no longer a pastor, he was still very well respected by the Christian Brazilian community of Atlanta. Nilton later started his own mechanic shop, which had become very successful in the area and was also an active member of the Atlanta Vineyard.

Being hosted by Nilton was like living in a piece of Heaven on earth. He was a single, middle-aged man with a beautiful three-bedroom home sitting on top of a hill. The house was surrounded by soaring trees, a small creek nearby, and short hiking trails. His home felt so safe and warm. It was our place of refuge in the midst of the raging battle we encountered on the streets every day. In Nilton's home, we were able to rest deeply in body, soul, and mind.

Alex and I were both given a room to ourselves and Alex's room had a queen size waterbed that he had the bliss of enjoying during our stay there. Nilton gave us free reign to use his laptop in order to write our blogs and check our email, his keyboard and guitar to worship, and, best of all, we were free to eat whatever we so desired as long as we washed the dishes we used. After sleeping on the street for three nights, sleeping on the floor of Greg's house in Orlando, and not knowing where our next meal would come from for several weeks, being hosted by Nilton was a dream come true.

Upon arriving from our daily evangelism, Nilton would almost always show us an inspirational video from Ravi Zacharias, Transformations, Diante do Trono, and many others. He also took us to visit and speak at various different churches and prayer meetings in the area and opened the doors for us to share our vision with several pastors.

My favorite part of being hosted by Nilton, however, was that every morning we would have a time of prayer together for about an hour. Alex and I would always spend a significant amount of time in prayer each morning, but there was something very special about praying together with our host. The blessing and presence of God would flood the three of us every time we sought God together.

So on our first day of evangelism in Atlanta, we spent about an hour-and-a-half praying together with Nilton in his home. The presence of God was so tangible that morning that it reminded me of Mt. 10:13, where it states, "If the house is worthy let your peace rest upon it." I realized that as Nilton joyfully welcomed us into his home the Lord found him worthy and allowed His peace to rest upon Nilton's home. Thus, I came to understand that this was what God would do for every household that welcomed and hosted servants of God with a joyful and loving heart.

Nilton then took us to his mechanic shop because there was a bus stop there that would take us straight to the MARTA, Atlanta's metro system. His house was several miles away from any form of public transportation, so every morning we would drive with Nilton to his shop and take the bus to the metro station.

At his shop, we met one of his good friends, Jerome Wilson. We soon became great friends with Jerome as we shared our story with him and he encouraged us with many testimonies and words from God for our lives.

Since he worked in downtown Atlanta he offered to give us a ride, so we gladly went along with him. On the way, I asked him if he had a family and he told me that he had never been married. He jokingly, yet seriously said that since he gave us a ride we were now obligated to pray for God to send him a wife, so when he dropped us off at our destination in the heart of downtown Atlanta we immediately prayed for God to send him a wife.

*

The street we were left at was hustling and bustling with people even though it was a Tuesday morning. I immediately walked up to an Asian girl who was waiting at the curb for the crosswalk to turn green. I opened up a conversation with her, but she bluntly rejected us by declaring that she was an Atheist and she didn't want to talk about religion.

Instead of being offended by her rude response or just walking away I asked her a few honest questions. Questions such as, "So you really don't believe in God at all? Have you ever sought God or even tried to know Him? So you believe that when we die we just go six feet under and nothing exists after death?"

She instinctively began answering my questions and before we knew it we were having a fantastic conversation. Alex and I explained to her several logical reasons why God exists, but she would quickly reject them by stating, "I don't believe in God. I'm an atheist." She wouldn't consider our arguments even for a brief second, but yet she continued the conversation. The entire time it seemed like a part of her just wanted to walk away, but another part of her wanted to stay and listen.

So we finally gave up trying to prove to her that God exists and Alex reversed the conversation by asking her to please prove to us why God doesn't exist. After all, she was so passionate about her atheism that she must have some mind-blowing explanations. This surprise reversal in the conversation threw her off course and she was at a loss for words for a few seconds. She stopped to think for a moment and then rebutted, "Well, you can't see God, so no one could truly know if He exists."

Immediately, God gave me an answer to her argument. This explanation had never crossed my mind in my entire life. It just happened to come out of my mouth in that moment and even I was amazed by the answer that I gave. I began saying:

> "You can't see love either. No one could put love in a test tube or laboratory and scientifically prove it, yet we see the effects of

love every day and it is the most real part of life that a person could ever experience. In the same way, no one can see God or scientifically prove Him, yet He is the most real aspect of life that a human can ever encounter. I believe the greatest proof of God are the lives that are transformed by Him. My life has been completely transformed by God and so have the lives of millions of people around the world. How is that possible if God does not exist? But one thing is for sure. If God does indeed exist then you are missing out on the greatest thing in all of life."

After I finished this illustration about God's existence she looked at me with a sense of amazement and sincerely stated, "What you said really made me think," and from that moment on she changed. She began to question her atheism and listened to us with an open heart. We finally were able to share the Gospel with her and at the end of it all we asked her if we could pray for her and she agreed. We prayed for her with all of our hearts and she was deeply touched. She thanked us for talking with her and we thanked her for her time. Alex gave her a tract to read and we went on our way. She walked away with a sense of awe and wonder in her eyes. It was evident that she had never heard what we had shared with her before and that she had encountered God in a supernatural way.

*

We continued walking down the street until we found Centennial Park. As soon as we stepped into the center of the park I thought to myself, "Jackpot!". The center of the park had an area with several beautiful Olympic monuments and there were easily a couple hundred people who were sitting around, relaxing on the benches and enjoying the shade under the trees. Alex and I looked at each other with excitement and we decided to split up since there were so many people. We spoke with dozens of individuals, but there was one conversation in particular that stayed impressed in my mind more than the others.

Sitting on the steps by the Olympic fountain, there was a tall, well-dressed African-American man named Anthony. I decided to approach him and share the Gospel with him. From the very beginning, he was unusually arrogant towards me and I couldn't understand why. As I went through the Gospel narrative, he treated me as though I was the most ignorant fool in the world for believing in what I believed. However, what shocked me the most was when Anthony boastfully declared to me that he was currently a seminary student earning his Master's in Theology and that I knew nothing in comparison to him.

We talked for over an hour and during the course of our discussion he clearly stated that he did not believe that Jesus was God, that Jesus was the only way to Heaven, and that the Bible was the infallible Word of God. Furthermore, he deliberately twisted every verse in the Bible that didn't concur with his own personal philosophies.

Throughout our entire conversation, I showed him Scriptures that proved his philosophies to be wrong, yet he would always pervert the interpretation of each verse I read or would simply reject the verse as useless. When I shared the Gospel with him he agreed with me until I made the point that because we were all sinners before God we would all be righteously condemned to Hell. As soon as that statement came out of my mouth, he began a violent diatribe against me and the Gospel. I explained to him that Jesus was the only way to salvation and that we could never be saved by our works, but by faith alone. However, he insisted that we are saved by our good works and a man could be saved without believing in Jesus.

I showed him John 3:18 where it says, "He who believes in the Son is not condemned, but he who does not believe stands condemned already because he has not believed in the name of God's one and only Son." Even though this was a very direct statement that salvation was found in Christ alone he attempted to create some strange interpretation for it that made no sense at all. I showed him several other Scriptures that were equally as blunt and every time he blatantly declared them to be false.

Finally, after he had denied the Bible, Jesus, and the Gospel while still claiming to be a holy minister of God I felt a tinge of the wrath of God in my soul. I clearly heard the Holy Spirit direct me to speak God's judgment upon him by reading aloud Matthew 7:22-23. I told him that God was giving him the following message at this very moment, "Many will come to me in that Day saying, 'Lord, Lord'...Yet I will say to them plainly, 'I never knew you. Away from me, you evildoers!'" At that moment, he stood up enraged and angrily asked me to please leave him because I was bringing him negativity and disturbing his aura. He accused me of acting like God. I replied that I was not acting like God at all, but only reading God's words to Him.

Alex was sitting close by listening to the end of the conversation, but not intruding because he saw that it was becoming quite heated. Once we ended our discussion Alex walked up to the man without saying a word and gave him a tract.

*

We were hungry, so we left the park to have our lunch break at CNN's food court. The food court was practically empty, so as we ordered and waited for our food we began chatting with the cashier at the fast food restaurant. It turned out that he was actually the manager.

When he gave us the change for our purchase Alex excitedly slammed a one million dollar bill on the counter saying, "Here's your change." He was very impressed with the bill because of how real it looked, so he asked Alex where he had obtained it. Alex explained to him that on the back it explained the Gospel of Jesus. This immediately blossomed into a great conversation about God.

The man was a middle-aged dedicated Muslim.

I began by asking, "Do you believe in Jesus?"

He immediately responded by saying, "Yes, I believe in Jesus as a prophet."

Alex then inquired, "Do you believe Jesus when he said that He was the Son of God?"

"No!" the manager exclaimed.

"Well," I asked, "do you believe in the Qur'an and Muhammad's teaching to be 100% true?"

"Of course," he quickly replied, "Muhammad's words are perfect!"

Thus, I began my short apologetic discourse geared to the Islamic worldview, "The Qur'an clearly states that Jesus never died, but ascended into Heaven to be with God and is still alive."

"Of course," he quickly agreed.

"However," I pointed out, "The Qur'an says that Muhammad died and you could go to his grave even today.

"Also," I continued, "The Qur'an teaches that Jesus healed the sick, but Muhammad never performed any miracles. So even according to the Qur'an Jesus is a greater prophet than Mohammed. Thus, how can one completely believe in Muhammad's teachings and not completely believe in Jesus' teachings."

He stood still for a moment. He didn't seem to know how to rebuttal this argument.

I urged him saying, "I encourage you to read the Gospels and treat them with just as much reverence as you do for the Qur'an."

However, at the end of it all he quickly brushed everything off declaring, "I will never study another religion besides my own. I will not read any other book besides the Qur'an."

At that point, he needed to go back to work and we needed to eat our late lunch. Although the conversation ended abruptly, Alex and I had faith that the pebble we put in his shoe would disturb him enough that it would force him to look into the Scriptures for himself.

*

We had to catch the MARTA back up to Doraville at 4:30 p.m. because Nilton would get off from work at 5 p.m. and he wanted us to participate in a prayer meeting he was hosting that night in his home. He gladly picked us up at the train station and when we got home we watched some amazing videos from Ravi Zacharias and a video of two former Muslims who help Christians to better understand Islam. It was so refreshing to hear teachings that were deepening our understanding of the discussions we had just encountered on that very day.

Once the men arrived, we met each one of them and promptly began the prayer meeting. Nilton opened us up in prayer and then asked me to share about our mission. I shared it with everyone and they were genuinely amazed and impacted. One South African business owner with several employees in his business was so impacted that he decided that, from that point on, he would share his testimony and the Gospel to every person he ever interviewed whether they got the job or not. And he said that he would regularly interview a lot of people.

The men's prayer meeting was truly glorious! This was the first prayer meeting that I had ever attended that was only men. Most of the time it is women who intercede and sometimes youth, but very rarely men. It was such a beautiful and powerful sight to see men praying, weeping, and crying out to God. I prayed my heart out and really felt the Holy Spirit flowing through me.

Jerome was also in the meeting and, afterwards, he shared with us how shocked he was by what had happened to him that day. He told us that fifteen minutes after we prayed for God to give him a wife his ex-fiancé called him out of the blue. They had ended their relationship two months before and he hadn't heard from her for three weeks, yet she happened to call the moment after we prayed for him and she was full of joy, love, and the Holy Ghost. Jerome was awestruck and he looked at Alex and I in disbelief. He couldn't believe that just minutes after we had prayed for him God had already begun to answer our prayers. To God be all the glory!

Open Hearts, Hungry Souls

On occasion, Alex and I had people from local churches join us for a day or two of evangelism. We were always overjoyed to have them come alongside us because we knew that they were the ones who were going to stay in the area, follow up with the people we witnessed to, and influence their local congregation to win the lost.

Sofia, who was the worship leader of the Brazilian church Tocha Viva, joined us and took us to her community college, Georgia Perimeter College. Also, Nora met up with us at Perimeter Mall later on the same day.

The college was quite empty because only summer school was in session. However, there were still enough people for us to talk to for a couple of hours.

After having a few short conversations, I walked into the main food court of the school. I noticed a young Hispanic man sitting by himself at a table, so I approached him and began a dialogue with him. He was very kind and polite and welcomed me to pull up a chair across from him. Hector was only nineteen-years-old and was originally from Venezuela, but was fluent in English.

As I took a seat, As I took a seat, I went straight to the point by asking him, "So do you have a relationship with God, Lucho?"

"Oh yeah, man. I love God," he confidently answered, "I even go to church occasionally with my girlfriend. Yeah...she's actually the pastor's daughter."

"Oh wow!" I exclaimed, "That great! So have you given your life completely over to Jesus?" In the back of my mind I couldn't help but laugh and sarcastically think to myself, "Another case of dating evangelism! This is great!"

"Yeah," he stated with a big smile on his face, "I have, but I always keep an open mind. My mom is New Age and I love and respect all religions."

"Well," I politely inquired, "could I ask you a question?"

"Sure," he said.

"Do you know why people believe that Jesus is the only way to Heaven?" I asked.

"Honestly," Hector responded, "I have no idea. I don't know why at all."

"Could I explain to you why many people believe that Jesus is the only way?" I kindly asked.

"Of course man!" he declared full of genuine curiosity, "I would love to know why."

I had never seen someone so excited to learn about why Christians believe that Jesus is the only way. Hector became giddy the moment I posed the question, his eyes became fixed on me, and he was completely attentive to every word I had to say.

I began sharing the Gospel with him step-by-step. The moment I explained to him that we are all sinners who would be justly condemned by God and that was why God had to send Jesus to die on the cross for our sins, his eyes lit up, he opened his mouth wide in amazement, and exclaimed, "Finally! I get it! Wow! Dude, now I totally understand! It all makes sense to me now!"

For a few brief moment, he just sat there in utter amazement. He had just had the greatest epiphany of his life and he was trying to soak it in.

"So do you want to give your life to Jesus and repent of your sins, Hector?" I asked with exuberant joy.

"Actually, Josh," He said with sincerity, "I've already given my heart to Jesus and repented of my sins. I really did and I meant it with all of my heart, but I just never really understood why I needed to give my life to Jesus until right now. Wow!"

I rejoiced together with him and prayed for him. However, I knew I couldn't stop there if he was going to go back home to a mother who was in the New Age movement. I lovingly warned him about the dangers of having an open mind to all religions. I explained to him what the New Age movement was and that even though his mom was involved in it he couldn't allow her to deceive him to believe in New Age.

Hector fully understood everything I shared with him and he humbly received it all with an open heart. He acknowledged that I was speaking the truth and firmly stated that he wouldn't allow New Age and other philosophies to deceive him.

Once I saw that he was genuine in his decision, we prayed together one more time, and I let him go.

Hector was just one example of a perfectly ripe and open soul who just needed someone to sit down with him and slowly explain the Gospel to him. If no one ever shared the Gospel with him he never would have understood it and possibly might have fallen into the Occult or another religion sometime later in his life.

After this glorious conversation with Hector much of my being was rejoicing, but a part of me was grieved. I couldn't believe that his girlfriend, her father, or someone else in their church hadn't taken the time or made the effort to share the Gospel with Hector at all. It was occasions like these that made me get on my knees and cry out, "Oh God! Awaken Your Church!"

*

We eventually made our way to the Perimeter Mall where Nora and I witnessed as a team and Alex and Sofia witnessed as a second team. If the conversation with Hector left me crying out for God to awaken the Church the first encounter we had at the mall left me wailing for revival in the Church.

Nora and I walked up to a table of five high school students. They were all dressed in the typical Abercrombie and Fitch paraphernalia that popular kids usually wore at that time and they were all freshmen. Every couple of seconds they would flirt with each other, make pointless comments, and laugh at any random thing.

"Ahh," I thought to myself, "typical freshmen. I remember those years and I am so glad they are over."

Anyhow, God still calls us to have compassion on preppy, immature freshmen, so I joyfully began to dialogue with them.

As soon as I brought up Jesus, they simultaneously blurted out different statements, "Yeah, yeah. We know." "We all go to the same church." "Yeah, we're Christians." "We go to the same youth group." "I'm baptized." "Yeah, I'm baptized too."

"Okay. I get the point," I thought to myself as I tried to recover from the barrage of statements the teenagers were throwing at me. So these were average American youth group kids who grew up in church, had been there done that, and knew all the Bible stories. I couldn't be more overjoyed because that was exactly the kind of kid I was growing up as a pastor's son in church. Therefore, I knew exactly how to talk to these kids and I didn't assume for one second that they were saved because I knew that I and most of my church friends growing up were not saved when we were their age.

So immediately I responded, "Great! That's awesome you guys! So could I ask you a serious question?"

"Okay," they said.

"If tonight," I began, "you were to die are you absolutely 100% sure of where you would go?"

All of a sudden you could hear a pin drop. Dead silence. I could see the guilt and uncertainty in their faces, but none of them had the guts to confess in front of their other "Christian" friends that they were not sure of their salvation. As we stood there in awkward silence, I remembered how taboo it was in my youth group to ever doubt one's salvation or be honest and transparent about one's doubts about Christianity.

At last, one of them finally mustered up the courage to confess, "No. I'm not sure."

Immediately, the rest of them all confessed that they were not sure of where they would go if they were to do that night.

In response to their uncertainty, I passionately shared the Gospel with them and they all quietly paid attention and listened with respect.

Once I finished sharing the Gospel with them I asked, "So do you guys want to genuinely give your lives to Jesus and repent of your sins?"

"No," they all said almost simultaneously. They seemed to hang their heads in shame. I could tell that each one of them had just now realized that they truly weren't saved and they had been merely wearing the mask of a "Christian." They were sincerely convicted, but something was still holding them back from making a decision to wholeheartedly follow Jesus.

"Why not," I asked them with concern, "What's holding you back?"

"I just don't know if it's the truth," one of the girls quietly responded. They all nodded their heads in agreement.

"I just don't know," one of the guys said, "I still have a lot of doubts."

"What are your doubts?" I sensitively asked.

"I don't know," he answered, "I can't explain it. I just don't know if I really believe in it all."

I lovingly asked the rest of the kids why they had doubts, but none of them could articulate their thoughts. I wholeheartedly encouraged them and prayed over them. Then Nora and I walked off and began looking for the next person to witness to.

It was in times like these that I would begin to wonder, "What is the church doing if we are not preaching the Gospel and being transformed by the power of the Holy Spirit? How can a group of young people grow up their entire lives in church, be baptized, and still not believe in the Gospel? How is this possible? When will youth groups seek to genuinely encounter the living God instead of trying to be the hippest, funnest youth group in town?"

*

Nora and I prayed under our breath as we strolled through the mall. We eventually rode up the escalators and as we got off, sitting alone on a bench, was a young African-American man named Darryl. We walked directly up to him and introduced ourselves. He was very polite to us and open to everything we shared with him.

He frankly told us that he did not go to church, was not a Christian, and did not believe in Jesus. However, he was on a quest to find wisdom.

I asked him if I could share with him the wisest teaching that Jesus ever taught and he happily agreed.

The wisest teaching that Jesus ever taught was obviously the Gospel, so I passionately preached the Gospel to him and he was deeply impacted by every word of it. He stared at me with such intensity and with a genuine hunger for truth in his eyes.

When I asked him if he wanted to surrender his life to Christ and repent of his sins he agreed without a moment of hesitation. Right then and there, we prayed together and he genuinely gave his life to Jesus.

Still somewhat shocked at how easily he had given his life to Jesus, I repeatedly reiterated the weight of his decision and exactly what it meant to give one's life to Christ. Every time I stated this, he would assure me that he fully understood the significance of his decision and that he was serious about his commitment. He even promised us that he would go to church that Sunday morning.

We prayed over him and went along rejoicing the rest of the day.

*

Alex and Sofia had a tremendous time witnessing as well. They spoke with three Hindus and two Muslims.

One Muslim young man was so impacted by his conversation with Alex that, a few hours later, he walked all throughout the mall searching for Alex in order to talk with him again. Eventually, he found Alex and they sat down for another hour or so to discuss the Gospel further. He was so hungry to hear about Jesus!

Athens: A City In Desperate Need Of God

The great city of Athens...Athens, Georgia. Throughout our stay in Atlanta we heard several comments from different people about a neighboring city called Athens. Comments about how wild the city was, how awesome the city was, and how desperately lost the city was, all depending on who was making the statement.

However, there was one person we met who would not stop talking about Athens. Nora used to live near Athens and had been praying for over eighteen years for a move of God to break out in the city. She also was so amazed by our radical mission trip that she decided to film a mini-documentary of our mission. She insisted that we go to Athens in order to film the documentary and reach some Athenians for Christ.

After several weeks of Nora's persistent encouragement to witness in Athens, we left on a Monday morning to the city. We drove about an-hour-and-a-half outside of Atlanta to reach the college town. The founding of the University of Georgia in 1785 was essentially the birth of the city of Athens, GA. Thus, the university and the city are thoroughly intertwined for better or for worse. The population of the city was only slightly over one hundred thousand, yet because the majority of the population consisted of young people the social and party life of Athens was outrageously vibrant.

As we drove into the city on a Monday morning, I was impressed to find that the streets and bars were reasonably busy with people. It looked like a Wednesday afternoon in any normal college town, only it was Monday morning.

As we drove through the city, prayer walked the streets, and preached the Gospel to dozens of individuals we were able to sense a thick, dark presence of evil that ruled over the city. It literally felt like the city was under the control of witchcraft and the New Age spirit. The only cities that I had been to that were comparable in regards to the level of spiritual oppression were San Francisco, New Orleans, and Venice Beach.

Yet even though we felt a deep darkness over the city, we held on to God's promise that where sin abounded grace abounded even more (Romans 5:20). Thus, Alex and I saw Athens as a goldmine for the Gospel, a city in desperate need of God that was ready to experience a great harvest.

*

We prayed together in the heart of the city that God would use us as His witnesses to share the Gospel with power and that He would send an outpouring of His Spirit on the residents of Athens. Alex and I felt led to split up to and begin engaging in one-on-one evangelism with the people walking around the streets and hanging out at the bars.

There was one bar in particular that caught my eye because it had about seven or eight hippie young adults sitting out in front drinking beer and smoking cigarettes. I thought to myself, "Now you gotta be hard core if you're drinking beer and smoking on a Monday morning." The name of the bar was "GLOBE" and, I later found out that according to Esquire Magazine, it was the number one bar in America at the time. The name of the bar was in all black caps and there was an outside fenced patio where the young people were hanging out.

I walked up to the group and shamelessly introduced myself. The only ones who gave me any sort of attention were the two guys I was closest in proximity to, David and Chris. The rest of the group either completely ignored me as they mockingly glanced at me or simply walked away into the bar.

I also introduced myself to a tall young man standing near the group right outside of the bar patio. I asked him what his name was and he obnoxiously exclaimed, "Jacob! I am god!" Then he quickly turned around and stormed off down the sidewalk.

"Welcome to Athens," I thought to myself. I turned my attention to Chris and David as we began our dialogue. However, David soon walked off and I was left alone talking with Chris.

As we talked, I was very intrigued, yet perplexed by Chris's story.

"So do you have a relationship with God, Chris?" I asked.

"I do. I have a great relationship with God," he answered as he kicked back in his chair with complete confidence in his voice, "In fact, I've been getting really deep into Buddhism lately. "

"Oh, wow! How is that going?" I asked with genuine curiosity. I was really interested to hear how someone deeply into Buddhism could be having a great relationship with God when Buddhism doesn't believe in a personal God.

"I love it," he answered with conviction, "I've been reading Buddha's teachings and just meditating on the deeps truths I'm finding in them. It's really helping to guide my life."

"So could I ask you," I began, "what do you think happens to us after we die?"

"We either go to Heaven or to Hell," he said matter-of-factly.

Now I was really confused. How could a Buddhist have a personal relationship with God and believe in Heaven and Hell? Also, at this point, David had returned to the table and was listening in on our conversation.

"Really?" I questioned with a bit of skepticism, "so you don't believe in reincarnation?"

"No way!" he exclaimed, "I would never believe in that."

"But I thought you believed in Buddhism?" I asked feeling very confused.

"I've been getting really deep into meditation and the teachings of Buddhism," he answered, "but I don't believe in reincarnation at all."

"Oh...okay," I stated with much confusion, "So could I ask why do you believe in Heaven and Hell?"

"Well..." he began with some hesitation, "I actually died once for thirty minutes and when I died I went to Heaven."

Both David and I stood there for a brief moment in disbelief and awkward silence.

"Seriously?" I said in unbelief, "So you really died and went to Heaven? You're not lying?"

"No. I'm totally serious man," he quietly answered. He seemed to have a deep conviction about it, so I listened.

Humbly and honestly Chris told us his story, "It happened on the most horrible day of my life. So many horrible things happened that day including that I found my wife cheating on me. I became so overwhelmed with depression that I grabbed a bunch of sleeping pills, mixed them with some other drugs, and overdosed. In that moment, I died and thirty minutes later they found me and they were able to resuscitate me back to life. But during those thirty minutes I was in Heaven."

"And what did you see when you were up there?" I asked with a mixture of awe and unbelief at the same time.

"I saw a bright shining light," he continued, "and I was guided up to Heaven by a bunch of angels. When I got there I saw my grandpa and several other loved ones who had died. Then I returned to my body. The doctors said that I would be a vegetable for the rest of my life and that my liver would never function again, but I'm perfectly fine now."

"Dude, Chris," David said out of nowhere, "I never knew that happened to you. That's amazing man!"

"Yeah, well, I don't tell you guys everything," he answered, slightly annoyed.

"Could I ask you a question Chris?" I asked.

"Sure," he replied.

"So after experiencing all of this," I lovingly asked, "have you come to believe and follow Jesus?"

"Of course," he stated with deep conviction, "Jesus is everything to me. I talk to Him every day. I love Jesus!"

"Actually, after my experience I searched online to see if there was a group in my local area who had gone through near-death experiences and, to my surprise, there was. So I attended the group and all of them were hard-core Christians who were super passionate for God. What's crazy was that I was one of the only ones who had gone to Heaven. Most of them had gone to Hell in their experience."

"So let me just try to understand this better," I slowly stated trying to unwind all the perplexities running through my mind, "Do you believe that Jesus died on the cross so that we could be forgiven of our sins and that He is the only way to Heaven?"

"Yes, I do," Chris answered.

"Do you believe that Jesus is God?" I continued.

"Totally," he replied.

"Do you read the Bible and believe that the Bible is the word of God?" I inquired.

"Yeah man," he said, "I read the Bible all the time."

"So why do you believe in Buddhism?" I kindly asked in a state of utter confusion.

"I really only believe in the meditation aspect of it," he explained, "and I really agree with a lot of Buddha's teachings. I think it's amazing. But I don't believe in any of the other stuff."

"So you don't worship Buddha, or believe in reincarnation, or believe in nirvana?" I asked, trying to clear things up.

"No, no, no, not at all," he emphatically replied, "I don't believe in any of that crap!"

All of Chris's supposedly contradicting statements were finally making some sense to me.

"Could I ask you another question?" I continued. He nodded. "So when you died...did you believe in Jesus then or follow Him at all?" "Nah," he said, "I was an agnostic then. I didn't really believe in anything."

"Hmm," I thought to myself. Either this guy was fabricating this story or he just told me that he didn't believe in God when he died and he still went to Heaven. I didn't know what to think of Chris's experience. All I knew was that this guy seemed to be genuine about his heaven-bound experience even though doctrinally it didn't seem to be possible. "So do you go to any church now?" I asked.

"Well," he explained, "after I had that experience I started going to several different churches, but eventually I got tired of all of their rules and divisions between themselves. They were really legalistic. So now I just go to a house church with a group of my close friends. I like it a lot better."

"So David," I started, "what about you? Do you have a relationship with God?"

"Yeah, I do," he replied, "it's kinda funny actually. I'm a lot more open to God now that I've graduated from UG then when I first came here. I was raised in a Christian home and always grew up in church, so when I came here God was the last thing I wanted to know about. I became a total atheist and I didn't believe in God at all for a couple of years. But the more I search for truth the more real I see that God is. He's everywhere and I'm really trying to seek Him more seriously now."

"That's awesome David!" I exclaimed, "I encourage you to keep seeking after God man. I'm sure you will find Him. God promises in the Bible that if you seek Him genuinely with all of your heart you will find Him. So what do you think about Jesus David?"

"I think Jesus was truly a holy figure," he began to explain, "and I really respect the Bible as a holy book of religious literature, but I don't think that Jesus is the only way or anything. I definitely think that Jesus and the Bible have reached the highest form of holiness possible, but I don't think that Jesus is God and I consider the Bible to be just one of many holy books."

"Do you know why Jesus said that He was the only way?" I asked. I posed this question because I had come to realize that many people who respected Jesus, but didn't believe that He was the only way to Heaven often assumed that Christians were the ones who created the narrow-minded claim that He was the only way. They usually were sincerely unaware that Jesus Himself was the One who had made this exclusive claim. However, after I would show them the scriptures where Jesus made these claims they would listen to the Gospel with a lot more openness.

"No, not really," David replied matter-of-factly.

"Could I explain to you why He claimed to be the only way?" I kindly asked.

"Sure," David said as he leaned back in his chair.

So, with much kindness and respect, I explained the Gospel story to David. He fully understood everything I shared with him, but he refused to agree on a few main points. He was not sure if he believed that there was a heaven and hell, that there would be a day of judgment, and that God was a literal being. He was convinced that God was a universal soul that we were all a part of, but he acknowledged that the universal soul did have a form of intelligence.

We continued talking for nearly an hour and when he found out that I was on a journey preaching the Gospel across America and living completely by faith he was awestruck and suddenly revered my words so much more. This discovery never failed to gain the wholehearted respect of so many sojourners and hippies throughout my trip.

As our conversation came to a close, David repeatedly thanked me for talking with him and commented on how thoroughly he enjoyed our profound discussion. He promised me that as a result of our conversation he would start reading the Bible again and, because I recommended it, he would read *More Than A Carpenter* by Josh McDowell. I prayed over David and Chris with great faith and joy in my soul and then let them be.

I soon met up with Alex and Nora and we began excitedly telling each other about the amazing encounters we had experienced thus far. Alex had brought an older African-American man to the Lord and Nora had been able to interview the man on camera. Throughout the day, Nora had been filming us preaching the Gospel. She would mount her camera on a tripod, stand on the opposite side of the street, and use zoom in order to capture the footage of us witnessing.

As we were joyfully sharing our stories with each other, we were rudely interrupted by a man about thirty feet away who began obnoxiously yelling, "I am god!" I turned around to see who it was and it turned out to be Jacob, the man I had quickly met at GLOBE. When he saw me look back at him he yelled to me, "...and you're god too!"

The dramatic scene he made was like a blaring red siren beseeching us to show him Jesus. Alex and I could not resist the draw to reach him, so we kindly walked up and greeted him.

Jacob and his friend were standing in front of a bar smoking cigarettes and drinking beer. The outside entrance of the bar was shaped in a semi-circle made up of a panorama of tall, black-tinted windows. Jacob's height intimidatingly towered over our small frames as we began our heated interaction.

The moment we approached Jacob, his friend bolted into the bar not wanting anything to do with us. Jacob kindly greeted us as we began talking and asking him spiritual questions. However, the response he gave to all of our questions was that he was god and that we were all gods.

A couple minutes into the conversation, he realized that Nora was filming us a short distance away. He immediately went ballistic and began angrily yelling at Nora threatening to break her camera. He started walking towards her to smash her camera, but she quickly pulled down the camera, walked away, and told him that she wouldn't film anything. Alex and I had to physically hold him back from attacking Nora.

Once the camera was put away, he regained his 'god' composure and peacefully talked with us again, "Where were we?...oh yes, I am god."

However, after a few minutes of calling himself god he suddenly switched and began claiming that he was Satan and began cursing Jesus over and over again. The more I shared the Gospel with him the angrier and more blasphemous he would become. Suddenly, he violently yelled in my face, "If you don't stop talking right now I am going to slam your head through the glass [window]!"

Well aware of the tall glass window a few inches behind my head and the great height advantage Jacob had over me I calmly looked him in the eyes and lovingly said, "Go ahead."

He was so shocked by my response that he marched right up to me and put both of his hands on the sides of my head. As his hands gained a firm grip on my head, I remained calm inside and out refusing to act out in self-defense. I began to brace myself for the worst...and then he kissed me on the nose and hugged me.

I felt relieved, awkward, and violated all at the same time.

I was still convinced that at any moment he would reverse his composure and violently bash my head into the window. However, as I was mentally preparing myself to be slammed into the window Jacob began begging me to give him a hug. At first, I refused to hug him because I was convinced that he either had a sexually perverse or violent ulterior motive for wanting a hug from me. However, when he threw his hands into the air in surrender, closed his eyes and, again, begged me to hug him, my heart melted with compassion for him because I realized that his request was genuine.

With some lingering hesitation, I finally gave him a strong hug. He let out a huge sigh of relief and thanked me for my hug. I held him for about five seconds and when I let go we stood in silence for a brief moment. There was peace in the air. The demons had lost control of him.

With complete brokenness and pain he began saying with tears in his eyes, "I have evil inside me." Before we could say a word he began telling us part of his life story.

In complete vulnerability, he shared with us that this year had been the worst year of his life. He was raised his entire life as a devout Jehovah's Witness in a very zealous Jehovah's Witness family.

Unfortunately, that year his dad passed away and upon his father's death he found out that his mother was not really his biological mother. Jacob felt betrayed by his father and "mother" for having lied to him his entire life about who his biological mother was. He was so deeply hurt that he concluded that everything his parents had ever lived for and taught him was a lie, including religion. In his eyes, his parents were the world's biggest hypocrites and he wanted nothing to do with them or their religion. In anger and disillusionment, He left his family and God and wished that he had never been born. As a result, he had become deeply depressed, suicidal, and, by his own confession, demonized.

We told him that Jesus could save him from the demons that were in him, heal him from all the pain he had experienced, make him a new creation, and give him purpose in life. I asked if we could pray for him and he desperately agreed.

As Alex and I prayed over him with authority and faith, he began to profoundly weep. We bound the demons that were in him, ordered them to leave his life, and asked the Holy Spirit to make him a new creation. At the end of the prayer he was in tears and he joyfully exclaimed, "I'm gonna give my life to Jesus! Thank you so much! I'm gonna give my life to Jesus!" He gave us both a big hug and literally skipped away full of joy.

Northpoint Mall

We began our wild hunt for lost souls at Northpoint Mall in Alpharetta, a suburb of Atlanta. We arrived at the mall around noon, so we decided to eat lunch before we began preaching.

As we were eating, Alex caught a glimpse of a long-haired, skinny teenager walking by and, for some strange reason, couldn't stop staring at him. Even after the guy had walked off beyond eye distance, Alex continued staring towards his direction. Eventually, Alex excused himself from the table even though he was only halfway done with his meal. About fifteen minutes later, he returned with a big smile on his face.

"Where did you go?" I asked him.

"I went to preach to that skinny guy," he answered.

He began to explain to me an amazing phenomenon that he had just experienced. The moment he had spotted the young man walking by, the Holy Spirit dropped a burden of compassion on Alex to share the Gospel with him. The burden was so strong that he was unable to continue eating. He had to stop in the middle of his meal and go talk to him.

Alex appeared dumbfounded as he explained the supernatural takeover of the Holy Spirit that he had just experienced. The moment Alex approached the teenager, words began flowing out of his mouth without him realizing what he was saying. Alex had never given a prophetic word to anyone in his life, yet, in that moment, the Holy Spirit began prophesying through him with words of knowledge, encouragement, and direction for this young man's life. It turned out that the young man was a believer in Jesus and he confirmed that everything Alex had spoken was accurate to what he had been experiencing at that very point in time in his life.

Alex, however, was freaked out because he had never been taken over by a supernatural force in such a powerful way. He had no theological grid for it, so he had no idea how to process what he had just experienced.

We split up after lunch and preached the Gospel to different people throughout that entire afternoon. When we met up again at the end of the day I asked Alex, "So how did the day go for you?"

"Weird," he responded with a perplexed look on his face, "The entire day the same thing would happen over and over again. The Holy Spirit would cause someone to pop out at me and when I would begin speaking to the person the words would flow out of me without me thinking about anything I was saying!

"I didn't use one method of evangelism that I've learned!" he continued in unbelief, "I would practically forget them all as soon as I would start evangelizing. I didn't preach at all from my mind, just from my feelings! Sometimes the fire within me was so overwhelming that I felt like yelling every word out with passion, but I held myself from doing it because I was scared of what the people would think."

Alex was still genuinely scared, confused, and weirded out from this supernatural takeover. He shared with me all of the qualms that were running through his mind. Were all of the methods of evangelism that he had learned wrong? Was this feeling truly from God? Were the people really impacted or were they just freaked out? Was God disappointed with him because he held back from letting God flow through him all the way?

I calmed him down and joyfully explained to him that what had happened to him was a beautiful occurrence. The Holy Spirit had seen that Alex was a surrendered vessel that He could freely flow through. Thus, He was able to wholly possess him in order speak directly through him to the people He wanted to reach.

I went on to share with Alex the times that the same phenomenon happened to me, "On occasion, the Holy Spirit just takes us over to an extreme degree," I elaborated, "Unfortunately, it's not like this every single time we preach the Gospel, but I sure wish it was. And don't worry, all of the methods of evangelism we have learned are still valid and useful, but when the Holy Spirit takes control He knows best how to reach the individuals He leads us to minister to."

Alex felt better after we processed his experience together, but he still remained somewhat bewildered by the day's supernatural events.

After encouraging Alex, I had the joy of engaging in one of the best conversations I had ever had in my life. It was with a young Palestinian man named Sayed who I had met sitting alone at a table in the mall. He was born in Palestine, came to the United States when he was nine-years-old, and was now in his early twenties. He was a devout Muslim who was still able to read and write Arabic fluently. He seemed to be somewhat open-minded, yet one hundred percent certain that Islam was the absolute truth. We began a respectful dialogue and, surprisingly, he listened with a humble, honest, and open heart as we candidly talked about Jesus and the Gospel.

I initiated our conversation in the same way that I would begin most conversations. I simply walked up to Sayed with a smile on my face and said, "How ya doin' man? My name is Joshua and I'm just going around today meeting people and encouraging people to have a relationship with God. What's your name?"

Sayed politely introduced himself and began confidently telling me about his relationship with God as a Muslim. I had never before heard a Muslim honestly describe their relationship with God, so I listened with an open heart and learners' ears.

I had recently been considering buying a Rosetta Stone course for Arabic because I was seriously praying about one day being a missionary to the Middle East, so I asked him all kinds of questions about the Arabic language and Arab culture. He explained to me the many differences between the different Arab countries in the Middle East and happily answered several more of my curious questions.

Eventually, we steered back to the subject of God and I began sharing the Gospel with him. I asked him, "Could I share with you the main teaching that Jesus taught in the Bible?"

"Sure," he replied with genuine openness and curiosity.

"Have you ever heard of the Gospel before?" I inquired.

"No. I haven't," he answered.

"Well, this is the main teaching of Jesus," I elaborated, "It simply means 'good news'."

So I explained to him the Gospel and why Jesus is the only way to heaven. I showed him why we can only be saved by grace and the absurdity of ever being so self-righteous to believe that we can be saved by our own works.

After explaining to him all of these truths I asked him, "So what do you think about everything I just said?"

"I believe in everything you just said," he calmly replied, "but I don't believe that Jesus is the Son of God."

"Well, do you believe that Jesus was a prophet?" I asked.

"Of course," he emphatically stated.

In response, I asked, "If there was a preacher who claimed that he was God would you consider him to be a prophet?"

"Of course not," he said.

"Well," I began, "Jesus claimed to be God and Islam claims that He was a prophet. So either He is a liar, a lunatic, or He is what He said He was: God. And how dare Mohammed call Jesus a prophet if He claimed to be God. Isn't falsely claiming to be God the highest blasphemy?"

This threw Sayed completely off guard. He was speechless.

I explained to him how even Jesus' murderers and secular, objective historians all wrote that Jesus claimed to be the Son of God. I showed him several passages in my Bible where Jesus claimed to be God including the verse where Jesus said, "Before Abraham was I AM." I even explained to him what I AM means and the story of the burning bush where it first originated from.

Sayed remained dumbfounded.

Then I compared Jesus and Mohammed and I explained how even throughout the Qur'an there was proof that Jesus is a greater prophet than Mohammed. I began explaining, "Jesus performed miracles, but Mohammed did not; Jesus never died, but Mohammed did; Jesus ascended into heaven to be with God, but Mohammed did not; Jesus will return to earth a second time, but Mohammed will not. These are all verses in the Qur'an that speak about Jesus."

Thus, I passionately asked him, "So if Jesus is such an amazing prophet why haven't you read His teachings?"

Again, he was speechless.

"Sayed, would it be okay if explained to you why I personally do not believe that Mohammed was a prophet at all?" I asked with a great deal of sensitivity. I was well aware that many Muslims were open to discussing the Qur'an and Islam, but when it came to the Prophet Mohammed himself they would often become belligerent and shut down the conversation.

"It's okay. Go ahead," he calmly responded. I could see that I had already gained his trust and respect.

Thus, I explained to him my qualms about Mohammed's lifestyle such as his practice of polygamy, jihad, pedophilia, his vain materialism, and his quest for political power. To my surprise, Sayed did not reply with one word or even a facial expression of defense for Mohammed, perhaps because he knew that all that I was saying was true.

I went on to explain why I believed that the revelation of the Qur'an that Mohammed received was a demonic deception that completely went against the Gospel of Jesus Christ. I even showed him the scripture in Galatians that says that even if an angel preaches another Gospel than the one that the apostles preached "let him be eternally condemned" (Gal. 1:8). Therefore, even if it was a real angel who appeared to Mohammed, that angel was now eternally condemned because he had preached a Gospel that completely went against all the teachings of Christ.

I continued my argument by asking that even if Mohammed had not believed in Jesus as Lord, but only as a prophet, why hadn't Mohammed at least kept Jesus' teachings? I showed Sayed several teachings of Jesus in the Bible that Mohammed had directly disobeyed.

Again, I kindly asked Sayed, "So what do you think about everything I just said?"

He smiled and replied, "I guess both of us have learned some new things today."

Sayed and I continued talking for another twenty to thirty minutes. I asked him some questions about the Qur'an and the Hadith and he kindly answered my questions.
I even confessed to him that the reason why I was interested in learning Arabic was because I was thinking about one day being a missionary in the Middle East. He laughed kindly and gave me some tips of what to do if I ever lived in the Middle East.

Before I left, I wrote down on a sheet of paper the website www.answering-islam.org for him to further investigate the similarities and differences between Islam and Christianity. He was very interested in the website and told me that he would definitely look into it. This was the best website I knew on answering Muslim objections to Christianity.

Finally, I prayed over Sayed and he was sincerely grateful for the prayer. He thanked me for stopping to talk with him and we went our separate ways.

*

We eventually had to bid farewell to beautiful Atlanta, a city that we had grown to love. We dearly missed the people, churches, and food of that amazing Southern metropolis, yet we had to continue moving forward to proclaim the Gospel to those who needed to hear it, believe it, and be saved. This was the nature of our lives as itinerant preachers. No matter how sweet a city or group of people may have been there were always more cities and more people who needed to hear the Gospel and be saved.

CHAPTER FOUR

CHARLOTTE

Welcome To Charlotte

We sat at the front of the Greyhound bus on our way to Charlotte poised to engage others with the Gospel. They were trapped with us for the next six hours, so there was no way that they could possibly escape hearing the Good News.

I began with the man sitting next to me. His name was Andres and he was a middle-aged businessman from Honduras who was spending his vacation time in the United States. We had a wonderful time of fellowship talking about Jesus and what He had done in our lives because it turned out that Andres was a thoroughly saved Charismatic Catholic who read the Bible daily and passionately loved Jesus.

Meanwhile, Alex enjoyed a great conversation with the man sitting next to him who was an ex-convict. The man openly heard the Gospel and received prayer from Alex.

After both of our conversations had ended and we had been on the road for a couple of hours, I asked Alex if he could pass out tracts to all the people on the bus. Quietly and assertively, Alex passed out the tracts to everyone on the bus. I watched as many people opened them up and read them intently as the bus ride progressed.

Towards the end of the trip, I felt the Holy Spirit strongly convicting me to stand up and preach the Gospel to everyone in the bus. I battled the fears and excuses that bombarded my mind as I hesitated to obey the Spirit's leading. I knew what God wanted me to do, but I couldn't gather the strength and courage to obey Him. At last, I felt God's supernatural strength empower me to preach. I stood to my feet emboldened with fresh courage and zeal, only to have my heart sink when I saw that half of the bus was deep in sleep.

Disheartened, I sat back down and, for the next hour, struggled within myself as to whether or not I would obey the Spirit's leading. "What should I do?" I wrestled within myself, "If I preach I'll feel like a jerk for waking everyone up and who knows if they would even listen to me after I rudely wake them up from their rest. But if I don't preach I know that I will have disobeyed God, the people won't hear the Gospel, and I'll feel miserable for the rest of the day." Time was running out and I had to make a decision fast. We were driving through greater Charlotte and I knew that we would arrive at the bus station at any minute.

Finally, I stood up and began preaching the Gospel. I didn't care anymore whether or not the people were asleep because they were all going to have to wake up at the bus station anyways. Also, I knew that if God had impressed upon me so strongly to preach the Gospel to them it was because He wanted to move in a mighty way. The anointing and grace of God was so strongly upon me as I preached that it felt as if God was literally speaking through me. Honestly, I didn't even know what I was saying. I had absolutely no train of thought or systematic thinking as I spoke. The message just flowed out of my mouth like a flame of fire. I don't know how else to describe it. Several people in the bus had their eyes fixed on me, paying attention to every word I said; yet several others were expressionless as they stared off in another direction. I finished sharing the Gospel in about eight minutes and then prayed fervently for everyone in the bus to encounter God and give their lives completely over to Jesus. As soon as I finished praying and sat back down, I was amazed to hear the entire bus explode in exuberant applause.

Two people who were sitting across from me began talking to me with such excitement. They told me that they were Christians and that they were deeply inspired and encouraged by my bold proclamation of the Gospel. They encouraged me to keep up the good work and committed to pray for me. Once we got off the bus, several more people approached me and complemented my preaching. Some of them were believers and some of them were not, but they had all been genuinely encouraged and impacted by my witness of the Gospel.

*

We walked out of the Greyhound station to find that we had arrived in the heart of downtown Charlotte. We were impressed at how charming the city was. We walked around downtown and had several one-on-one conversations with people for the next few hours.

Around 8:30 p.m., the nightlife of the city began to become quite lively. Several bars opened up and a good number of scantily dressed young people began walking the main street.

We soon passed an outdoor bar that had about sixty people sitting down, talking loudly, and having a good time. It was martini Wednesday so everyone was ordering martinis. The opportunity was just too tempting to pass up.

I immediately felt the presence of the Holy Spirit giving me the words to speak and the anointing to stand in the middle of all the tables and boldly preach, but, again, I hesitated. For one hour, I struggled within me to obey God. In the end, I walked away defeated. Goliath beat David. I felt like the ultimate coward and such a disobedient son. I tried to comfort myself by believing that the same bar would be packed on Friday or Saturday night and I would have a second chance to open air preach. However, every time we walked by that bar for the rest of the week it was practically empty.

I had missed my opportunity. However, one lifelong lesson that I learned from that day and from the trip in general was that I was not superman. I would succeed and I would fail; I would obey and I would disobey; I would be bold and I would be cowardly. That day was a day of both victory and defeat, yet God's grace covered it all and all the glory belonged to Him in all circumstances. What was important was that I didn't give up or get discouraged, but that I continued to joyfully deny myself, take up my cross, and follow Jesus. He was and is worthy of it all.

Searching For Morning Star

On our second day in Charlotte, we wanted to connect with a local church as we always did whenever we entered a new city. I had heard great things about a church called Morning Star, so we decided to attend their youth service that night. We rode the city bus to the farthest point it would take us and then began walking the rest of the way. According to the map we had looked up online, the church was only three miles from the final bus stop. We assumed that we would arrive at Morning Star in about one hour, but instead, we ended up getting lost and walking for well over four hours with no church in sight.

A man driving past us in his truck took pity on us and gave us a ride to the area where he thought the church was. Sure enough, we found Morning Star around 9:45 p.m. It was in the middle of nowhere, surrounded by dense forest and a lake. The moment we stepped into the youth service the worship team was singing the final phrase of the closing song. They dismissed the congregation and everyone left the building. We were deeply dismayed and physically drained. After spending the entire day and night trying to find Morning Star we ended up missing the entire service and not building a relationship with anyone at the church.

We introduced ourselves to the youth pastor, told him our story, and presented the idea of partnering with Morning Star to bring unbelievers to be discipled there. He seemed to be uninterested in what we had to say, but kindly suggested that we check out The Cause and The

Call base to see if we could get involved with them. He also mentioned to us that they had a 24-hour house of prayer. Immediately, I thought to myself, "Well, maybe we could pray at the house of prayer for a few hours and then sleep there for tonight. If that doesn't work out, we'll just sleep in the woods."

Alex and I walked around The Cause property for a while but no one was around. There were no city or house lights on, so the area was pitch dark. Suddenly, we saw a man quickly walk into a trailer, so we decided to knock on the trailer door to ask him where we could find the house of prayer. He kindly answered the door and we began our inquiry, "Excuse me sir. We're so sorry for disturbing you so late at night. We heard that there was a house of prayer here and we were just wondering if you could tell us how to get there?"

The man politely began giving us directions on how to get there. Suddenly, he stopped mid-sentence and asked us, "Are you guys thinking of walking there?"

"Yeah," we replied.

"Oh, you can't do that," he said as he shook his head, "It'll take you a good while to get there if you're walking. Let me just take you in my truck."

"Okay. Really?" I asked in shock, "Wow. Thank you sir."

"My name's Chuck Mervin," he stated as he extended his hand for a handshake and came down the front steps of his RV.

We introduced ourselves to Chuck and hopped into his truck. As we rode in his truck he asked us where we were from and what we were doing at Morning Star. We told him about our mission trip and then he suddenly stopped his truck and said, "Wow. God must really love you guys because He's telling me right now to let you guys stay in our cabins for free for as long as you need."

Out of all of the people we could have bumped into that night, God had orchestrated for us to meet the director of The Cause and spoke to him to provide us with free lodging. We had been mentally ready to sleep in the dense forest that night, but God surprised us at 10:30 p.m.

with a beautiful cabin to stay in. The cabins were huge habitations with about six bedrooms, a large living room, several bathrooms, and several people living together in community.

During the couple of weeks we stayed at The Cause we would spend our mornings praying by the lake or walking through the forest, our afternoons preaching the Gospel on the streets of Charlotte, and our nights in rich fellowship with the radical young people at the base. We loved living in a healthy, Jesus-loving community while going out preaching every day on the streets. We were living the dream!

Gospel Proclamation To Crowds

The Cause, the Call, and Morning Star functioned as a dynamic hub that pulled in several incredible ministries from the Charlotte area. One of these ministries was Bound 4 Life, a ministry dedicated to praying for the ending of abortion in America. So one Saturday morning we heard that Bound 4 Life was going to "siege" an infamous abortion clinic in Charlotte, so we decided to join them. This specific abortion clinic was where the woman in the Supreme Court case of Roe v. Wade had received her abortion, so it had extreme prophetic significance as the place where the first legal abortion in American history had taken place.

For four hours, about fifty of us stood across the street from the clinic with red tape over our mouths and the word "LIFE" written on it as we silently cried out to God for the ending of abortion. This was our form of protest, a silent siege against Satan's stronghold that loudly reverberated in the halls of Heaven. It was truly a life transforming experience that instilled in me a loud cry for the ending of the mass genocide that has been taking place every day in America for the past 40 years. Since that day we have been united with Bound 4 Life to pray, "Jesus, we plead Your blood over our sins and sins of our nation. God, end abortion and send revival to America!"

Once the siege was over, Matt Lockett, the director of Bound 4 Life, dropped us off at the Carolina Place Mall so that we could commence our work of evangelism. As we walked out of the car, Matt slipped us ten dollars for us to buy lunch. Years later, he told us that it was all the money he had left at the time.

*

We decided to rest and call our family members for a couple of hours before engaging people with the Gospel message. We were exhausted from the long week and four hour siege.

Once we began preaching the Gospel, we had a few good conversations, but the highlight of the day did not take place until the early evening. As Alex and I enjoyed a few slices of pizza in the food court, God moved upon Alex in a supernatural way. I'll let Alex tell you the story:

Josh and I went to the food court and bought pizza for dinner. It was delicious. The food court was jam-packed. There were barely any seats left. Josh started talking to me about David Hogan and we were having a pretty good time. We needed a break from all the preaching we were doing because it could get very exhausting at times. But right in the middle of the conversation I started to feel a little strange. Josh kept talking, but I couldn't understand the words that were coming out of his mouth. I wasn't really sure what was going on. All of a sudden, the Holy Spirit dropped right on me in the middle of the crowded food court!

Josh looked at me and saw that something was up. I looked at him, he looked right back. He instinctively knew what I was about to do. Josh locked eyes with me and encouragingly said, "Go for it man." He bowed his head and began to pray for me. I told Josh, "The Holy Spirit wants me to say something." Immediately, Satan infiltrated my thoughts trying to convince me to stay put, but I rebuked the thoughts in the name of Jesus!

I walked over to a table, stood right up on the chair, and let the Holy Spirit say what He wanted to say through me. I said to the crowd,

"Excuse me everyone!! The Lord wanted me to speak to you all today."
The place went dead silent. You could hear a pin drop. I had no fear.

The Holy Spirit moved so powerfully. One guy began recording
me as I spoke. The Holy Spirit wanted me to tell them all to repent, put
their faith in Jesus, to stop putting it off or waiting for another day, and to
put away their disbelief. I quietly began to pray in tongues, and when I got
down from the chair the Holy Spirit told me to keep praying in tongues.

Josh and I walked out of the mall full of joy because of the
powerful breakthrough that had just taken place. My eyes were welled up
with tears of joy. Suddenly, a few security officers stormed out of the
mall entrance rushing towards us.

They questioned us, "What were you guys doing in the mall?"

"God spoke to him to preach the Gospel to the people, so he
obeyed and did it," Josh responded.

The men were taken aback by Josh's response because I think
they were church-goers and they didn't know how to respond. They came
up with some lame explanations as to why we are not allowed to preach
the Gospel in the mall.

They said, "There are many people with different religions and
beliefs and you need to respect that."

"I understand," Josh replied.

"You cannot go around making a mess like this," the security
continued, "If you guys ever want to return here you need to behave
like adults."

"No problem," Josh responded.

"If you guys ever do this again here you will be permanently
expelled from the property," the officer emphatically declared.

"We understand. Thank you sir. God bless you," we said.

We left the mall rejoicing that we finally had the honor of being
somewhat persecuted for the sake of the Gospel. We fully understood
the request of the security guards, but we chose to fear God rather than
man. The Lord directed us to preach the Gospel at the same mall a couple
more times and we gladly obeyed. Each time we went the security

followed us around and kept a close eye on us, but since each group willingly talked with us they were not able to kick us out. In fact, the security interrupted a conversation with one of the first groups that we met. They asked the group if were bothering them and the crew of young people all said that they were thoroughly enjoying our conversation and were not bothered one bit by us.

*

Once Alex and I left the mall, we decided that it was time to walk to The Cause base since the sun was about to set. It was about a three-hour walk to the base, but we had no other option since we didn't have a car and there were no bus lines in the area. After having got lost the first time, we had memorized the route well enough that we were confident that we would find the base the second time around. The sun soon went down, the paved road eventually ended, and all signs of civilization disappeared. We were filled with joy as we made our way down the gravel road in the middle of a tall pine forest without flashlights and no destination in sight.

A little over two hours into our walk we ran into the first sign of civilization. About twenty Hispanic men and women were sitting down in a circle in the front yard of a quaint home with carne asada on the grill, beers and soda in hand, guitars strumming, and people singing. They were all from different parts of Latin American and none of them spoke English.

As we were passing by this scene I felt the Holy Spirit tugging my heart to go and share the Gospel with everyone at the party. Alex's example at the food court had inspired me and now was my chance to do something equally as crazy as he had. I hesitated for a second, especially since I had never preached to a crowd of unbelievers in Spanish before, but Alex knew what was going on in my spirit without me vocalizing a word and he encouraged me saying, "Yeah man! Do it! Do it!"

So I did it. Alex and I walked straight up to the group, I introduced the two of us in Spanish, and I candidly told them that God had spoken to me to share the Gospel with them. Upon listening to our introduction, the first thing they did was offer us food, something to drink, and a chair for us to sit down and join them. We were shocked by their hospitality and welcoming spirit towards us. Most groups of people would have awkwardly listened to us or just told us to not disturb their party, but this group welcomed us with open arms and great respect. We were lost for words.

We had just eaten dinner at the mall, so we only accepted some cold water to drink, which was much appreciated after walking for two hours. All eyes were fixed on me. No one was talking to each other anymore and they were all attentively waiting for me to speak. I began by asking them several questions about their salvation and relationships with God and they answered them all respectfully and honestly.

They explained to us that most of them were migrant workers who worked hard all week and Saturday night was one of the only times they had free to rest and spend time together. So they always got together to eat, drink, play music, and relax. They made it clear that none of them get drunk or party hard and a couple of them were Christians.

After hearing where they were at in their individual walks with God I asked if they would allow me to share with them what Jesus taught we had to do in order to have an intimate relationship with God. I shared the message of the Cross and urged them to put their faith in Jesus and repent of their sins in order to have an assurance of salvation. They listened to everything with great respect, but they also actively gave their opinions and asked challenging questions as I explained the Gospel. It was so enriching to have such an interactive and open conversation with a group of people who ranged from being Evangelical Christians to nominal Catholics to Atheists. Everyone contributed and was quite frank in their opinions about the Gospel, yet they always respectfully permitted me to give straightforward answers in response to their questions and comments. All of this was done within an atmosphere of honor for one another, friendliness, and even some jokes. At the end of our time together, I asked them if it would be alright for me to pray for them and they all kindly agreed. I prayed for them with all of my heart to encounter Jesus and be saved and then we bid them all a good night.

As we were about to turn around and walk away, several of them insisted in giving us a ride to The Cause base. Along the way, the driver openly told me about his journey with God and his doubts. He explained that he was a Catholic who was not sure of what he believed, but he had some good friends who were Christians and he was open to Christ. He made it clear that he would love to have us come over to their house whenever we wanted because they welcomed anyone who spoke about God and the Bible.

Alex and I learned something very important that day: no matter how hard it seemed to obey God's command, all we had to do was have the boldness to take the first step and God would be faithful to complete the rest.

How God Provides

A person who lives by faith, at least in my dictionary, is essentially a person who has left behind their money, house, material possessions, and job, in order to obey the call of God on their lives. They simply hear and obey God's command knowing that He will be faithful to provide them with clothing, shelter, food, money, and/or a job.

I have read many books about, heard about, and even met people who have lived by faith, but it always frustrated me that they would just tell me one or two isolated accounts of how God provided for their needs and the rest of the time they would just say "Well, God provided."

"How did God provide?! Tell me!" I would always think to myself, "I want to know the nitty-gritty details. How did you eat every day? Where did you sleep each night? On the street? In a person's house? How did you get around? What about your wife and kids?"

Well, since I have always been curious to know the ins-and-outs of what happened to people when they lived by faith, I decided to be faithful in telling how God provided for Alex and me when we put our faith in Him alone. So I would like to provide a chronological account of every provision God gave us up to this point in our journey. I will briefly repeat a few of the past stories that I've told in detail only to present a full picture of God's faithfulness during the first half of my journey.

First of all, I did have money in the bank when I started my trip, but God spoke to me specifically to trust in Him alone. So I left both my credit and debit card behind and never accessed my bank account once throughout my entire six-month journey.

Moreover, I made a rule with God for our trip. The rule was that we would never ask anyone for food, money, shelter, a ride, an offering or anything else. We would simply be faithful to daily preach the Gospel and obey the Spirit's lead and we would trust Him to be faithful to provide for our daily needs. I reasoned that if I could trust a sinful, worldly boss for a paycheck at the end of two weeks after working for him a certain amount of hours, how much more could I trust the most faithful Boss in the world to supply all of my needs if I was truly working for him every day of the week.

The first financial provision I received began with a wonderful temptation several months before the trip had begun. A close friend of mine informed me about the possibility of being sponsored by a cycling company and several Christian businesses if I rode their bicycle and wore their clothes as I trekked the United States. Besides providing me with a free bicycle and clothes, all of my food and lodging expenses would be covered as well. The opportunity seemed too good to be true, but I knew that if I accepted it the element of living by faith would be gone. However, what if this was the way God wanted to provide for all of my needs? How could I reject God's gracious provision just because I wanted to take the more rugged route of having no financial security at all? I hadn't asked for this sponsorship. It was freely presented to me.

For over a month, I sought God for His direction, but I never received clear guidance from Him concerning the decision. I had to make a final decision soon, so I was forced to give God an ultimatum: If He didn't want me to accept the sponsorship then He must provide me with enough money to buy a bus or plane ticket to Orlando by August 11th. The money could not come from a family member or from someone who knew the circumstances of my decision. It had to come from an outside source. If the finances did not arrive by August 11th then I would simply assume that God wanted me to accept the sponsorship. God had three weeks to provide.

The three weeks quickly passed by without anything happening. Finally, on the morning of August 11th, I reminded God that it was the last day that He had to come through with the money and I expectantly prayed for the miracle to take place. As I arrived slightly late for church that Sunday morning, my friend's dad, Tony Wilkins, stopped me in the hallway and asked me if he could speak to me for a moment. He walked me over to an ATM and told me a story. Him and his wife, Maira, had been earnestly praying for me, especially after they had heard about the mission trip I was planning to embark upon. As they prayed, the Holy Spirit spoke to them to sow into my ministry. Once he finished the short story, he had $120 in his hands that he had pulled out of the ATM. Then he said, "So here you go Joshua. This is for your ministry."

I was speechless and overflowing with gratitude. God had spoken! He did not want me to accept the sponsorship. He wanted me to go completely by faith. I saved the money until it was time for me to leave for Orlando. I used it to purchase my Greyhound ticket and then gave away the change.

So on the day I left for Orlando, my only possessions were my backpack with clothes and toiletries, my Bible, a cell phone, and two empty pockets. However, when I was about to step onto the Greyhound Bus my mom, with tears in her eyes, pleaded with me, "Here Joshua. Take this son. Please take this!" Although I had not wanted any help from my family on this trip, I humbly took the $40 because I could not bear to reject my nearly weeping mother.

Ultimately, then, I started this trip with $40 in my pocket. And boy did it help. Those forty dollars enabled me to have some food to eat for a couple of days.

The first night I was in Orlando I slept on the street and the second and third night I slept in a lush field. During those three days, a few of the members of Tabernaculo de Vida lovingly gave me $45.

On the fourth day, a paralyzed man named Greg approached me in conversation and after nearly one hour of fellowshipping with each other he invited me to stay at his house. He lived very humbly, so he wasn't able to provide me with much food to eat. Thus, I paid for lunch and dinner every day when I wasn't fasting and I was constantly paying for bus fares.

By the end of the first week, God had provided me with a place to stay and money for food and public transportation. However, I only had $25 left and it seemed like I was going to be broke within a day or two. I was beginning to be anxious that Sunday morning, but on the bus ride to church I prayed with faith for God to provide. As soon as I walked into the church, Lourdes gave me a big hug; served me breakfast; and gave me two loaves of Cuban bread, a box of Argentinean pastries, and $20. The church served free lunch that day and Lourdes invited me over for dinner. After dinner, she gave me another $20.

On Monday, Greg gave me $100. I was shocked, extremely humbled, and felt unworthy of receiving such a sacrificial offering. I strongly refused to take his money, but he insisted that I take it with tears in his eyes saying that what I was doing was the only ministry he fully believed in and wanted to give his money to. Here was a paralyzed man who had already cared for me far beyond anyone else had on my trip thus far, yet he wanted to support me even more. He had three homeless people living in his apartment, was unemployed, and lived off of disability paychecks every month due to his condition. That donation was certainly the holiest $100 I have ever received in my life.

On Tuesday, I received a package in the mail. I had foolishly forgotten to bring a jacket on my trip, so my mom sent me one through the mail. In the jacket pocket was $70, sixty from my mom and ten from the lady working at the post office who was deeply moved by my mission when my mom told her about it.

On Wednesday, I preached to a group of African-American and Caribbean guys playing basketball at a park. One of the guys was a devout Christian. He really respected me for preaching the Gospel to all the guys at the court that day, so he gave me $20.

Thus, on Sunday I only had $25 and was worried that I would soon be penniless, but three days later I had more than $200. Praise God!

After being with Greg for six days Lourdes' pleaded with me to stay at her and her husband's home. She spoiled me with fresh pastries every morning for breakfast and homemade gourmet meals every night for dinner. I felt like I was living in a five-star hotel. I was given my own room with a queen size bed to sleep on. Throughout this time, I was daily spending money for lunch and bus fares. I rode the bus everywhere. I ended up buying a $12 seven-day bus pass, which saved me a lot of money. When I left Lourdes' house a week later she gave me a $25 gift certificate for Wal-Mart.

For the next week-and-a-half that I spent in Orlando no one gave me any money. Thus, by the end of my time there I had a little over $100 remaining. I was going to spend it on a bus fare to Jacksonville, but then my parents offered to pick me up in Orlando and take me with them to Atlanta. They weren't going to Atlanta for my sake. It was for a completely different reason, but it ended up that I just happened to be conveniently on the way to their destination. Thus, I didn't have to pay for a bus fare, saving me about $70. Also, Alex came along with my parents, so he didn't have to pay for transportation either.

In Atlanta, the entire first weekend was paid for because my family was with us. They didn't let us pay for anything.

On Monday, my parents left and Alex and I were invited to stay with Nilton. Nilton took us to a meeting that he hosts at the Atlanta

Vineyard that night. We preached there and someone came up to us at the end of the meeting and gave us $50.

Nilton served us breakfast each morning and took us out to restaurants several times. In fact, in Atlanta, we actually gained weight and were treated like kings. Our stomachs were constantly full because people would take us out to eat or they would feed us at their church or home. We stayed in Atlanta for over a month and we probably only paid for six or seven meals. We spent a good amount of income on bus and metro fares as we daily used public transportation, yet all the money we spent was overshadowed by the huge blessings that God had in store for us.

On Tuesday, Nilton hosted a men's prayer meeting. We shared our vision with the men and they were greatly touched and challenged. At the end of the meeting one man came to me and gave me an envelope with $40 in it and another man came by and slipped me an envelope with $200 in it. We couldn't believe it. We were totally shocked.

If I were to add up all of the donations given to us up to this point on the trip without subtracting the money we spent it would come out to be $620. Thus, in three-and-a-half weeks we had already received $620. We were overwhelmed by God's faithfulness.

From Tuesday until the next Wednesday we received nothing, but we already had quite an abundance of finances, so we were not worried one bit. However, God soon decided to bless our socks off.

On a Thursday night, we preached at Videira, the largest Brazilian church in Atlanta. However, since it was a weeknight only about eighty people were in attendance. The congregation was extremely impacted by our testimony and radical message. Then the pastor did something that I would never have expected or even dreamt of happening. He asked the church to take up a love offering for us. The people joyously gave to us. Alex and I just stood there in complete unbelief and awe as people lined up to put money in our hands. That night we received a total of $554. We were utterly overwhelmed by their love and generosity. We felt so unworthy to receive their sacrificial offerings, yet they would have felt mocked if we had refused to receive it. Alex and I were deeply humbled by Videira's generosity towards us. I realized that this money was sacred and should never be misspent, so we only used it when we had genuine needs.

We attended Videira's Sunday night service that same week and they decided to give us another large offering even though we didn't speak at all that night.

Furthermore, Tocha Viva, a small, Presbyterian Brazilian church that we had preached at four times during our stay in Atlanta, gave us an offering.

Also, a few individuals gave us very generous offerings.

Thus, when we left Atlanta we had over $2,000. Never once did we ask for money or send out newsletters, yet God decided to bless us beyond belief.

We decided to open up a savings account so that we didn't have to carry around so much money with us. We only kept a portion of the money with us to use as spending money.

The first day we arrived in Charlotte we weren't offered a place to stay, so we spent the night in a cheap motel. I couldn't justify sleeping on a street corner when our brothers and sisters had given us over $2,000 to provide for our basic needs. On our second day in Charlotte, connected with Morning Star and The Cause and God provided a cabin for us to stay in for two weeks through Chuck Mervin.

That weekend, we went to Morning Star for their Sunday morning service. We sat next to an elderly man and introduced ourselves to him. He asked me where we were from, so I told him that we were from Miami and we were traveling around the country preaching the Gospel on the streets. Towards the end of the meeting, he smiled at me and handed me a one hundred dollar bill.

Finally, The Cause invited us to join them on God's Summer of Love Tour from Nashville to San Francisco. We felt that God was leading us to join them with the aim of preaching the Gospel as they prayed and worshipped across the country. The cost of the Tour was $400 per person. We realized that this was the reason why God had blessed us so abundantly; He wanted Alex and me to join God's Summer of Love Tour. We also gave our tithe to The Cause since they were the church family we were a part of during this time. In fact, we always tithed into the local church we were partnered with in each city and we often gave offerings to ministries we encountered and individuals we met.

Some might consider me foolish for being so candid and transparent about the financial aspect of our trip, but I don't mind. I believe that there is practicality in spirituality. It would be dishonest for me to only describe the spiritual side of our trip without showing the practical side of it as well. The church has a right to know where their offerings go and I want to be very real and transparent about every dollar we received and spent. God was always faithful to provide for us and we give Him all the glory!

GOD'S SUMMER OF LOVE TOUR: TIME OF TRANSITION

God's Summer of Love Tour had been set to begin in Nashville, TN after The Call Nashville and would end one month later in San Francisco, CA for the 40-year anniversary of the Summer of Love. The purpose of the trip was to pray and worship in every city along the way asking God to saturate the nation with His presence. The goal of the tour was to make a prophetic declaration throughout the country and especially in San Francisco that the artificial, immoral summer of love of the 1960's was over and God's summer of love now ruled and reigned.

The young people in our cabin told us about the tour as soon as we arrived at The Cause. We weren't sure if we were supposed to join them because the tour didn't have a focus on evangelism and they were traveling to the West Coast while we had planned to go up the East Coast. However, after a couple weeks of prayer, God clearly showed us that He wanted us to join the tour. Chuck made us a promise saying, "I'll let you guys loose to preach the Gospel while the others worship and pray."

Once we knew that we would have the freedom to preach the Gospel every day we felt peace to join the Tour.

We carpooled with The Cause to attend The Call Nashville on 07/07/07. The solemn assembly was historic and was one of the most powerful prayer gatherings I have ever attended. After praying at The Call, we kicked off God's Summer of Love Tour beginning in Nashville and began our road trip to the West Coast.

Since the Tour was open to the public, my brother, my cousin Andre from Brazil, and my girlfriend all decided to join. I was overjoyed to spend time with Brooke after not seeing her for several months and it was great to travel with my brother again. I was really happy that Andre was finally going to experience American culture, make friends with American people, and see our beautiful nation. He had spent nearly a year in Miami as a foreign exchange student only to learn more Spanish than English and be immersed in Latino culture more than American culture. Now he would be able see and experience a much grander picture of the culture and beauty of our great nation.

God's Summer of Love Tour was a blast for Alex and me! There's nothing like going on a road trip across the country with 250 lovers of Jesus who live in community, worship and pray every day, and are burning for revival. While most people on the tour considered this to be the craziest trip of their lives, for us it was a time of rest and refreshing. Alex and I got to bask in the presence of God every day and renew our strength. We felt like batteries that were being recharged to last for the rest of our journey.

Besides praying and worshipping as a community, The Cause would rent a prime venue for one or two nights in the downtown area of each city we visited. They owned a semi-truck that transformed into a professional performance stage and had several anointed worship bands who were on tour with us. The bands included Mark Mathis, John Mark McMillan, Sarah McMillan, Joel Khouri, Kevin Prosch, Leonard Jones and Luke Skaggs, the son of Ricky Skaggs. So on these nights, one or two of the bands would lead worship for three or four hours straight and all

250 of us would worship God like maniacs. We would invite churches and people from the community to attend for free and we usually had about 100 to 200 people show up for each worship night. Also, the live music and undignified dancing and singing unto the Lord would attract dozens of people as they walked by. Towards the end of each worship night we would pray for the visitors standing around us, and God would often touch them with His Holy Spirit.

Tragically, the Gospel was never preached from the stage nor was an invitation to follow Christ ever given. This deeply frustrated me, but I still loved the tour and knew that God was moving in and through it. The theme of the tour seemed to be what one of the singers declared on a particular night when she passionately proclaimed, "We don't need to preach the Gospel anymore. There's a better way. All we need to do is love." In fact, when Alex and I preached the Gospel to unbelievers there were a few times when our friends at The Cause rebuked us and told us that there was a "better way." This left me hurt and somewhat jaded with The Cause for a few years, but the Lord later healed me and I could now honestly say that I love The Cause and everything the Lord used them to do through God's Summer of Love Tour.

Although Alex and I loved worshipping, praying, and living in community with The Cause, we were extremely frustrated that we did not have the opportunity to preach the Gospel very much while we were on the Tour. We were a massive group that was hard to accommodate, so at every city we visited we would camp out at a field or church that was several miles away from the main city. Our campsites were never close to a bus stop and the only way to find any people to witness to was by driving or walking for ten to twenty miles. We didn't have a car and every time we asked the people who did have cars for a ride they were unwilling to drive us out to the city because everyone was tight on gas money.

We toured with The Cause for two weeks through the following cities: Nashville, TN; St. Louis, MO; Wichita, KS; Amarillo, TX; Albuquerque, NM; Sedona, AZ; and San Diego, CA. We were able to preach the Gospel in Nashville, Wichita, and Sedona, but even then we only preached a handful of times.

Once we arrived to the West Coast I felt the Holy Spirit leading me to leave the tour and continue my mission of preaching the Gospel throughout the United States. Alex, however, sincerely felt that he needed to go all the way to San Francisco to finish the tour with The Cause. We both felt peace about the direction God was leading us, so we agreed to separate for two weeks and then meet up in Los Angeles.

The day before I left the tour an astonishing miracle took place. I was sitting down on the front lawn of the church we were camped at when, out of nowhere, a random woman ran up to me and smacked two hundred dollars into my hand! I was in total shock! Who has ever had a complete stranger enthusiastically throw two hundred dollars cash in their hand while relaxing on a grass lawn doing absolutely nothing? If that doesn't prove that God is real I don't know what will.

The middle-aged woman who had just blessed me financially began joyfully telling me the story of why she just handed me so much cash. She was from the state of Washington and she and her husband happened to be in San Diego on vacation. They knew all about God's Summer of Love Tour because they had attended The Call Nashville.

So as they were driving around San Diego enjoying the scenery during their vacation, they drove by the church we were camping at and saw our huge bus that said "The Cause" on it. They got so excited when they realized that they had caught us in the middle of our tour and immediately the wife heard the Holy Spirit tell her to go to the bank, withdraw two hundred dollars, and give it to one of the people at The Cause who the Holy Spirit would guide her to.

She joyfully obeyed the Holy Spirit. She went to the bank, withdrew the money, drove up to our campsite, and loudly inquired, "Who is the leader here?"

One of the main leaders replied, "I'm a leader. How could I help you?"

The woman said, "Is there anyone here who needs money?"

"That guy does," the leader responded, pointing to me, "He's about to leave the group to preach the Gospel on the streets alone, so he probably needs it more than any of us."

"Perfect!" the woman exclaimed.

That is when she walked right up to me and exuberantly placed the money in my hands. I have two words for that: Jehovah Jireh!

*

In conclusion, our time spent with the Cause was amazing and God truly worked in our lives, but it was time for me to leave the tour so that I could continue focusing on witnessing to the lost. In fact, the tour was absolutely necessary for us to be a part of for many reasons.

First of all, towards the end of our time in Atlanta, Alex had seriously begun to consider giving up and returning home to Miami. He had felt inadequate in evangelism and had begun to seriously doubt if God had really been the One who had directed him to go on the trip. He eventually decided that he would go to Charlotte with me, but if God did not empower him to breakthrough in evangelism and did not clearly guide him to continue on the journey he would return home. I tried my best to encourage and pray for Alex to continue the journey because I knew that God was the One who had called him to carry out this mission trip. I was convinced that Alex was both called and fully capable of preaching the Gospel with power and I also knew that I would be not be able to finish the trip alone. Thus, The Cause was an answer to prayer because it was only after we joined them that Alex finally experienced a personal breakthrough in his walk with the Lord and call to evangelism. Once we left the tour, Alex never wavered again in his confidence and we successfully completed the mission trip together.

Moreover, Alex and I had started to become somewhat annoyed with each other. It wasn't anything too serious; just the common annoyances two roommates in college would have with each other. I would get into arguments with Alex about his cleaning habits, bad manners, and staying up late on the computer usually because he was researching apologetics and Scripture. Alex would get into arguments with me about being too controlling, talking on the phone for too long with my girlfriend, and spending an unnecessary amount of time in prayer every morning when we could be out winning souls. So being with The Cause was the perfect scenario for us to remain as mission partners, yet also have 250 other people to hang out with throughout the week. Thus, we would spend most of each day with The Cause community and only one or two hours with each other. This brought healing, maturity, and peace to our relationship. Once the tour was over, we rarely argued again for the rest of our trip.

CHAPTER FIVE

SAN DIEGO

Inspiring A Long Term Laborer

San Diego was hard ground. God had led me to focus on the
upper class areas of the county such as La Jolla, Pacific Beach, Scripps
Ranch, and downtown. A typical day of witnessing entailed getting
rejected over and over again, having a few mediocre conversations, and
perhaps one or two good conversations. I would spend at least an hour or
two of each day idly sitting down on a bench or standing up against a wall
too intimidated to approach these well dressed, refined Californians
puffing their cigars and sipping wine as they strutted along the beach.

The majority of my fruitful encounters were with Asian
immigrants and young people. Quite frankly, most of the wealthy Anglo-
American adults that I encountered were simply unwilling to speak with
me and they were offended and hostile at the very mention of the name of
Jesus.

The two weeks I spent there, however, were extremely fruitful
because San Diego was the only place in my entire journey where God

used me to inspire a man to begin preaching the Gospel every Saturday in the darkest place in all of San Diego county: Pacific Beach.

His name was Fabian Silberberg. Fabian was a Jewish Argentinean man who was brought to Christ when my dad shared the Gospel with him in the early 1990's. When he was working as a door-to-door salesman he just happened to knock on the door of our home. My dad invited him in, gave him a meal to eat, and shared the Gospel with him. He soon gave his life to Christ, became a committed member of our church, and married a Brazilian woman named Elaine. Fabian and Elaine have been passionately following Jesus ever since.

Thus, when Fabian and Elaine found out that I was in San Diego they immediately invited me to stay with them for as long as I needed. They had been praying for me and following my blog throughout much of my journey and they were overjoyed to have me with them in their city.

After witnessing in San Diego for a few days I heard by word-of-mouth that Pacific Beach, also known as PB, was where the main club scene of the county was to be found. So I resolved that I would preach the Gospel there on a Saturday night.

I mentioned the idea to Fabian to see what he thought and to see if he might even want to join me. To my surprise, Fabian was quite scandalized by the idea and tried to convince me never to go to such a wretched place.

"What?!" He shouted, "Why do you want to go to there?! PB is a baaad place. You should never go there, Joshua. It is too sinful."

"Fabian," I responded as I burst out in joyful laughter, "That is exactly why I want to go there; because it is such a sinful place."

"Are you going to go during the day?" He asked, "If you go during the day then that might be okay."

"I could go during the day," I replied, "but I have to go at night too."

"No, no, no, no, no," Fabian pressed on, "you cannot go at night. It is too sinful at night. They have clubs and bars everywhere and it is just too dark at night."

"Fabian," I stubbornly persisted, "I'm going to go at night. Jesus didn't command us to go to the nice and safe places. He commanded us to go to the dark and sinful places to save lost souls and help those who are spiritually sick.

"So Fabian," I asked, "Do you want to come with me to preach the Gospel this Saturday night at PB?"

"No way!!!" he passionately yelled with a high-pitched shriek in his voice, "I am not going to that place! I cannot do that! It's too worldly!"

He abruptly stopped to think for a moment. Then, after several seconds of awkward silence, he calmly said, "Even if I did go...Kevin (Fabian's son) would not be able to go. He is too young."

He continued his thought process some more until he eventually remarked, "Well, maybe I'll come. I'll pray about it and see. But Kevin definitely can't come."

A couple days later Fabian confirmed to me that he had prayed about it and felt peace from the Lord to join me in Pacific Beach for a night of evangelism.

*

Saturday came along and I took Fabian's advice by taking the bus to PB during the day to evangelize. I was so pumped to preach the Gospel in such a decadent place. When I arrived at the beach, it was packed with girls in bikinis laying out in the sun and buff guys playing volleyball and frisbee while swiggin' some beers and blasting their boom boxes. The boardwalk was buzzing with cruiser bicyclists, rollerbladers, power walkers, joggers, and an amazing crew of unicyclists. Instead of having shops and restaurants lining up the boardwalk there were multi-million dollar homes where parties were being held, the front yards being the boardwalk.

I walked up and down the boardwalk asking for the Lord to fill me with boldness to preach the Gospel, but the boldness never came. My mind was filled with excuses:

'No one will stop to talk with me on the boardwalk.'

'I'm not going to go and preach to those girls in bikinis laying out in the sun. They're going to think I'm hitting on them and I'm going to have difficulty not thinking bad thoughts while I'm witnessing to them. That would be horrible!'

'The guys won't stop in the middle of their volleyball or Frisbee game to talk to me. Maybe in between their games I could approach them.'

"All these people are White and rich. They don't want to hear the Gospel."

As I began to believe these thoughts I became gripped with fear and intimidation. I was paralyzed and unable to start a conversation with anyone for a good while.

Finally, I mustered up the courage to talk to a couple volleyball players only to be immediately rejected by them.

I struck up a conversation with a man sitting down listening to his boom box. We talked for a little bit, but our conversation went nowhere and he soon made it clear that he didn't want to be bothered.

Thus, my fears were reinforced and I remained paralyzed in fear for most of the day. I finally just gave up for the day and decided to read my Bible and pray until Fabian arrived for night evangelism.

*

At last, around 9:45 p.m., Fabian arrived along with eleven others whom he had invited from his church, Abiding Place Ministries. Seeing twelve brothers and sisters in Christ join this defeated soldier refreshed my spirit and filled my heart with faith. It felt like I had just received military reinforcements to help win the battle for souls that night.

We gathered around in a circle and began to fervently pray and intercede for the people partying in Pacific Beach (PB) that night. We cried out to God for His mercy and for His saving power to encounter the people we were going to speak to. We were all filled with faith and joy as we sought God and praised Him together for over an hour.

Four of the people in the group were German teenagers who were visiting the United States for a few weeks. They had never been evangelizing on the streets before and they were pretty weirded out by our intense prayers. Once we concluded our prayer time we split into groups and went out to preach the Gospel. Two of the Germans, Lisa and Patrick, came with me.

I was in constant prayer in my spirit as we walked down the main strip of clubs and bars. We asked the Lord to guide us to the people He wanted us to speak to that night and stayed sensitive to His leading.

Eventually, God led us to speak to a teenager who was sitting on the sidewalk with his back up against the wall of a building. He had a nice BMX bicycle with him and his clothes were pretty dirty, but what drew me to him was the expression of utter despair that he wore on his face. You could see the hopelessness and pain in his eyes and it was obvious that the young man had already given up on asking for help. He was homeless, but he wasn't begging at all. He was trying to sell his shiny bike for thirty dollars.

So I immediately knelt down next to him, gave him a dollar, and began talking to him about Jesus. Even though he was suffering from deep depression he didn't seem to be an alcoholic or drug addict. I asked him if he had family who could help him and he explained that his family lived in New Jersey and, for a reason that he did not care to elaborate upon, they couldn't help him.

He wasn't sure if he believed in God and he didn't really seem to care whether there was a God or not. He just wanted help and love. I spoke to him from the depths of my heart offering all of the hope that I could give in that moment. I told him about my few days being homeless in Orlando and how I was so close to God in those days because I realized that He was all that I had and He was all that mattered. I prayed for him and poured my heart out to him. He was touched and impacted by my prayer and words of encouragement and he was really touched when I ended up giving him five more dollars at the end of the conversation.

I was saddened that I couldn't bring him to my house since I didn't live in San Diego and that I didn't know of any believers in the city who would be willing to take him in to lovingly restore him.

*

We had a few other short conversations with people as we walked down the strip. Then my new German friends decided to use the restroom at McDonald's. I was standing outside waiting for them when I felt led to preach to a group of eleven adults who were sitting around a McDonald's table right outside the door of the fast food restaurant. Most of them were drunk and I could tell that they had been partying for several hours already, so I walked up to them and joyfully said, "How ya guys doin' tonight!?"

"Great!" They all exclaimed.

Immediately one of them said, "So do you want to preach Scripture to us?"

It must have been obvious because I had a Bible in my hand.

"Yeah man!" I responded.

So the two men who were the most hammered piously petitioned, "Read us a passage of Scripture." They both claimed to be Christians and believed that they were saved, yet they were the most drunk in the whole group.

I began talking about Jesus to them all, but eventually one of the girls influenced everyone else not to listen to me. However, the two 'pious' Christians wanted to listen. I preached the Gospel and shared with them what it really meant to repent of one's sins. They understood everything that I shared with them, but they still thought they were great people who were all going to Heaven.

In the middle of the conversation one of the two men took off his shorts and just stood around in his boxer briefs in front of the girls. Then he came back and told me about how good of a person he was. I tried to convict them through the Law, but it didn't really work. So I just prayed for them and left. I felt like I had just thrown my pearls to a bunch of swine, but only God knows what really went on in their hearts when I shared His message with them.

The Germans were amazed that people would actually stop to have a conversation with me and listen to the Gospel. They said that in Germany no one would have the politeness or interest to ever talk to a stranger about God. I told them about my vision for BUILDERS and it deeply inspired them. Lisa was convinced that the vision would work in Germany as well because there were plenty of dedicated Christians who would love to be a part of such an evangelistic ministry.

*

As we began making our way back to the beach, I began talking with three rich young Mexicans who were on vacation from Mexico City. They were all nominal Catholics who never really put much thought into following God. We talked in Spanish for about forty minutes and had the most fruitful conversation of the night. They were so hungry and impacted by every word that came out of my mouth. It felt like I was speaking to spiritually starved children who were finally being given fresh bread to eat. They seemed to be shocked as they realized how ignorant they were of God and the Bible and they committed themselves to seek and follow God. We prayed with them and let them go. Hispanics are some of my favorite people to talk to because they are almost always extremely open to and hungry for God.

At 1 a.m., our evangelism teams suddenly collided with each other from all four directions. We hadn't planned to finish evangelizing at a certain time or place, but when we all bumped into each other on the boardwalk we felt like the Lord was saying that our mission had been accomplished. We decided to call it a night and I left with Fabian to his house.

Little did I know that God had marked Fabian's heart that night. Once I left San Diego a few days later, Fabian made a covenant with God that he would preach the Gospel every Saturday at Pacific Beach until the Lord told him to stop. By the grace of God, Fabian continued to faithfully preach the Gospel in Pacific Beach every single Saturday since July of 2007 and when his family moved to Orange County in 2011 he dedicated himself to preach the Gospel in Huntington Beach every Saturday. As I am writing this book, Fabian is still preaching the Gospel every Saturday. God still hasn't told him to stop.

California, The Land I Love

California is truly a melting pot of all nations. Every time I rode the bus I would hear conversations all around me being spoken in numerous languages. Such languages as Tagalog, Hindi, Mandarin, Japanese, Korean, Arabic, Spanish, and many others would flood my ears as I walked through the crowds of people and rode on public transportation. In fact, it was impossible for me to open air preach on the bus because so many of the people didn't speak English at all!

The realization of unreached people groups living in our midst hit me like a brick wall during my time in California. Millions of immigrants from unreached nations and people groups were now living amongst us and what were we doing to reach them with the Gospel? We have the greatest opportunity in American history to reach the nations for Christ because God has brought them to our own backyard. During my trip, I had several fruitful encounters with unreached peoples and I had the joy of experiencing firsthand how easy it was to witness to them here at home.

As I walked around a mall in San Diego, I spotted a young Asian man in his twenties sitting alone in the food court. I felt compelled to speak to him and when I introduced myself to him he very kindly reciprocated the introduction with telling me that his name was Jao. He shared with me that he was from the northwestern region of Thailand

and he had been in the U.S. for eight months now. He was only going to be here for a total of two years in order to learn English and then return to Thailand.

The more we spoke with each other the more I realized that I was speaking to a completely unreached individual from an unreached nation of the world. Jao had never heard anything about Jesus, the Bible, Heaven, Hell, judgment, or Christianity. He had heard the name Jesus before and he knew Jesus was a religious/historical figure, but he had never even heard of him dying on a cross. What's most tragic about this is that he attended a Catholic school during a few years of his childhood where he attended multiple chapel services, but he never understood why people went to church or what it was that people did in church.

How could the church go through so much sacrifice in sending dozens of missionaries and spending thousands of dollars to spread the Gospel in Thailand, and yet children were able to attend one of their schools for several years without ever hearing that Jesus died on the cross for them? This was a discovery that was sickening to my stomach and grievous to my soul.

As we talked about God, Jao told me that he didn't believe in God and that he was a Buddhist. From the depths of my heart I started to tell him that there was a purpose to life and it was found in knowing, loving, and following God. We were not put on the earth just to make money, go to school, and die. God created us to have a relationship with Him. I expounded on the reality and existence of God as Jao sat mesmerized by the truths that he was hearing.

I asked him if he understood what I was saying and he laughed and said, "I cannot change religions. I am Buddhist, my parents are Buddhist, my grandparents are Buddhist, and my ancestors too." I was impressed by his response because I never once mentioned Buddhism or Buddha nor did I ever insinuate that he had to convert to Christianity when I was talking to him. However, he immediately understood that he would never experience God in the way that I was describing to him if he stayed in Buddhism and that in order to know God in this way he would have to leave Buddhism. I didn't have to say one word about conversion. He simply understood that that is what it would take to know God.

"It's not about religion," I responded with conviction in my voice and my eyes locked with his, "It's about truth. Truth must exist and it is found in knowing and following God."

As I described this reality of finding truth in God, his eyes began to water. I explained the Gospel to him in detail and he genuinely understood it. I encouraged him to visit my friend's church, Abiding Place Ministries, and handed him their business card.

He promised me that he would visit the church and then asked me with a mixture of anguish, shame, and honest desire, "Is it okay to change religions?"

"Of course," I answered, "Because it is not about religion. It is about God and truth."

I prayed with Jao and then we parted ways. I could only imagine the battle that was going on in his soul just for him to ask me such a question. I could see in his eyes that he was deeply longing to experience the living God in the way that I had just described to him, yet he knew that if he chose to follow God he would be betraying his family and ancestors because he would have to leave Buddhism behind. However, he still took the courageous step and asked. My prayer for Jao was that God would complete the good work that He had begun in him and bring him to eternal salvation.

CHAPTER SIX

GREATER LOS ANGELES

Labor Day

Alex and I spent Labor Day in Moreno Valley at the home of my old friends Danny, Alejandrina, and Emilio Cervantes. In the early 90's, Emilio was the leader of one of the Blood gangs in South Central L.A. Through a series of incredible events, my father led him to Christ and discipled him for many years. He soon brought his younger siblings, Danny and Alejandrina, to Christ and they began their journey of following Jesus together as a family. Emilio later became a youth pastor and evangelist, married a pastor's daughter, and had two beautiful children. When he offered to host Alex and I at his home in Moreno Valley, he was one of the head elders of his church and was passionately in love with Jesus. Furthermore, Danny and I were about the same age, so we had grown up together as close friends. Alejandrina was one of my favorite Sunday school teachers in the church I had grown up in.

So it was a great joy for me to see my old friends again whom I hadn't seen for about eight years and it was even more amazing to see all that God had done in their lives. Now we were spending Labor Day together with them and several others. They spoiled us with a traditional Mexican barbeque with carne asada, tortillas, rice, beans, onions, cilantro, Tapatio, and lime. My nostalgia for authentic Mexican food was definitely satisfied after being deprived of it for several years in Miami.

Even though Labor Day was a holiday for most of America, Alex and I decided that it would not be a holiday for us. We felt peace to enjoy some fellowship and delicious food with our brothers and sisters in Christ, but we knew that sometime during that day we would get up, leave the party, and preach the Gospel.

We arrived at Emilio's house around 12:30 p.m. and by 4:30 p.m. everyone in the house was stuffed, tired, and trying to survive the scorching heat of Moreno Valley. We were all seated around the living room and kitchen in a state of silence, satisfaction, and slight boredom, when I began to feel a rumbling in my spirit.

"Now, Joshua," I heard the Holy Spirit say inside my soul.

I knew exactly what He wanted me to do. I raised my voice and, with excitement, I challenged the group, "Hey, let's go evangelize at the park!"

I could feel the resistance in the air after making my statement. Everyone was tired, stuffed, and feeling very lazy. No one wanted to leave the comfort of the couch they were sitting on in an air-conditioned home to confront the 105 degree dry heat outside and witness to a bunch of strangers on their day off from work. Even though all the people in the house were radical Christians, evangelism was the last thing on their minds on a lazy Labor Day afternoon.

"C'mon you guys," I insisted trying to encourage them to overcome their carnal nature, "There are a ton of people at the park down the street. This is the perfect day to evangelize because everyone is relaxing and spending time with their families. We could go there for one or two hours and then come back."

Alex and I stood up, ready to go. Everyone else was wiggling uncomfortably in their chairs fighting with their flesh to decide whether or not they would go. Soon Emilio and Danny stood up and said they were in and, eventually, all the guys in the living room arose to their feet.

One of the girls said, "It's cool. You guys could go. The girls are just gonna stay here at the house."

"No problem," we agreed.

So all the men got in a circle, held hands, and began to fervently pray. We passionately cried out to God to fill us with His Holy Spirit and anointing, to use us to win lost souls, and to touch the lives of the people we were going to speak to at the park. After about twenty minutes of intense prayer we all felt ready to go.

As soon as we finished praying all the women came around us and told us with conviction in their voices, "We're going too. We want to go with you guys."

"Awesome!" we exclaimed encouraged at the women's confident response, "Let's do this!"

So we all held hands again and prayed for another 10 minutes or so with all the women. There were sixteen of us in total, so we divided into four groups of three and one group of four with at least one woman in each group.

When we arrived at the park we quickly divided the park into zones and each group began witnessing to the people in their zone. As we strategically witnessed to each group in the park we felt like we were conducting a military takeover of an enemies fort. It was so encouraging because as I was witnessing to a table full of people I could see out of my peripheral vision Danny witnessing to a group of people on my left, Alex way in front of me preaching to some teenagers, and Emilio on my right praying over an entire family as they committed their lives to Christ.

The people at the park noticed too. They were seeing what was going on and they knew that it was only a matter of time until we reached them as well. However, instead of closing up and becoming defensive towards us they seemed to be even more open and ready to listen once we got to them.

As we witnessed in unity, we received a supernatural boldness to witness like I had never felt before. Normally, I did not have the boldness to approach a table of more than 5 or 6 people to preach the Gospel to them. However, here we were approaching entire families of twenty or thirty people at a time and sharing the Gospel with them all simultaneously. We were amazed to see these families quietly sit around their picnic tables and lawn chairs to hear us with respect and attentiveness. What surprised me the most was that the older men and women who were fathers, mothers, and grandparents, listened to 19, 21, and 23 year-olds with utmost respect. They even allowed us to pray over their entire families and some of them gave their lives to Christ.

Alex and I were overwhelmed by the supernatural power we all experienced by preaching the Gospel in unity with the body of Christ. There had not been one day in our entire mission trip that had been as powerful as this one. There had been about 200 people in the park and in less than two hours we had witnessed to every single person in the park. Nine people gave their lives to Christ on the spot and dozens of people gave us their phone numbers so that we could follow up with them and invite them to cell groups in their area. None of the outreach teams were fearful of sharing the Gospel with others because they were all emboldened by each other and filled with the Spirit of God. I had never experienced anything like it before.

Moreover, I had gone witnessing with large groups of people on a number of occasions, but never had I evangelized with a group of such deeply rooted, passionate Christians. Typically, in a large outreach group there are a few very strong evangelists; several people who love God, but have never evangelized before in their lives; some people who are lukewarm Christians; and a few people who are on the verge of backsliding, but came to the outreach just because they had to. In this group, however, every individual was burning on fire for God, living a lifestyle of consecrated holiness, seasoned in evangelism, had strong prayer lives, and knew the Word of God very well. Many of them were leaders of their own cell groups and most of them had powerful testimonies of God redeeming them from a lifestyle entrenched in sin. These were all genuine, no-nonsense Christians who loved God and knew what it meant to preach the Gospel and make disciples. All of them were being personally discipled in their church and most of them were already discipling others.

When we returned to Emilio's home, everyone was beaming with light as we shared our stories with one another about what God had done through us. Inexpressible joy, exploding faith, and shouts of praise were bursting out of our souls and written all over our faces. Each person went on and on about how their lives had been deeply impacted by this evangelism experience. They had never realized how much authority and boldness they had in Christ to witness to the lost and especially to their elders who reverently listened to and received everything they had to say. They all agreed that this experience had raised them up to a whole new level of evangelism and zeal for God and they thanked Alex and me for challenging and pushing them to step outside of their comfort zone and witness on their day off from work.

What was so encouraging about this experience was that since everyone who participated that day was part of a church with cell groups we knew that whoever had received Christ or had given us their contact information would be followed up and brought into a local cell group to be discipled. This was a perfect example of how we desire for all of our itinerant preaching trips to function. We win the souls and the local churches follow up and disciple them.

To conclude the night, we spent another thirty minutes or so praying that the Holy Spirit would seal the work of evangelism that had impacted the lives of so many individuals and families that day, including our own. Then we all relaxed and laughed our heads off as we watched Mr. Bean's newest movie, Johnny English!

The Story Of Lee Phan

I lost my cell phone when we were witnessing in Little Tokyo. For a whole week I had been praying for God to supply me with a phone because the cheapest phone at T-Mobile was $115 and I was not willing to spend so much of the money that others had sacrificially given us just to buy a phone. I didn't want to ask any of my friends for a phone either because I wanted God to provide.

After a week of not having a phone I became a little desperate, so I asked Silvia, our hostess, if she had any extra phones. She didn't have any, yet God, in His mercy, decided to provide me with a phone on that same day when my faith was weak.

Silvia dropped us off at Ontario Mills Mall to evangelize and as I was walking through the mall a really suave-looking twenty-seven-year-old Vietnamese guy named Lee walked up to me to sell me a T-Mobile plan. He reminded me of Jinn from Tekken because of his slick hairstyle and well-built physique. I explained to him that I already had a T-Mobile plan, but I was actually in need of assistance. I told him the story of how I lost my phone in L.A. and asked him if there were any phones that I could buy for cheaper than $115. I described my mission trip to him as he looked up the information on his computer.

Lee eventually sighed and confessed to me that they had nothing cheaper than $115, but then he kindly looked at me and said, "Well, you seem like a really nice guy. I have an extra phone at my house. I'll sell it to you for $20."

"Are you serious?!" I asked him in a state of shock.

"Yeah man, no problem," he replied.

"Thank you so much!" I exclaimed with joy. Then I shifted the topic of the conversation, "Hey, Lee. I wanted to ask you something. Do you have a relationship with God?"

"I don't know God, but I really want to," he replied, "Maybe you can invite me to your Bible study and I could learn more about God. Yeah man, I could go to your Bible study."

"I live in Miami," I explained to him, "But I do have friends here at the church I'm with who have awesome Bible studies in the area."

He was really excited, so we swapped business cards. He gave me his T-Mobile card and I gave him my mission trip card. I told him about the three-day Encounters the church would often hold and he said that really would love to attend one. He said that he would bring the phone to the mall the next day and I could come pick it up. I explained to him that I would be leaving to Orange County the next day and since I didn't have a car I had no way of getting to the mall. So he decided that he would mail me the phone wherever I stayed and he trusted that I would mail him back the money. I wanted to pray for him, but he had to get back to work.

I immediately gave Lee's contact information to my friend Danny so that he could invite him to his cell group that met in the area.

On Thursday, I tried to contact Lee in order to give him our host's address in Anaheim, but he couldn't talk because he was at work. On Friday, I called him around 1 p.m. and he happened to not be working that day. I began to dictate the address to him when he abruptly stopped me and told me that he wanted to come to Anaheim to give me the phone. I told him not to inconvenience himself with the long drive, but he said that he didn't mind the drive and he kept insisting that he wanted to come down and give me the phone. It's a forty-minute drive from Ontario to Anaheim without any traffic.

He said that he would arrive by 4 p.m. but ended up arriving around 5 p.m. Why would a guy drive over an hour just to sell his phone to some stranger for $20? It was obvious that the real reason Lee was coming was because he was hungry for God. As soon as I saw him, he told me that he would give me the phone for free as an apology for arriving an hour later than he had promised. I insisted that I wanted to pay for the phone, but he stood his ground and ended up giving me the phone for free. I welcomed him into our hosts' apartment, gave him something to drink, and we started talking.

The first words out of Lee's mouth were, "So what do you want to talk about? Do you want to know about me?"

"Of course," I said.

Alex sat with us and Lee began telling us a little bit about his life, his family, and his struggles. He confessed to us that he was very ashamed of himself because he had been smoking marijuana for some time now. He also told us that he had been entertaining the idea of committing suicide.

Suddenly he asked with a glimmer of hope in his eyes, "Can God change people? I heard that God changes people. I would like Him to change me."

"Of course," I answered, "God will totally transform you when you give your life to Him."

He kept insisting that he was too bad of a person for God to change him, but I explained to him that God could change anyone who commits his life to Him. Then Alex told Lee some of his testimony about his former lifestyle of drug abuse and alcoholism and how God had faithfully delivered him from all of his vices.

Lee was satisfied with Alex's testimony and quickly understood that his sin could be overcome by the transforming power of God. So he began asking us several questions about God and we answered them all. Eventually, he asked us if he could have a Bible. He told us that he would really like to read it and he had plenty of free time when he was at home.

I asked our hostess, Meire Viana, if she had an extra Bible and she just so happened to have recently bought a high quality NLT study Bible at a used bookstore, so she gladly gave it to Lee as a gift. He was extremely thankful. When he skimmed through the pages he said, "I could probably finish this in a couple of weeks."

"It might take some months," I replied with a kind laugh, "but go for it man. Eat it up. Read it like crazy."

Lee's countenance had changed from someone in the depths of depression to someone with optimistic expectation for what the future held. He giddily asked us, "Would you guys like to go somewhere to hang out. I don't have many good friends to hang out with and really want to introduce you to my people!"

"Of course!" we excitedly replied, "We would love to Lee."

So he drove us out to Little Saigon in Westminster and took us out to eat. It was quite a cultural experience. We went to a Vietnamese restaurant where the menu was all in Vietnamese and none of the waitresses spoke English. Most of the people in the restaurant were eating from large soup bowls that had all kinds of plants, meats, noodles, and sauces coming out of them into their mouths. I wasn't sure what we had just gotten ourselves into, but I was thrilled by the experience. It felt like we had just exited the United States and stepped into a side street of Vietnam. Lee ordered the food for us because we had no idea what or how to order and he taught us how to properly eat the meal. When the food arrived it was very different, but very delicious. The name of the dish was Pho (Fuh) and he said that this place had the best Pho in town. So since we were in the heart of Little Saigon, the largest Vietnamese community outside of Vietnam, and this was the best Pho in town we could arguably have been eating the best Pho available in the world outside of Vietnam. Since then, we fell in love with the Vietnamese people and their delicious signature soup dish filled with rice noodles, thin slices of meat, vegetables, bean sprouts, and mint leaves.

Throughout our drive and dinner we mostly talked about music and our hobbies. Lee told us about his side job as a DJ and I told him about the worship music that I composed for the Lord. He really wanted to hear my songs, so I agreed to play him a song when we returned to Meire's house.

On the drive back to Meire's house I explained the entire Gospel to him. He was spiritually starving to hear everything I had to say. He was blown away by the beauty and power of the Gospel and was genuinely convicted of his sins.

However, in a last ditch effort to keep his old philosophies he asked, "What about Buddha? Can't Buddha change your life?"

We could tell that Lee didn't really care about Buddha, but he was testing us to see what we would say in response. Also, being a

Buddhist was obviously part of his cultural heritage as a Vietnamese man and he wanted to hold onto his heritage as much as he could.

Alex quickly responded to his question, "Lee, Buddha's a real cool guy who had some cool philosophies, but he can't save your soul. He can't transform your life. Only Jesus could change your life and save your soul."

"That's true," Lee laughed, "you're right. Maybe I should give my heart to God."

Although Lee was evidently hungry for God we felt like we were not supposed to push him to make a decision to receive Christ. Something inside of us told us that we needed to let it happen naturally.

Upon arriving at Meire's house, Lee was anxious to hear one of my songs and I was excited to introduce him to worship, a world he had never before encountered in his lifetime. During the drive to Little Saigon, Lee had showed us his favorite songs that he claimed 'ministered' to his life in some way. They were such shallow, lame songs from artists such as Sugar Ray, Orgy, and Gwen Stefani and I couldn't wait for him to experience the power of worshipping God and dwelling in His presence.

I joyfully grabbed my guitar and prepared myself to worship Jesus because I knew that this would be the first time he had ever witnessed someone wholeheartedly worship God. I passionately worshipped the Lord with a song I had written called "Holy Sacrifice" and when I opened my eyes at the end of the song Lee's eyes were red and at the verge of breaking out in tears.

I felt moved to pray, so I began pouring my heart out in prayer to God and sang one more song that I had written. When I finished the second song, I looked him straight in the eyes and told him, "Lee, there are many songs about life and love. I've even written some love songs for my girlfriend, but nothing can ever be as deep as worship to God."

"I can see," he responded awestruck as his eyes locked with mine, "I can see the passion you sing with to God. I've never seen someone sing with such passion."

Then he asked Alex to sing a song he had written, so Alex grabbed the guitar and sang a really creative song that he had written. It was melodically genius and Lee was really touched by it too as he soaked it in and listened.

After this rich time in worship, prayer, and dwelling in God's presence, Lee began genuinely saying, "I want to know God. Maybe I should give him my heart." We could see that Lee was now saying this out of a healthy place in his heart. He was not saying this just so that God could save him from depression, because he thought we were cool, or because he wanted to try out a new religion. He had tasted and seen that God was good and he wanted more of Him.

"Yes, give Him your heart," we finally encouraged him, "Do you want to give your heart to him tonight?"

"Yes, I do," he gladly answered, "But I heard that when someone gives their life to God they need to be baptized. Is that true?"

"Yes, it is true," I told him, "You need to be baptized when you dedicate your life to God. Do want to be baptized? Meire has a pool back here. We could baptize you right now!"

"Oh, I don't know. It's probably really cold right now," he said with a bit of hesitation.

I explained to him the meaning and significance of baptism so that he could comprehend why it was essential to carry out in order to become part of the body of Christ. Once he understood the power of baptism, he immediately stated with giddy excitement, "Alright then. I'll get baptized!"

Alex and I jumped for joy inside. We couldn't believe what we were hearing and experiencing. We felt like Phillip in the Bible when he encountered the eunuch, led him to Jesus, and baptized him in a nearby pond. Kent, Meire's husband, allowed us to borrow some swimming trunks in order to do the baptism. Meire brought out the photo camera and Kent brought the video camera.

I asked Lee for his permission to capture this moment on camera. He felt uncomfortable with the idea at first, but when I explained that we wanted to record this event in order for him to remember this significant milestone for the rest of his life, he readily agreed to it.

Alex, Lee, and I held hands by the pool. Alex prayed a powerful prayer over Lee and then I said a prayer over him as well. After completing my prayer I said to him, "Now you pray, Lee, to give your life to Jesus."

"I don't know how," he responded.

I asked him to repeat a prayer with me. I led him in an intense prayer of salvation and repentance that had nothing to do with the traditional cut and dry sinner's prayer. It was a powerful prayer and we could see that Lee was praying it with genuine faith in Christ and repentance of his sins. We walked down the steps with him into the pool and I prayed for him one more time. Then Alex and I baptized him. It was one of the most glorious moments of my life.

When Lee rose up out of the water, he was so filled with joy that he began shouting to the Lord, "God thank you for allowing me to be a part of your life! I want to know you God! Thank you God!"

This was the first prayer that Lee Phan ever prayed to God in his life; a twenty-seven-year-old man who was born and raised as a Buddhist in Vietnam and lived in the United States for over ten years without ever hearing the name of Jesus. After hearing the Gospel for the first time in his life, seeing the love and fire of God in our lives, and experiencing God's tangible presence, he couldn't resist giving his life completely over to the living God who truly loved him.

Both Alex and I praised God with jubilation. Our hearts were jumping for joy within us. Words could never describe the joy I felt in that moment. If we had gone on this entire trip just to bring Lee to Jesus it would have been worth it. We swam in the pool for about twenty minutes because we were all so happy that we didn't know what to do with ourselves. Then Meire came over and told us that Kent wanted to buy us pizza to celebrate Lee's salvation.

Lee, Alex, and I were all blown away when we heard that Kent had just ordered pizza because Lee had been craving pizza the whole day.

When we went to Little Saigon he wanted to eat at Pizza Hut because he was hungry for pizza, but we insisted on eating Vietnamese food with him. Also, when we had returned to Meire's house, Lee had said that he wanted to order some pizza, but we told him that we were still stuffed from the Pho. He concluded that he would order it in a couple of hours when we weren't so full. However, now Kent had ordered pizza for him without knowing anything about how much Lee was craving pizza that day. We were in awe of God's sense of humor and how much He cared about Lee, even in the little things.

We dried off with towels, changed into our dry clothes, and sat together in Meire's living room. While we waited for the pizza to come Lee began pouring his heart out about several issues he was going through with his family. He told us about the physical abuse he had experienced as a child and he sadly stated that no one had ever truly loved him in his life. In fact, he had never once had a birthday party in his entire twenty-seven years of life. He explained to us many negative things about Vietnam and Vietnamese culture that had affected his life growing up.

Suddenly, Meire walked in with the pizza and exclaimed, "We have pizza, I bought soda, and we have cookies for dessert!"

Lee commented excitedly with a huge grin from ear-to-ear, "Wow! It feels like it's my birthday or something!"

"It is your birthday Lee!" we exclaimed with joy, "Today is your spiritual birthday. The day your spirit was born to God."

I looked at my watch to see the exact date.

"It's September 7th, 2007," I announced.

"Write that down for me," Lee asked.

We ate together and continued fellowshipping with each other. Alex eventually went to bed and I stayed up talking with Lee for at least another hour giving him counsel, guidance, and encouragement. We planned to go together to the church Alex and I were partnered with in Riverside where I would introduce him to my friends who would disciple him.

Meire gave him his first Christian CD and I gave him a list of good Christian bands for him to listen to. I prayed for him for the last time and he left exuberant with joy. He said, "I'm going to listen to this CD on my whole drive back home and sing along with it."

On our last night in Southern California, Lee came to spend some time with us because he loved us so much and he promised that he would hang out with us on the last night that we were in town. He bought a bucket full of KFC chicken for us and presented each of us with a gift.

Then he suggested that we watch a Jesus movie together. It was already 11 p.m., but he was determined to watch a Jesus movie with us before we left. He had never watched a movie about Jesus in his life and he wanted to know more about Jesus. Meire had "The Passion of the Christ" and the Jesus film. I explained both of them to him and he insisted that he wanted to watch "The Passion of the Christ". I warned him about its graphic nature, but he was so hungry to see and understand the depth of who Christ was and what He had done for him.

I explained the death of Christ and the meaning of the Gospel once again to Lee, so that he would truly understand what he was watching. We prayed together and then began watching the movie at 11:30 p.m. None of us fell asleep or felt tired at all. We were all totally gripped by the power of what we were witnessing, including Lee. At the end of the movie, we prayed together and had a wonderful time talking. We both prayed for Lee and then he spontaneously began praying for Alex and me straight from his heart. We were amazed that he offered to pray for us and prayed so naturally from his heart to God. Finally, around 3:00 a.m. he went home.

HALLELUJAH! ALL GLORY BELONGS TO GOD FOR THE GREATEST MIRACLE OF ALL, A REDEEMED SOUL! There is truly no greater feeling than to lead someone to Christ who has never heard the Gospel, never read the Bible, never stepped inside of a church, and knows virtually nothing about the Father, Son, and Holy Spirit. We were overwhelmed by the honor of being used by God to bring an unreached soul to the feet of Jesus.

A Day On The Streets Of L.A.

Alex and I were wiped out physically, emotionally, spiritually, and mentally. We didn't have one drop of energy left in us and we really didn't want to preach the Gospel at all. We laid out on the grass in a small park in front of Oliveira Street just to waste some time. I logged in my journal, "I'm tired. I'm tired. I'm tired. I want to go home."

That is exactly how I felt at that moment, yet God was still stirring me with compassion for the people around me. Finally, I mustered up the strength and motivation to speak to two homeless men who were laying down a few yards away from us.

Their names were Andres and Diego and they were both migrant workers from Mexico who were trying to find jobs. We began talking in Spanish about God and Andres opened up to me quite a bit.

He told me that he had been living in New Jersey for many years and had been spiritually born again three years ago in a Pentecostal church. He had been faithful both to God and his church until three months before I had met him. He confessed to me that he had begun drinking and smoking cigarettes again and, as a result, lost his job. So he moved out to Los Angeles in hopes of finding employment, but instead had been homeless for six days. He'd concluded that the jobs in L.A. County were already picked over, so he decided he was going to try to find employment in Oxnard.

After hearing his story, I implored him to return to God before he went completely overboard in his spiritual walk. I shared about friends of mine who had backslidden and now were living purposeless lives and beseeched him to not go down the same path.

Andres went from being a listless man who's love for God had been hopelessly extinguished to someone who's heart's embers were being suddenly reignited. Life appeared in his eyes again. He shamefully confessed to me that that same day he had been contemplating throwing away his Bible because it was weighing too much in his backpack.

"I never read it anymore," he explained, "So why should I bother lugging it around? That's what I thought at least. But now..." he continued as his eyes brightened up and a short grin appeared on his face, "...not only am I going to keep my Bible, but I want to start reading it again."

Diego had walked off the moment I began talking with Andres, but after talking with Andres for about forty-five minutes he had finally returned. I asked him what his story was and he explained to me that he had just come straight from Mexico and was planning to find work in the state of Washington. He said that he was a non-practicing Catholic who had no relationship with God and hadn't been to church in years.

I preached the Gospel to him and implored him to believe in Jesus and repent. After hearing me share the whole Gospel he claimed to believe in the message that I had shared with him, but he insisted that it was unrealistic for anyone to truly repent of their sins. He had no problem believing in the Gospel, but thought it was entirely useless and dishonest to repent of one's sins because no one was capable of living a sinless life. I explained to him the depths of God's grace and patience with our sinfulness even after we are saved. I shared that God does not require us to be perfect, but rather He requires us to believe in the sinless One who took our sin upon Himself and sent the Holy Spirit who empowers us to live holy lives.

Finally, I challenged him to give his life to Christ in that very moment. And to my surprise, he did! I prayed with Diego right then and there and he gladly received Christ into his life. After we prayed, Andres butted in excitedly insisting that he wanted to give Diego his extra New Testament as a gift.

*

After a few more hours of witnessing, the sun began to set and we realized that we were going to be sleeping on the streets of downtown Los Angeles that night. The last time that I had slept on the street was in

Orlando and it already seemed to have been so long ago. Since then, the Lord had always provided us with a place to stay, so it was quite sobering for me to have to sleep on the street again.

Alex, on the other hand, hadn't been with me in Orlando, so he was thrilled to finally get to experience what it was like to sleep on the street. He had begun to feel like we were more on vacation than on a faith journey because of the extravagant hospitality that our hosts were continually lavishing upon us.

I personally knew several families in the Greater Los Angeles area who I could have easily called and who would have gladly given us a place to stay, but that was against the rules I had made with God to never ask anyone for anything and to trust in Him alone to provide. Even if our closest friends had lived a few miles from the street we were about to sleep on, we could only accept their hospitality towards us if they offered it.

To our surprise, around 8 p.m. a food line formed at the rotunda of Oliveira Street where we were witnessing. Since we realized that we would be staying on the street that night we thought it would be fine for us to eat the food they were providing for the homeless.

While we were waiting for the meal to arrive I spotted an extremely raggedy-looking young girl sitting on the ground with her legs crossed Indian style. She was abnormally fair-skinned and had cut her hair very short, almost appearing to be a boy. Her clothes literally had the appearance of being filthy rags that someone had just used to wash the rims of their car. They had black spots all over, were torn at the ends, and had holes everywhere.

My heart broke for her as I watched her sitting on the cement floor by herself with her head hung low. I couldn't even begin to imagine what this young white girl had gone through as she struggled to survive alone on the streets of Los Angeles.

I quietly walked over to her and very sensitively sat down on the floor a short distance away from her. I wanted to respect her space and I didn't want her to feel threatened in any way.

"Hello," I began, hoping to initiate a conversation with her. She didn't look up or say anything in response.

"My name is Joshua," I said gently and politely, "What's your name?"

"My name's Jessica," she responded.

"How are you doing today?" I calmly asked her.

"Not so good," she replied.

"Where are you from?" I asked.

"I'm from the East Coast," she said, "I was born and raised there."

As I continued to ask Jessica questions about herself to get to know her better she seemed to realize that I actually cared about her as a person and was interested in knowing who she was. I wasn't trying to get something out of her, pester her, or hurt her in any way. I really cared. Once she understood that she looked directly at me and began to open up her heart and tell me her life story.

I asked her if she had a relationship with God, but she somberly stated that she didn't believe in God. She explained to me that she had been born and raised in church for most of her life, but everything changed for her when her boyfriend got her pregnant as a teenager. She was sincerely excited about having the baby and didn't want to abort the baby at all, but instead, she ended up having a miscarriage. The miscarriage filled her with anger towards God for allowing her to lose her baby and from that point on she concluded that there must not really be a God. If there were a God, she wouldn't have miscarried.

My heart broke for Jessica. I could not begin to imagine the depth of her pain and feeling of betrayal towards God. Although I was incapable of empathizing with her sorrow, I lovingly explained to her that God is not the author of suffering and He was not the One who caused her baby to die. Suffering and death entered into the world through sin and the Devil, not by the will of God. God wants to heal us, transform us, free us, and give us abundant life, but the Devil is on a mission to kill, steal, and destroy and sin has caused the whole world to become corrupted, including little babies. I kindly pleaded with her to not blame God for the death of her baby, but to realize that God was weeping together with her when she lost her baby.

I told her about the Good News of Jesus and the everlasting love that God has for her. She was deeply touched and I could see that I had just answered some hard questions for her that had blinded her vision of God for years. She never thanked me with words, but I could feel her gratitude as she looked me in the eyes as I made my final remarks about God's love for her.

Our conversation came to an abrupt end when the food arrived. A church group had popped out of nowhere and had set up a few tables with covered hot plates of food in a matter of seconds. It was obvious that this was the spot they had served food in for years. Upon their arrival, everyone jumped to their feet and formed a line to receive their hot meal. The volunteers joyfully and respectfully provided us with a surprisingly delicious homemade meal of tacos, rice, beans, and an orange. Once everyone finished eating, they went their separate ways to get settled in their sleeping spots for the night.

Some of the Mexican men we had met while eating our food gave us advice about safety and street smarts when they realized that we were going to be sleeping on the street that night. We were planning to sleep in a large grass area directly in front of Oliveira Street, but the men told us that the cops never let anyone sleep there and would probably ask us to leave as well.

After looking around the area for a good place to sleep, Alex and I decided that we were going to sleep on the grass regardless of whether the cops asked us to leave or not. This tiny park was the only patch of grass that we could find in the gigantic concrete jungle of downtown Los Angeles and we were determined not to sleep on bare concrete.

We went to sleep around 9:30 p.m. and, by God's grace, Alex had brought two small blankets with him, so we were both warm and cozy as we curled up in our blankets and used our backpacks as pillows. The grass was comfortable and the streets quieted down a bit at night, so we were able to sleep deeply. However, around 11:45 p.m. a cop woke us up and politely told us that we were not permitted to sleep in the grass area because they needed to turn on the sprinklers and another cop kindly escorted us to a Catholic church about one hundred feet away. The second cop respectfully explained to us that all the homeless people within that vicinity of the city were required to sleep on the church's property for safety reasons.

I was surprised to see dozens of homeless men sleeping together in a straight line on one long, skinny sidewalk in the well-lit parking lot of the Catholic Church. In all of my experience with homeless ministry, the most common piece of advice the homeless would give me about sleeping on the streets was to find a place where one was well hidden from cops and other homeless people, yet here we were surrounded by them both. However, I was amazed to see that the police officer, who had kindly escorted us to the church, stood watch over us all night long to ensure our safety and prevent any illegal activity from taking place. I had always heard of how savagely the police treated the homeless in Los Angeles, but the behavior of this particular officer revealed to me that there were officers who sincerely cared about the homeless.

I felt very safe with the officer watching over us, but I was still only able to sleep for about an hour throughout the entire night. The sidewalk we slept on was about two-thirds the size of a regular sidewalk with a metal gate built on one side of it and a small paved road on the other side. My body just barely fit the width of the skinny sidewalk and I constantly felt like I was about to roll off onto the paved road. It was hard to have peace of mind in such a position. Furthermore, sleeping on concrete was miserable because it was impossible for my body to warm up the floor. During this trip, I learned that the human body naturally heat up grass, dirt, cardboard, cotton, and most other natural materials it comes in contact with. Thus, it's not so miserable to sleep on the street if our body is sleeping on a natural element that will eventually become warm. However, concrete is either very cold at night or very hot on a warm day, but our bodies are not capable of warming or cooling it down.

Thus, I was cold all night long as we slept on the sidewalk. It felt like the concrete was sucking the warmth right out of my body and the cracks in the sidewalk were very uncomfortable to sleep on as well.

The police officer had told us that we were not allowed to sleep on the grass at night, but we were allowed to sleep on it during the day. Therefore, as soon as we spotted the first glimpse of sunlight, Alex and I, along with about a dozen other homeless men, walked over to the grass area and slept another three hours or so. We had finally rested and were now ready to begin our next day of evangelism.

The Day I Jumped

The following is an entry from Jon Fish, one of my closest friends. We met up during my time in Ventura County to preach the Gospel together at the Westlake Promenade. This is the account of Jon's one-day evangelism experience with me in his own epic words:

One of the most influential people in my life sat across from me at Starbucks. I had not seen him in four years. He told me of his journey across America. He wore boldness like a mane around his neck. His love for the One was deep and true. I was drawn to the beauty of his testimony as one is drawn to water after a long, exhausting hike. He looked deep into my eyes and asked me if I would preach Christ crucified with him on the following day.

"God, You be glorified!" were the last words that left my lips as Josh and I sat in the courtyard of the Westlake Promenade praying fervently that God would be with us as we shared the 'Good News' with the people there. After my bold statement left my lips my stomach sank. There were a lot of people in front of me. Each person was engaged in their own world: talking to their loved one, on their cell phone, reading books, smoking cigarettes, making sales calls, or shopping. I was afraid. My heart started to pound as I stood up from my chair. Josh began walking ahead of me to a group of elderly people. I split from Josh and walked to the most vacant part of the mall. I sat on a fountain and prayed.

The words, "I will be ashamed of those who are ashamed of Me," screamed in my head. I felt so torn. Everything within me wanted to scream the gospel at the top of my lungs, but my body would not respond. I was paralyzed with fear.

I began walking around again and found Josh. He was talking to a Hispanic fellow. He looked at me and asked how I was doing. Sheepishly, I laughed and told him that the first few steps are tough. He flashed a picture that a cartoonist had drawn of him. I asked him who had drawn it. He pointed to the elderly couple that he had been talking to earlier. I walked over to the table of elderly folks and asked who the artist was. A man wearing a trucker hat and a Star of David pendant raised his hand. I struck up a conversation with the elderly group and told them I was an artist as well. I told them about the two years I had spent up at a college in Washington and the next thing I knew I was sitting with literally old friends. We were laughing and talking about life. Naturally, Jesus was brought up into the conversation. I told them how much He meant to me and how He alone had changed my life. I spoke to them that they, the promised ones, were loved of God. That Christ did not reject them but longed for their hearts. I could tell that the artist was having a hard time with what I was saying, but by the end of the conversation they were totally drawn to my message. I ended with inviting them to the church that meets in houses. They laughed and said that they would come if they were younger. I didn't blame them for not wanting to come. One of them told me not to get discouraged if someone turns me down when I talk to them about Jesus because for every one that does turn me down ten more will be eager to listen. I was so encouraged by our talk. I blessed them and told them that I hoped to see them again.

*

Upon finishing the conversation with my elderly friends, I spotted Josh standing across from me. He was talking to some young teenagers. They looked totally astonished; like someone was laying news on them they had never heard. I walked over and introduced myself to them. I felt God tell me to preach the gospel to someone else, so I moved.

I saw a woman in pink sitting at a table by herself, so I asked as I pointed to the chair next to her, "Hi, is anyone sitting there?"

"Please, sit down," she politely replied as she gestured towards the chair.

"How is your day today?" I kindly asked her.

"Quite good," she responded in a foreign accent that I couldn't quite get my hand on.

"Where are you from?" I inquired.

"I'm from South Wales," she stated with a smile on her face, "I am visiting some friends here in California for a few weeks."

The next thing I knew I was in another awesome conversation with a total stranger. She was telling me about herself as if we were old friends. Right when I began to explain why I was talking to her, her friend showed up. I started to tell them both about Josh and my conviction to speak the gospel. Their eyes grew wide as I shared the whole story with them. The first woman's friend told me that they were both Christians. I laughed and told them that that was a relief. After I explained what part of the church I was from we parted and went our ways. I had totally encouraged some fellow sisters in the Lord by just striking up a conversation with a stranger.

*

The last conversation I had was with an elderly woman in a bookstore. She was looking at a sci-fi book that I was familiar with. I casually walked up and talked to her about the book as if I was an employee. The next thing I knew I was in another conversation with a long lost friend. She began telling me about her hometown she had grown up in and how she ended up in California. Her daughter had recently moved out to join the Peace Corps. She had traveled the world and ended up in Rwanda where she met the love of her life, an Egyptian man. They moved to Egypt and have lived there ever since. Her daughter happened to be in town at the time and her grandson was standing across from us in the bookstore. She called him over for me to meet him. He was going to Portland State University this year and seemed like a really great guy. I soon started to talk to them about Jesus and it turned out that the elderly woman was Jewish and her grandson was a Muslim! I spoke to them about how amazing Jesus is and that they should both look into the teachings of Jesus. The grandson seemed interested and agreed with me that Islam teaches that Jesus is a great prophet. I emphasized that and told him to search in the Koran for God's character and who Jesus is. They eventually had to leave so I bid them farewell.

When I walked out of the bookstore I found Josh preaching to a group of Indie kids. After he was done, he walked over to me with a huge smile on his face. "That was glorious," he said as he embraced me. As Josh and I drove away from the promenade I realized the similarities to cliff jumping and preaching the gospel. Cliff jumping involves you using ten percent of your body to jump off a cliff and ninety percent gravity to pull you down to the water. Preaching the Gospel involves you using ten percent of your body by talking to someone and ninety percent the Holy Spirit drawing the person to Him.

Jon <><

Camarillo Outlets

As I strolled around the Camarillo Outlets in prayer I was drawn to a group of four Mexican teenagers from Oxnard who were dressed in the typical Mexican gangster attire. They had on plaid collared shirts with only the top button closed, a white undershirt, and extra large blue jeans that were sagging down their rear end. Three of them were Catholic and one was a Christian named Marcos. Marcos claimed to be a member of Victory Outreach, but confessed that he had not attended church in a long time, while the three Catholics had almost never attended church. None of them had ever read the Bible and none of them understood the Gospel.

As I began sharing the Gospel with them, Marcos butted in to ask me a question, "No offense," he began, "But I just wanted to know how long this will take because we need to leave soon."

"Five minutes," I told him.

"Alright", he said.

The three Catholic teenagers were captivated by the Gospel message and were engaged in dialogue with me as I shared it with them. Thus, when five minutes rolled by I was still not done with teaching the Gospel. Nevertheless, Luis put on his macho face and attempted to end the conversation, "Alright, we gotta go, man. It's been five minutes."

"You can go man," I quickly responded.

"No. We're all going," He stubbornly declared with his chin raised high in the air.

Then his three friends simultaneously looked at him and said, "We're not going. This is real interesting."

Shocked, he exclaimed, "You hear this stuff in church all the time!"

"Not like this man," they simultaneously replied, "He's answering important questions that we have. He's telling us about deep things. Real things."

Luis couldn't believe his ears. Embarrassed, he finally gave up, sat down, and listened. I explained the Gospel to them and they were truly impacted and convicted. They all realized that if they died in that instant they would go to Hell because they were living in their sins, but God loved them and desired for them to repent and come to Him. They all listened, but three of them were still checking out girls, cussing, and cracking jokes during the entire conversation. However, one boy named Xavier was so hungry for what I was saying that he stared at me as if he had never heard these things before. He appeared to be in a state of shock as he listened with an open heart. Xavier later confessed that he had always assumed that he was right with God, but now he realized how far he was from Him.

I asked Xavier if he wanted to give his life to Jesus and truly repent of his sins. He responded, "Yes, I really do. I really do man." I asked him if he wanted to do it right now, but he said, looking into my eyes, "I'll do it tonight when I get home. I just don't want to do it with these guys right here acting like that." I understood. His friends were acting like rascals and he didn't want to make a sacred commitment to God in such a dishonoring atmosphere. So I prayed over all of them and continued on my mission.

*

As I walked past the food court, I met a Korean man named Samuel who owned two kiosks at the outlet and who spoke just enough English to maintain a conversation. He was relaxing on a chair calmly smoking a cigarette when I approached him. It turned out that Samuel was a Korean Catholic who regularly attended a Catholic church in Oxnard. He strongly believed in helping the poor, but he admitted that he had not fully repented of his sins. I urged him to fully repent and follow Jesus wholeheartedly. He proudly showed off his large Korean Bible, but then admitted that he rarely read it because it was too heavy and big. I prayed that God would revive his faith and give him a hunger for the Word of God. Following the prayer, he went back to work on the kiosk and I went to work amongst the ocean of men and women around me.

*

Later in the day, I met three Koreans who had come to the U.S. to take English classes over the summer at UC Berkeley and were scheduled to fly back to Seoul in three days. Their names were David, Andy, and John. Andy was born and raised in a Christian home, but was living a very worldly lifestyle, David was the only Christian in his family and was deeply rooted in his faith, and John was an atheist. I spoke to all of them, but I spent most of my time talking with John. He was impacted by all that I taught him about Jesus and when I challenged him to seek God and read the Bible for himself he sincerely promised me that he would. I jotted down the book titles of *More Than a Carpenter* and *The Case For Christ* for him to read as well and he really seemed eager to check them out. I prayed over the three of them, but as I prayed John wore an expression of extreme curiosity. From the look on his face, it seemed as if no one had ever prayed for him before.

After the prayer, David and Andy began asking me a ton of questions about my mission trip. They were inspired by what I was doing and wanted to know all about it. Finally, we ended our time together and parted ways.

Nevertheless, about fifteen minutes later, David showed up again and asked if he could speak with me in private. I agreed and we began a rich time of fellowship that ended up lasting for two hours. David opened up to me and confessed that in Korea he had been a strong Christian, but during his summer at UC Berkeley it had been extremely difficult for him to maintain his walk with Christ. He had grown very weak in his faith because he hadn't been able to find one Christian at UC Berkeley and even though he visited several churches in the city none of them seemed to have any spiritual power. He claimed to have gone through the entire summer without speaking to one Christian. Thus, he was spiritually starving for genuine fellowship with another believer. David was overjoyed that I had preached the Gospel to Andy and John because he had been wanting to preach to them since the beginning of their trip together, but had never found the courage to do so. He confessed that he had come to the U.S. hoping to discover his mission in life, but hadn't found anything. He was moved to tears as I prayed for the Holy Spirit to awaken him once again.

Andy joined us at our table after David and I had been talking for a long time. I asked him if he genuinely followed Jesus with all of his heart. He admitted that he didn't wholeheartedly follow Jesus and he was convinced that it wasn't necessary to be so passionate about God. He claimed that he knew about God, and loved God and he was satisfied with that. I asked him if he'd ever been in love with a girl. I explained to him how falling in love with a girl and falling in love with God were very similar in nature. I shared my testimony with Andy and David about how I had been a lukewarm, hypocritical pastor's son who, through a one year transformational process, fell passionately in love with God and had been following Him ever since. I left them with a stirring challenge to fall in love with God and they both took it to heart. David and Andy were speechless at the end of our conversation. As we went our separate ways, David and I exchanged contact information so that we could remain in communication with each other.

*

As I made my way over to the food court to buy some dinner, I observed Samuel intently studying his large Korean Bible at a table next to his kiosk. I stared at him from a distance for quite a while, but he never noticed me because his eyes were fixed on the pages of the Bible.

CHAPTER SEVEN

SAN FRANCISCO

The City That God Loves

San Francisco was the most beautiful city I visited on the West Coast. It was much more metropolitan than Los Angeles, boasted an excellent public transportation system, was exploding with exquisite cultural experiences, and was filled with breathtaking landmarks. Although to the natural eye San Francisco was an enchanting metropolis, in the spiritual world it was the most dark and demonically oppressed city I had encountered in my journey across America.

In order for someone to even begin to comprehend what we faced while we were there one would have to physically go to San Francisco for the purpose of praying and preaching the Gospel there for at least a few days. Never in my life had I seen a city that so adamantly hated God and embraced sin to the point of becoming one with it. It was truly Satan's playground.

San Francisco is the birthplace and headquarters to many of the world's most powerful spiritual strongholds. The first official Church of

Satan in the world was established in San Francisco. The Beatnik movement began there, which was the forerunner for what later exploded into the Hippie Movement. America's drug culture first exploded in San Francisco, making the use of marijuana, LSD, mushrooms, and other drugs common in the Western World. The Sexual Revolution began there and was majorly responsible for spawning sharp rises in divorce, fornication, adultery, prostitution, pornography, nudist colonies, pedophilia, homosexuality, and every other form of sexual immorality that now pervades American culture. The largest LGBT community in the world has made San Francisco their home and also the headquarters for their global movement. Lastly, regardless of what one's biases are towards the United Nations, it is notably significant that it was birthed in San Francisco as well.

The district that we spent most of our time in was Haight Ashbury, the birthplace of the hippie movement and still one of the main centers of hippie activity in the United States. When we first stepped foot onto the intersection of Haight St. and Ashbury St., we felt like we had been transported back in time to the late 1960's when the hippie movement had first begun. Virtually all the shops were New Age, Hindu, and/or hippie in their ethos. Naked women were painted on the walls, the smell of weed was in the air, and hippie art was everywhere. Posters for meditation classes led by Hindu gurus were on light posts; the locals were talking about the next classic rock concert; and tons of hippies, gutter punks, and drug addicts were sleeping on the streets and in Golden Gate Park. Homeless hippies played folk music on the sidewalk and aggressively begged for money as people indifferently passed them by. The New Age worldview was the most commonly held by the people, hookah bars were common, and bongs were openly displayed and sold. Sex with virtually anyone seemed to be an attainable reality and drugs were so common that I was asked if I wanted to buy drugs or if I sold drugs on numerous occasions.

On the other hand, there were several new cultural scenes in Haight Ashbury that proved that we were indeed living in modern times.

Somehow, they all had found a way to contextualize themselves into the New Age, hippie culture that spiritually and culturally dominated the district. Some of these modern trends included tattoos covering the bodies of countless individuals, artistically skilled graffiti on dozens of walls from the hip-hop culture, and gutter punks being present in far greater number than the hippies in the area. Gutter punks are essentially punk kids who normally have tattoos, numerous piercings, wild hair, grungy clothes, and a much more hostile attitude than the stereotypical, fun-loving hippy. Their main philosophies are rebellion and rage against any authority and most of them have run away from home or were kicked out of their homes and voluntarily chose to live on the streets.

Upon walking down Market Street, in direction to the Financial District, the demographics completely changed. Diversity abounded and thousands of people walked up and down the streets every day of the week and at all hours of the day. Hippies, punks, potheads, and thugs were not nearly as common to see on Market Street as they were in Haight Ashbury. Instead, most of the people were wealthy and dressed either in formal business attire or in the latest and most expensive designer clothes imaginable. Yet even in this posh atmosphere most of the people were bound by the New Age and atheistic philosophies that arose out of Haight Ashbury during the Hippie Movement. Market Street is the heart of downtown San Francisco, the center of business for the city, and the center for fashion and shopping. In fact, when I would walk down Market Street it felt like I was strutting along the streets of Manhattan.

The Mission District was predominantly Latino, while simultaneously courting to a newly thriving hipster scene. The Tenderloin District was flooded with the homeless, drug addicts, and was predominantly African-American. It was somewhat equivalent to L.A.'s Skid Row. The Castro was home to the most highly concentrated LGBT community in the world. Fisherman's Wharf was always swarming with tourists and was the part of town that most San Franciscans tried to avoid. Chinatown and Japantown were also significant cultural centers of the city filled with extravagant restaurants and shops pertaining to their respective ethnicities. I'm sure there were many more sections of San Francisco, but these were the only ones that we became familiar with during our time there.

During our time witnessing in San Francisco, we found that some people were open to Jesus, but the vast majority were not merely closed to the Gospel, but were openly hostile to it. I wouldn't have been surprised if while we were there we had gotten physically beaten for preaching the Gospel. For the first time in my life, being a martyr for Christ didn't seem like a far-fetched daydream; it felt like it could become a living reality at any moment.

In spite of all the sin and spiritual darkness over the city, there was still a small remnant of ardently sold-out saints of God living in San Francisco. I had great respect and admiration for each believer I met there. Not many Christians seemed to last in that city. Most of them would end up either totally backslidden in the world or they would become discouraged and depressed by the prevailing sin and obstinacy towards God and eventually move to another city. I wouldn't blame those who left because after two weeks of preaching in San Francisco I was relieved when it was time for me to leave and go back home.

We fell in love with and our hearts broke for the people of San Francisco. God's heart beats for the transformation of this city and we believe that its day of salvation is near.

Welcome To San Francisco

Alex and I took the Greyhound bus from Sacramento into the heart of San Francisco on Monday morning. We stepped off the Greyhound and immediately hopped onto a city bus in order to get to the Haight Ashbury district. As we drove through the city, I perceived numerous mentally insane, demonized, and violently hostile people wherever my eyes turned. The bus we were riding on had a man wearing disturbingly small shorts that only a slutty woman would normally wear, a transvestite man-turned-woman, and several punks. However, the strangest person I encountered on the bus was a man who was dressed in a black suit and wore a leather satchel at his side. The moment he caught sight of me, his eyes became full of rage, he began heavily venting through his teeth, and he stood in a stance that implied that he was about to attack me. "Where am I?" I thought to myself. I was on Market Street in downtown San Francisco.

We got off the bus on Haight Street and began engaging people with the message of the Gospel. After about an hour of talking with people about Jesus, an older hippy named Eric walked up to us insisting that he had met us before. We were certain that he had never seen us because we were from Miami, but it turned out that he had recognized Alex from God's Summer of Love Tour.

He asked us what our story was and what we were doing in San Francisco. After we told him about our mission trip he explained to us that he was also visiting the city, but knew of a friend who might be able to help us find a host home. So he called his friend, Adam Hood, and it just so happened that his friend was walking down the same street as us.

A few minutes later, we met Adam Hood and he just couldn't stop talking about two squirrels that he had found in Golden Gate Park. Once he finally calmed down about the two squirrels, he asked us to tell him our story. The instant we shared our mission with him he flipped out and exclaimed, "Oh my gosh! No way! You guys are the two squirrels in my friends dream!"

Alex and I were utterly confounded. "What in the world is this guy talking about?" I thought to myself. Then Adam began to unfold a storyline that blew our minds and left us in awe of the sovereignty of God.

Adam's roommate had had a dream the previous night. In the dream, there was a master with two squirrels in his hand. The master walked up to a large door, but the door was locked. Immediately, the squirrels began to bark at the master and, in response, the master handed them a key. With the key, they were able to open the large door. When they walked into the master's house there was a contract titled "Youth Movement" laying on a table and the master signed it.

So Adam's roommate woke up that morning and shared the dream with Adam. They talked about it and prayed for the interpretation. They decided that the interpretation of the dream was that there were going to be two young people who God was going to give the keys to a youth movement and His blessing would be on it.

Adam went about his day completely oblivious of the dream. He decided to visit Golden Gate Park and when he was there he spotted two squirrels. He remembered that he had some bread in his backpack, so he took some out to feed the squirrels. The squirrels ran up to him, but he didn't throw the bread to them. Rather, he kept the bread on the palm of his open hand and insisted that they climb on his hand to get the bread. Eventually, the squirrels began barking at him. Adam was in shock. He didn't even know that squirrels could bark in real life. Then, all of a sudden, he remembered the dream. "This is crazy," he thought to himself, "two squirrels are barking at me just like in the dream. What is going on?" To top it all of, one of the squirrels actually jumped onto Adam's hand, grabbed the bread, and took off.

At that very second Eric called Adam. Adam picked up the phone and told Eric about this crazy occurrence with the two barking squirrels. He walked down Haight Street to meet us and when we met he couldn't stop talking about the two squirrels. Finally, he asked us what we were doing in San Francisco and after we told him he was dumbfounded because he realized that we were the two squirrels in the dream. Then he looked at us in all seriousness and declared, "You guys are staying at my house!"

We stayed with Adam for a little over two weeks. Part of the time we slept at his house and part of the time we slept in their church, Promised Land Fellowship, because it was in the center of the city. Throughout our time in San Francisco and throughout several years of friendship, the theme of squirrels continued to resurface. God has an amazing sense of humor.

Haight Ashbury

The weather on Market Street was gloomy and depressing. The entire sky was overcast, a cold wind was blowing, and it was slightly drizzling. Not one sliver of sunlight could be seen through the thick layer of clouds. Although it was morning, the darkness of the day made it feel like the sun was already setting. The weather reminded me of several stories that I had heard where the climate in a city or region literally changed as a result of revival. I began to wonder if San Francisco's nasty weather might possibly be a reflection of its spiritually ominous state. I began to imagine that if revival came perhaps the weather would miraculously change. Thus, as I ate breakfast at the "Caffe Trieste" and read *That None Should Perish* by Ed Silvoso I began to have hope for revival in San Francisco.

As Alex and I walked out of Caffe Trieste to make my way to the bank the Lord spoke to me to begin praying over Market Street. Thus, I began to fervently pray for revival as I walked down the street and about five minutes into my prayer I looked straight up to the sky just in time to to see the clouds begin to open up directly above where we were standing. As I continued praying, the clouds rolled back more and more until not a single cloud was left in the sky and the sun was shining bright through the clear blue skies. Some might think that this incident was sheer coincidence, but I believe that it was a sign from God that He was opening up the spiritual heavens and bringing breakthrough to San Francisco on that very day.

Alex and I decided to walk all the way up Haight Street in order to prayer walk that area as well. After walking for quite a while, another man had begun walking alongside us. I struck up a friendly conversation with him and we had the joy of hearing his glorious testimony. He told us that his first wife was a Buddhist and his second wife was a New Age Yogi and it was only at this late point in his life that he had firmly come to believe that Jesus was truly the only way. What a hopeful story in the midst of such a daunting city. I challenged him to bring his family to Christ and then Alex and I prayed for him.

We walked by a beautiful park along the way, so Alex decided to take a pause in his day by going into the park to spend some time in prayer. We split up for a while and I tried to talk to two young people at the park, but they quickly rejected me. I continued to prayer walk Haight Street until I crossed Masonic St. and realized that I had just entered into the heart of the Haight Ashbury district. There was a crazy tattoo shop called Mom's Tattoo Shop right on the corner of Masonic and Haight. As soon as I passed by it, I felt God telling me to go into the shop and preach the Gospel to everyone who was inside. I was extremely intimidated because it was one of the most evil, demonic looking tattoo shops I had ever seen. All the tattoo artists were covered in tattoos from their faces all the way down to their ankles. Their tattoos weren't the fun, creative kind of tattoos. Their tattoos were as demonic looking as they get. I stayed outside for about twenty minutes praying and battling against fear, but eventually I gained the courage to enter the shop. I went inside and began innocently looking at the pictures of tattoos on the wall.

The girl at the front desk could see that I was obviously out of place, so she asked, "Could I help you?"

"Hi, my name is Joshua," I introduced myself and began to candidly explain what I was doing in their store, "I was just walking down the street praying over the city and I felt God tell me to go inside this shop to encourage you and the others here to seek God."

She looked at me listlessly in return without muttering a word.

"So could I ask you...do you have a relationship with God?" I inquired.

"Don't worry about me," she bluntly replied, "I'm all good. I don't need to hear you preach to me."

"That's fine," I conceded and then asked, "Would it be okay for me to encourage everyone in the shop to seek God?

"Go ahead," she passively responded, "I don't think you'll get a good response, but go ahead if you want."

The moment was surreal. I couldn't believe that this receptionist had just given me permission to open air preach in their tattoo shop. This had to be God's favor and I had to obey His voice.

I confidently walked up to the seven people who were in the shop, six tattoo artists and one customer. I began the dialogue by loudly asking, "Hey, what's up you guys? How you guys doing?"

"Alright," some grumbled.

"My name is Josh," I said kindly, "I was walking up Haight St. praying for the city and I just felt God compel me to come in here and encourage you guys to seek Him."

I paused, then said, "I challenge you guys to seek Him, He's real. He's alive."

"We don't need f#?%ing God!" one of the guys violently yelled, "Get the f#?@ out of my store."

All of them started simultaneously screaming and swearing at me.

"But He's real! He's not fake! You gotta seek Him!" I cried out.

They all screamed even louder and cussed me out even more. The guy closest to me stood up, stretched out his hands to grab me and got in my face exclaiming, "You want me to escort you out of here?"

Most of the other tattoo artists had stood up by now, had begun walking towards me and were beginning to surround me.

I began slowly taking small steps back towards the door while saying, "God bless you! I encourage you to seek Him. He loves you and wants you to know Him, but you have to seek Him with all your heart."

I gently opened the door behind me and walked out of the shop as a diatribe of swear words were being thrown at me by the tattoo artists. I prayed over the owners, workers, and customers of the shop directly outside their door and then continued on my way.

*

I soon took a quick lunch break and ate an amazing slice of pizza while spending some time reading the Bible. After lunch, I met a tall, White-American Rastafarian guy who had long, unkempt dreadlocks and was wearing a bulky army green jacket that made him look much bigger than his actual size. He was smoking a cigarette and had a somewhat foul body odor, but it was tame compared to most of the people who lived in the area. His appearance was very normal for the district he was in, but what was special and also intimidating about him was that he had a large fighting dog as his pet and he held it with a short, homemade rope leash.

As we began our conversation he was very respectful towards God and the Bible. This kind of respect for God and Christians was highly unusual in this part of town, so I was sincerely impressed. He seemed to have a genuine love for and belief in God and we discussed God for a good while. However, as we talked, I had a strange feeling inside of me that something was not right with the guy.

Eventually, he began expounding on why he believed that weed was God's holy herb and he explained how Rastafarianism was founded. He also began quoting Rasta scriptures such as the book of Enoch and others, and he even claimed that the Bible says that the incense that was burned to God in Solomon's Temple contained cannabis as one if its ingredients.

I responded to his quotations of Scripture and other revered books by explaining what the Word of God says about drugs and why the Bible is the actual Word of God. The moment I began elaborating on the truth of God's Word he began to warp and become filled with anger. He started exclaiming that the Bible was trash and that no one could trust it because the Romans had defiled it.

So instead of arguing about the validity of the Bible I steered the conversation back to the One we both had initially agreed upon: Jesus. I asked if I could explain to him what Jesus taught and he calmly conceded my request. Thus, I began explaining the Gospel to him step-by-step. The second I stated the phrases "Jesus died for you on the cross" and "the blood of Jesus" he lost control of himself and began acting like a wild lunatic. Within a few seconds, he went from being a kind, respectful young man to an enraged, out-of-control person who was deeply huffing and puffing, screaming all kinds of incoherent obscenities, and yelling at me, "Get out of my sight, Satan!"

I was shocked by his sudden transformation in behavior, yet I was well aware that he was not the one who was ranting and raving at me. I knew that a demon was in him and it was manifesting aggressively against the Gospel I was sharing. In my heart, I began rebuking the demon and binding it in Jesus' name.

I continued to attempt explaining the Gospel to the man, but he was simply unwilling to accept that Jesus died on the cross for our sins. Every time I tried to explain the meaning of Christ's death on the cross he would scream and yell even louder. At one point, I honestly thought that he was going to sic his dog on me and, I must confess, I was scared to get attacked by that dog. It was a beast!

Out of nowhere, a homeless man walked by us asking for money. I said one quick statement to the man and the Rasta man used the opportunity to quickly walk away.

I didn't care much to chase the guy down for the sake of continuing our antagonistic conversation, so I approached a junkie woman who appeared to be utterly broken and lost. She listened intently as I shared the Gospel with her and she seemed to be touched by what she was hearing. In the middle of our conversation, the young Rastafarian returned to the exact spot where we had been talking before and stood by us with his dog. Once I finished talking with the woman I began talking with him again.

We had a more wholesome conversation the second time around, but he eventually walked off angry again. I wasn't discouraged, however, because I knew that the real reason he became so angry and walked away each time was because the demons in him didn't want him to hear the Gospel. That man sincerely confounded me because throughout our hour-and-a-half conversation he was perfectly sane and cool, but the moment I reached the central points of the Gospel, which are the cross, the resurrection, and Jesus' atoning blood, he became completely demonized and threatened to beat me up. I was honestly amazed that he didn't sic his ferocious dog on me.

*

Alex was starving when we joined up later on in the day, so we decided to go to the same pizza place that I had eaten at earlier in the day. We were moved with compassion for three gutter punks who were sitting on the sidewalk with an empty glare on their faces. The moment we mentioned Jesus one of them walked away, but the other two, Sky and Fred, didn't mind talking with us. Alex passionately shared the Gospel with them because he himself had been an anarchist punk before he had come to the Lord, so he felt a deep compassion for them and was able to relate to them easily. We were amazed at how hungry and open they were to the Gospel. I could see that Sky was especially hungry since he repeatedly looked into my eyes as if he were desperately crying for help. He confessed to us that he had just been released from prison and he had nothing to live for and no one in his life who cared about him. He was utterly lost and desperate even though he was only in his early twenties. Once I saw that he was ripe for salvation, I asked him if he wanted to give his life to Jesus. Without a moment of hesitation he agreed to surrender his life to Jesus, so Alex led him in the sinner's prayer and then I prayed over him. He was practically moved to tears after receiving Jesus into his life and receiving prayer from us. At the end of our time together, we invited him to church, gave him a hug, and continued our journey to the pizza parlor.

As we were walking, we felt compelled to speak to two other guys who were standing around on the sidewalk. Even though we were hungry for food, we had become so conditioned to be moved with compassion for the lost that we would stop to talk with whoever God led us to no matter how hungry, tired, or busy we were.

One of the young men was nicknamed Tortoise and the other guys' name was Jesse. Once we opened up the conversation and began sharing about God, Jesse felt the liberty and trust to share his life story with us. He began telling us that, as a teenager, he was a hard-core gutter punk, drug addict, and alcoholic. He had never met his parents in his life and he led an absolutely miserable existence in every way.

However, as he was living on hippie hill along with all of his other gutter punk and hippie friends some people from the Prodigal Project began witnessing to him, giving him free food, and praying for him. Eventually, their love, message, and lifestyle won him over and he gave his life completely over to Jesus.

He committed to attend their communal discipleship school that was located a few hours north of San Francisco in a small forest town. For four months, he lived in a cabin in the middle of the woods, cultivated a garden, ate organic foods, and lived in a community of believers all free of charge: a hippie's dream. The leaders of the Prodigal Project discipled Jesse thoroughly in the Word of God, his character issues were dealt with, and he became passionately in love with Jesus.

He eventually gained a strong desire to find his parents and re-unite with them. Once he found out exactly where his mom lived in Pennsylvania, he decided to leave the ministry in order to find her. When he finally found his mom, it turned out that she was a lesbian and a drunkard who wanted nothing to do with him. Upon seeing how spiritually lost his mom was, he passionately preached the Gospel to her and told her to repent of her sins. She became enraged, called the police, and had him put in jail.

Jesse stayed in jail for several weeks until one day his never-before-seen father arrived at the jail to bail him out. After bailing him out, his father disappeared once again from his son's life. Jesse never saw him again. Nevertheless, Jesse ended up finding a good job and living in a one-bedroom apartment by himself for four years. He eventually backslid into the world again, became bored out of his mind with his routine life, and decided to return to San Francisco to live on the street again. He unashamedly declared that he loved being a gutter punk, smoking weed, drinking, and leading an unstable life. However, in spite of this major downfall in his walk with God, he still fully believed in the Gospel and still loved God. He firmly believed in repentance and that Jesus was the only way, but he didn't believe that smoking and drinking were sinful. Thus, despite our appeals to his conscience he felt no conviction to repent of such things. He still loved reading the Bible and personally considered himself to be a true Christian.

This was the state in which we encountered Jesse. We talked with him about Christ, urged him to repent of his sinful lifestyle, and invited him to attend Promised Land Fellowship with us. After he shared his story with us, we told him that the Prodigal Project still existed up north. He became ecstatic with joy when he found out that they were still functioning as a ministry and he said that he would love to go back there again. He thought that the ministry had died out because it no longer owned the house on Haight Street. So after he committed to go back to the Prodigal Project we prayed for him and told him that we would help reconnect him with the ministry.

That Sunday he visited Promised Land Fellowship with us and he really loved it. He said that he would continue attending the church even after we left. We were blown away. He definitely needed to be delivered from many demonic strongholds in his life, but even he acknowledged that he knew God was calling him back to Himself.

*

We finally arrived at the pizza parlor and delighted ourselves in a few slices of ultra cheesy pizza for dinner. While we were eating, I preached the Gospel to one of the baker's who was standing around doing nothing and to the girl on the cash register. They didn't speak English, so I preached to them in Spanish. The baker was about fifteen feet away, so we had to speak loudly to each other in order to hear one another. Thus, everyone else in the little pizza shop who understood Spanish heard the Gospel as well.

I was so pumped from having had such an awesome day that when we stepped onto the bus to head back to Promised Land Fellowship for the night I stood up and open air preached in the bus without I split second of hesitation. I had become fed up with being full of fear, hesitation, excuses, and distractions. So, for once, none of those things were in my way. However, when I began preaching I felt like I had run into an impenetrable spiritual wall that I couldn't break through. As I spoke, no one seemed to care about what I was saying. There were even people rolling their eyes at me in disgust. My mind was going blank on what to say and my words were not coming out with fluidity and authority. This had never happened to me at any other time that I had open air preached during our mission trip, so I knew that it was a spiritual attack.

Halfway into my message one guy randomly yelled, "Hey boy, who won in Iraq today, Allah or Jesus?"

"None of them," I replied, "Jesus isn't fighting. He's there trying to bring peace."

"Well," he arrogantly continued, "You don't need to be telling these people anything when you don't know how to live."

Nothing he said affected me, but my mind had gone totally blank and no one was paying attention to my message, so I concluded the message by encouraging everyone to seek God for themselves and then sat down. Nevertheless, throughout the bus ride, the same man would sporadically make loud remarks against God that he thought were clever. Every time he said something I would immediately answer back with an answer that would disprove his statement. He would then get frustrated, make a fuss about it, become silent, and then come up with another random statement against God, which I would immediately disprove again.

When we left the bus, God showed me that my preaching had in fact touched someone, it had touched that man. One thing I had learned on the trip was that whoever opposed the loudest was the one who was the most convicted by what was being preached. This applied to open-air evangelism even more than it did for one-on-one evangelism. The reason that people were sometimes so violently opposed to what we were saying was usually because we had touched a wound or vice that was deeply ingrained within their soul.

Once we arrived at the church, Adam Hood asked us if we could lead the prayer set from 12 a.m. to 3 a.m. We joyfully accepted the honor of praying all night for the city that we had just preached in all day. The people that we had encountered were still freshly imprinted in our minds and the reckless compassion and intense warfare we had experienced were still being felt in the depths of our souls. It was our honor to join the united effort of the body of Christ in the city to cry out to God for an awakening to take place in San Francisco.

The Castro

The new JHOP team had just arrived. Roger and Gabrielle Joyner had brought a solid crew of Jesus lovers to live in the heart of Haight Street. Adam Hood, being the legend that he is, was going to train their them on how to witness in the Castro because we were all planning to preach the Gospel together in the Castro that night. We arrived at the JHOP house a few hours early because Adam wanted to fellowship with Roger before the meeting. So Alex, Eric, and I walked down to Haight Street to preach the Gospel. Alex decided to witness on his own and I decided to tag along with Eric for the sake of company and because I was sure that I could learn a few things from him since he was a full time missionary to hippies and still a true hippy himself.

As we walked through hippie hill, a young man was about to walk right by us when he recognized Eric. He slowed down and jovially declared, "I'm going to commit suicide today. You wanna come and watch me commit suicide?"

The young man's friends who were walking with him jokingly responded, "No man. We don't want to see that," as they laughed off his remark and walked away from him.

Eric lovingly put his arm around the young man as any real friend would and began walking with him down the sidewalk. I stayed alongside them as they caught up on life speaking to each other as if they were long lost friends. Eric told him a little bit about how his life had been going, but most of the time he just listened to how the young man's life had been recently.

Eventually, Eric found a somewhat private spot next to a tree and some tall bushes where he sat down with the guy to talk more deeply with him about what was really going on in his life. At this point, I did not feel at liberty to be a part of the conversation because Eric already had a past friendship with the guy and I didn't want to intrude in the trust that they had already built with one another. Thus, I sat down on the grass a few yards away and prayed that God would use Eric and that He would touch this young man's life.

After a good while, Eric ended the conversation and met back up with me. His eyes were red and his face was somber as he approached me and quietly told me that the young man wasn't joking at all. He had been serious about wanting to commit suicide that day. When Eric sat down with him to talk the young man immediately broke down weeping and poured his heart out to Eric telling him why he considered life to be worthless and why he had resolved to end his life that day. Eric ministered to him and prayed over him for about an hour. He felt much better after Eric had ministered to him and said that he now had the strength and peace to carry on with his life.

At 6:15 p.m., I went over to JHOP for the meeting that was supposed to begin at 6:30 p.m. I hung out with the JHOP team as we waited for the meeting to start, but it never did. Adam was stuck in the room talking with Roger and it didn't look like they were going to be ending their conversation anytime soon. So at 6:50 I decided to go back to the streets and spend my time evangelizing in Haight Ashbury until everyone was ready to leave for the Castro at 9 p.m.

*

Within the short time I had spent in JHOP, the atmosphere of Haight Street had morphed into an entirely different reality. The sun had set and darkness cloaked the city like a thick blanket. People carried hostility in their gaze and aggression in their cryptic walk. If during the day it could have been described as a strange hippie scene where sexual immorality and the New Age flourished, at night it could have been called a demonic hellhole where every fear and nightmare would come alive as an inevitable reality.

Well over two hundred punk rockers flooded the streets dressed in their chaotic regalia of metal spikes, patches, and tall, steel-toed boots. Mohawks, liberty spikes, and hot pink hair were the common hairdos on these tattooed, pierced-up rebels. Most of them were crowded around Amoeba Music angry that there was no more space to see their coveted punk band. The posters of the band were splattered all over the walls and electric posts of the city depicting a punk rocker vengefully stabbing a pig-faced cop through the heart. I have had many friends who are punks, including Alex, who used to have thirteen piercings on his body and a multi-colored Mohawk before coming to Christ, and even I have had liberty spikes before, but never before had I seen such a hostile, aggressive crowd of punks. Not only were they mean, but they were old. These were not your usual high school punk rock kids. These were grown men and women in their mid-twenties to mid-thirties who had stayed true to their punk roots. Some of these people had to have been original punks from the 80's.

Although punks were the most numerous crowd, they were definitely not the only crowd. Dozens of gangsta-looking youth were littered throughout the night's scene. Many of them were openly selling drugs on street corners, others were walking into clubs with their arm around a lasciviously dressed girl, and still others were just chillin' trying to enjoy the dark culture all around them.

What took me by surprise was the solid number of preppy high school girls walking with their jock boyfriends to clubs or bars. Abercrombie and Fitch and letterman jackets just didn't seem to fit into this misfit picture and yet, there they were, more abundantly present than in the sunshine hours. I couldn't help but wonder what their parents would think of them hanging out in such a dangerously sketchy place, but, then again, it was San Francisco.

A small number of hippies and homeless men were scattered down Haight, but their presence was nothing like it usually was during the daytime. It was obvious that Friday nights on Haight Street was not the Hippie hour. It was the hour of the punks, thugs, and partygoers. The main activity I saw the homeless and hippies engaging in at night was quietly creeping up to the thugs to buy some drugs. Perhaps the reason they weren't hanging out on the main street was because the late hours of the night was when they blazed it up somewhere in Golden Gate Park. Also, throughout the night, several people tried to sell me drugs while several others asked if I had any spare drugs I could give them.

So, there I was, in the middle of this sinful hellhole with very mixed feelings of overwhelming intimidation by the darkness that surrounded me and exuberant joy at knowing that this was exactly where Jesus would have been if he were in San Francisco that Friday night. I felt like I had hit the jackpot! I had always dreamt of finding the places in the world that were so desperately wicked and lost that the only hope for them was the Gospel of Jesus. I longed to see the light of the Gospel shine in these places because I knew that where sin abounded, grace abounded even more. Haight Ashbury was definitely one of those places.

I met up with Alex and we fervently prayed together, preparing ourselves to go to war against hell side-by-side. As we were witnessing such deep darkness all around us, I began to meditate on the genuine truth of the Gospel and how deeply I believed it. I began inwardly weeping for the lost souls in Haight Ashbury and longed to preach the

Gospel to them all the more. I knew that ff only these people could encounter God and see Him for who He truly was it would be impossible for them to resist His goodness and truth.

So as these inner meditations were taking place in my soul, Alex and I turned the corner and spotted two young couples seated on the stairway to the entry of McDonald's. They were dressed like cool hipsters and seemed to be very intellectual. Upon initiating the conversation I asked them if they believed in God. Three of them said they were not sure if God existed and one of them said that she definitely did not believe in God. A burning fire welled up within me and I found myself passionately expounding upon why I personally believed that there was a God and I encouraged them to genuinely seek Him because He was a rewarder of those who diligently sought after Him. I then articulated the Gospel to them with a burning conviction pleading with them to seek God, repent of their sins, and give their lives to Him. I wanted to proclaim the message from the rooftops.

When I first began sharing with them they seemed to be quite skeptical and dismissed much of what I was saying as mere religious dogma. However, once they saw that I truly believed in what I was saying and it made good sense to them, they became much more attentive and respectful. After explaining the Gospel to them I said to them, "I'm not telling this to you guys just because it's a nice story and a good religion. I'm telling this to you guys because it's totally real and I pray that you would come to see how real it is."

"I believe you man," one of the guys suddenly interjected with genuine conviction in his voice, "I could feel your passion for God coming out of you. But I want to know how did you become so committed to God?"

As soon as the young man asked that question all three of his friends fixed their eyes on me and agreed that this was what they wanted to know more than anything else I was talking about. They were amazed that a young man around their age could be so passionate about God. "How could this guy be so convicted about something we don't even believe in? Is he right and we're wrong?" Those were the questions I could see revolving in their minds as they stared at me with fixed eyes of desperation. They were hoping that what I was describing was true, but they were hesitant to believe in it.

I told them my testimony of how I fell passionately in love with God when He transformed my life at twelve years of age. They were blown away by my story.

"Have you ever felt or encountered God," they hungrily asked.

I recounted to them the encounter I had with God when I was baptized in the Holy Spirit at ten years of age. They were in awe of my story and I could see that they too wanted to have a genuine encounter with God. They hadn't found it in churches, but on this dark night on Haight Street they were finding it through an encounter with a strange young man who claimed to know God. Who would have thought that Haight Street would be the place where they would draw near to God? We prayed for them and they greatly appreciated it. They weren't ready to surrender their lives to Jesus in that moment, but their spiritual hunger had been awakened.

*

It was now a quarter to 9 p.m. and we were supposed to meet with Adam Hood and the JHOP group at nine o'clock for prayer before heading out to the Castro. We hopped onto a bus and headed for Promised Land Fellowship.

The group was made up of about twelve JHOP'ers, Adam Hood, four or five others from Promised Land Fellowship, Alex, and myself. Everyone was burning on fire for Jesus, full of compassion for the lost, and mature in their walk with God.

When we first began walking up the hill on Market Street, our surroundings were similar to most places in San Francisco: chic restaurants, occasional bars, random shops, and uniquely designed houses. However, little by little, the scenery began to change until it had completely warped into a full-blown, sexually promiscuous, homosexual atmosphere. Everything became sexually perverted and rainbow colors burst out of every place imaginable.

Gay porn magazines were plastered on the walls inside a barber shop so that when the customers were getting their haircuts they could relish in images of gay sexual acts. The logo and motto of a certain gym was an illustrated poster of a shirtless, muscular man ripping his shorts off and the words in large print directly over the man's private part saying: "Get Buff... Take Off Your Clothes." Bus stops had large marketing posters of gay men intimately embracing each other with a message of caution to always use condoms while another bus poster had the head shots of four different men who had been tested for HIV; three of them were tested positive, but the one who tested negative had a blurb that said, "I'm still available!" Sexual perversion pervaded every facet of society in the Castro. It was inescapable and overwhelming to the point that I felt like I was going to vomit, much like when a rancid smell of rotten waste hits your nostrils and there is no way of getting away from the toxic smell. My eyes and soul were being defiled to the point of weeping, but my love for the people we were about to encounter motivated me to continue walking into the darkest neighborhood that I had ever seen.

As we journeyed further into the Castro District, we saw more and more people walking up and down the streets and when we finally reached the heart of the district the streets, bars, and restaurants were teeming with people. What shocked me beyond belief was that, to the best of my recollection, I did not see one heterosexual person throughout our entire outreach that night. I am sure that there must have been some heterosexual men and women in the midst of the crowds, but from what I perceived I was unable to find them.

Couples and groups would walk by grabbing each other's hands, waist, shoulders, or butts. Even the men who were walking alone carried themselves in an openly flamboyant manner. At one point in the night, a man without one article of clothing walked by greeting random people and shaking their hands, including people in our group. The city dwellers didn't seem to be the least bit surprised at the sight of a bare naked man walking down the street. Perhaps it was a common occurrence there. I never thought that I would personally encounter a modern day Sodom and Gomorrah in my lifetime, but now I had.

Our group of about twenty people gathered on the corner of a main street. Adam gave us some simple instructions and we began worshipping God. We had two guitars, one djembe, and several voices. Some of us sang, some prayed, some talked with people who walked by, and others just wept. Our hearts were bleeding with compassion at the pain, deception, and depravity of the souls round about us. The sight of thousands of men and women bound by homosexuality inflicted a deep sense of despair and hopelessness in our hearts while being simultaneously certain that God was more than able to redeem and transform each individual in the Castro. But in such a deep trench of despair where should one even begin? We began with prayer and worship.

For the first thirty minutes or so I played the djembe and worshipped with all of my heart. However, I soon began to itch to talk to someone. I wanted to understand them better and be able to bring the Gospel to them in a loving and powerful way and the best way to learn was to jump right in and start swimming.

I initiated three or four conversations with different people, but none of them cared to talk and they soon walked away. From time to time someone would clap their hands to the music, stop and listen for a few seconds, or shout out a "Hallelujah!" Eventually, a well-built Latino man stopped right in front of me and began gleefully dancing to the music. He was obviously a little drunk, but he was genuinely happy to hear worship music on the streets of the Castro.

"I love you guys," He exclaimed as he danced flamboyantly, "I love this music!"

"Finally," I thought to myself, "someone who was open to our message." I immediately introduced myself to him and began talking with him about Jesus. His name was Eddie and he claimed to love Jesus and told me that his whole family was Christian. He repeatedly stated that his family would love me for preaching the Gospel to him because they were all praying for him to return to God. He naturally brought up his homosexual lifestyle into our discussion and confessed that he knew that it was wrong. I urged him to repent because God loved him so much and wanted to forgive and transform him, but he insisted that he enjoyed his lifestyle way too much and didn't want to stop.

Suddenly, Eddie's boyfriend, Jake, showed up and began talking with him. I quickly brought him into our conversation and he respectfully listened to everything I shared about Christ. He was not hostile towards me or the Gospel and kindly listened to me as I presented the Gospel.

After about five minutes of talking, Jake abruptly said to me, "Hey, we're gonna go get a drink. Do you want to come with us so you could talk to us more? C'mon, I'll buy you a drink."

"Well," I replied with some caution in my mind, "I would love to continue talking with you guys, but I don't drink beer and I can't drink anything because I'm fasting today."

Kind of taken aback by abnormal statement he said, "Alright. Whatever man, just come."

"Oh!" I said, "I just realized that I can't go in the bar because I'm only 20-years-old."

"Don't worry," he replied, "You're with me. No one will ask you for anything."

There were no red lights flashing in my spirit and I felt God's peace and security with me, so I decided to go with them into the gay bar. The rest of the group continued worshipping, praying, and ministering to people on the street corner while I walked about thirty feet down the road into a nearby bar with this couple.

I had never entered a gay bar before, so I had no idea what to expect. As I walked through a maze-like entryway with fuzzy black walls I came into a fairly large room with dim lighting and dark colors painted on the walls. Several rainbow flags were hung on both sides of the bar in the same manner in which a dozen American flags would be hung on the porch of a traditional, patriotic home in the South. Everyone inside the bar was male, except for one lesbian couple, but this was not too surprising since the ratio of gay and lesbian couples outside of the bar was virtually identical with the ratio inside of the bar. There were no seats in the place except for one row of cushioned stools up against the bar and everyone else stood around four-foot tall tables resting their drinks as they talked with one another. Eccentric indie rock music played at a high volume while strange music videos were shown on two large flat screen TV's. The scene around me was quite awkward and strange, yet well designed and fashionable. I felt like I had randomly walked into the set of a bizarre movie.

       Jake continued to push me to accept some alcohol, but I firmly insisted that I would only drink water. Embarrassed, he asked the bartender for water and I continued preaching the Gospel to him as I gratefully drank my water. He seemed to acknowledge that I was speaking the truth and I could tell that he was somewhat convicted, but he ultimately didn't seem to care. As we were talking he interrupted me for a moment to compliment my hair. A couple of times he told me that I was such a nice guy. I brushed off all of these comments as distractions and as common remarks that gay men made to each other in conversation. About twenty minutes into our discussion he tried to put his arm around my shoulder, but I quickly threw it off sternly exclaiming, "Don't put your arm around me! Respect me!"

       That disturbing gesture caused me to finally wake up to the fact that Jake was actually hitting on me and his openness and kindness towards me was just part of his filthy scheme to get with me. Upon realizing that I was being strategically hit on by a grown, gay man in a gay bar in the Castro, I was struck with one of the most disgustingly awkward feelings I had ever experienced in my life. What confounded me the most was that he was acting this way with his boyfriend standing right next to him. Nevertheless, I continued compassionately preaching the Gospel to him praying that the Holy Spirit would somehow convict him through His Word. What happened next, however, was an even greater paradox to me.

Eddie walked over to the bar and flamboyantly approached the only lesbian couple in the room. The more feminine of the two women was sitting on a stool at the bar while her partner stood closely behind her with her hands on her shoulders. Surprisingly, he began flirting with the lesbian woman seated on the stool and soon was rubbing his whole body up and down her front side as she giggled with excitement. I was confused and repulsed. Here was a gay man openly flirting with a lesbian woman in a homosexual bar while the man's boyfriend and the woman's girlfriend calmly stood around as if their partner's provocative infidelity was perfectly normal and acceptable. The atmosphere both in the bar and in all of the Castro seemed to be so sexually charged that any sexual act was encouraged regardless of one's sexual preference or relational status.

Eventually, Eddie invited us over to meet the lesbian couple. We both walked over and I politely introduced myself to Elizabeth and Debbie. Elizabeth, the more masculine of the two who had been standing, asked me if I was their friend. I explained to her that I was here just talking with them about Jesus and, suddenly, she became very interested in talking with me. Her partner tried to discourage her, but she responded, "No. No. This is good. We might be able to win him over to our cause."

Elizabeth possessed a formidable presence as she stood lean and tall in her men's business attire. Her mannerisms and eloquent speech were evidence of her high level of education. We naturally engaged in a respectful, yet candid conversation where both of us were mature enough not be offended by each other's strong statements.

She was curious to know who I was and what I did for a living. After I explained to her the nature of my mission trip across America she bluntly asked me, "So where do you stand on homosexuality?"

"I love people who live in homosexuality," I sincerely explained, "I respect them. I care about them. But I honestly believe that their lifestyle is utterly sinful."

"So do you think that homosexuals go to Hell?" she inquired, as she looked me straight in the eyes.

This question led me to share the Gospel with her. I explained that regardless of which sin we commit we all will be judged by God for our lives and will all be found guilty of sin. Thus, all of us justly deserve to go to Hell and that is why Jesus came to redeem us from Hell and our sin by taking our place of judgment on the cross.

"Okay, I see," Elizabeth nodded with understanding, "Let me tell you my story."

"I was raised in a white collar family. We were an affluent family and I had the opportunity to have relationships with many wealthy men, but I never felt true to myself being with a man. It just wasn't me.

"I eventually realized that God made me as a lesbian and I thank Him for making me this way. Once I told my family that I was a lesbian my whole family rejected me. They don't want anything to do with me and I'm fine with that. I'm happy now because I am who I feel that I am."

I listened to Elizabeth's whole story without interruption and respected all that she had to say. I was amazed that she had opened up her heart to me so quickly by sharing about her journey of self-discovery as a lesbian. My heart broke for her because I saw that she was thoroughly convinced that this was her true identity. It would take a miracle for her to see that she was deceived and that God knew her identity better than she knew her own.

So with utmost compassion and faith I told her, "I fully respect your story, but I want you to know that if you surrender your life to God the Holy Spirit has the power to come into your life and make you a new creation. All you need to do is believe from your heart, acknowledge that you have sinned, and repent, and God will completely transform your life."

I could see the disappointment on her face. She thought that she was winning over a convert to the LGBT cause and once she saw that I would not budge she gave up on me. She quietly rolled her eyes at my final comments about the Holy Spirit's power to make her a new creation. To her, it was just a bunch of empty religious philosophy that had no real power to change her.

So our conversation came to an abrupt end as she turned around to ask for another drink. It was evident that my time in the bar had come to a close and it was time for me to leave.

I bid farewell to Elizabeth and went over to say goodbye to Jake. Debbie and Eddie returned to the bar as I was talking with Jake. During my conversation with Elizabeth, they had slipped away to the bathroom area of the bar and had been gone for at least twenty minutes. I tried to say goodbye to them as well, but they were too lost in their sensual giggling and drunken stupor.

Jake was upset that I was leaving so soon and he tried whatever he could to stall me from leaving. He asked me if he could buy me another drink and offered to buy me food. He was desperate to have me stay a moment longer.

Realizing that it was late, I looked at my watch to see what time it was. It was five minutes past midnight. I could break my fast!

"Well, my fast just ended because it's midnight," I told him, "I guess I'll accept some food if you insist."

He smiled and joyfully walked me over to a hip pizza stand right outside of the bar. As we were waiting in line to order the pizza he asked me, "Do want to come over to my apartment to hang out?"

"No, man," I refused as politely as possible, trying not to let the disgust I felt in my gut reveal itself in a facial expression.

I was finally given the two huge slices of supreme pizza that Jake had ordered for me and I was so happy. Although God provides in the weirdest ways sometimes, He definitely was faithful to provide me with a great meal to break my fast that night. I thanked the Lord for the food and gratefully took a bite into a slice of pizza.

"Mmhmm!" I exclaimed with satisfaction, "This is so good. Thank you so much Jake. Well, I gotta get back with my group. It's getting late. It was great talking with you."

Jake thought that I was going to spend more time with him because he had bought me pizza, but it was late and I had to leave. Once he realized that I was really leaving he became a little frantic.

"But, but, but…that's it?" Jake stuttered in a last ditch effort, "Wait…please…are you sure you don't want to come over to my apartment?!"

"God bless you Jake," I said as I walked away.

When I returned to our group I noticed that about half of the people had already left, but I was relieved to see that those who had stayed were still deeply engaged in worship, prayer, and evangelism. I was a little worried that they might have left or been looking for me, but they were fine. No one even commented on the fact that I had been gone for so long. Alex was on the street corner talking to an older man with a hefty beard. Later he told me that the man he was witnessing to was a Druid high priest. San Francisco never ceased to amaze me.

There were only two cars between everyone in our group, so they had filled them up to drop people off at their homes. They would soon return to pick up the rest of us.

I enjoyed my pizza for a moment as I sat on the sidewalk with my back up against the wall. I reflected deeply on the events of the night and the continuing sin that I was witnessing before me as I ate my meal. It was too overwhelming to dwell upon. I had never witnessed such a deep, pervasive depravity in one place in my entire life. South Beach, Buckhead, Athens, Venice Beach, and Pacific Beach combined could not even come close to the darkness we experienced in the Castro and in Haight Ashbury that night. And to think…this was only one random Friday night in the nightlife of San Francisco. I could not even begin to imagine how insidiously depraved it must be during special events such as Halloween and the Gay Pride Parade.

After finishing my meal, I joined the group in prayer and witnessed to a couple more people. Adam arrived to pick us up around 1:30 a.m. He took us home and we had a very restful night of sleep.

What a day. What a night.

I later thanked God for protecting me from Eddie and Jake. I had not thought it through in the moment, but later on I realized that they were two tall, buff gay men who took me into a bar with many more buff gay men who were mostly drunk. They could have easily beat me up, forced me to go to their apartment, or have done something much worse. After looking back on the event, I realized how naive I had been in going into the bar with them. Although I still do believe that it was God's will for me to have gone in and talked with them, I should not have gone in alone. I praise God that His grace was sufficient to protect me in my foolishness.

UC Berkeley

I must confess that I had preconceived judgments about UC Berkeley. I had seen too many videos and photos of Berkeley students in the 1960's and 70's and had assumed that the ultra liberal protester spirit of UC Berkeley still lived on. Since I had discovered that the hippie scene was still alive and well in San Francisco, I assumed that the Berkeley campus would be littered with hippies and potheads playing guitars on grass fields and perched up on trees as they were being trained to become the world's future ultra liberals.

To my chagrin, all of my presupposed judgments were proven wrong as soon as I stepped foot onto the UC Berkeley campus. I was surprised to discover that the student body was just as typical as any other student body in many high-ranking universities on the West Coast of the United States. The majority of the students were East Asians and White Americans; there were a good number of Indians and Arabs; and only a handful of Blacks and Latinos. The common cliques of nerds, jocks, hippies, and several others were spread throughout the campus. It was obvious that the students came from all walks of life, held to many different beliefs, and had distinct cultural backgrounds. I only spoke to seven students, but each conversation was so profound and comprehensive that they lasted me the whole day.

Before visiting the campus, I had woken up at six in the morning and spent a solid four hours in prayer, worship, and Bible reading. It was honestly one of the most glorious times of prayer I had spent with God during my entire trip. I was spiritually renewed and inwardly strengthened as I worshipped Him with total abandonment, meditated on the mysteries of His Word, and dwelt in His intimate presence. So even though I was somewhat intimidated by my false presuppositions about UC Berkeley's ultra liberal culture, I felt empowered by the Holy Spirit burning inside my soul.

Upon arriving at the campus, I walked and prayed as I surveyed the area trying to find where the main crowd of students were gathered. I soon felt compelled to approach a well-dressed, good-looking young man whose name was James. He was a white American from Northern California who was raised in a Presbyterian and Congregational background. His grandfather was a Presbyterian minister and his mother, at one time, was a nun. He confessed that around the age of thirteen he had stopped attending church and his parents had now stopped attending as well. We talked for a good while and then I explained the Gospel to him. Surprisingly, he had a rich understanding of the Gospel, but he had chosen not to follow God at all. I could see that there was a deeper reason for why he wasn't following God, so I asked him if he actually believed in God. He confessed to me that he was not sure of God's existence. I gave him some reasons for why I believed in God and I told him to seek God humbly because God rejects the proud, but draws near to the humble. After talking for about thirty minutes, he informed me that his class was about to begin and he had to be on his way.

So as we closed our conversation James looked my in the eyes and sincerely thanked me saying, "Thank you very much for this conversation Joshua. You've opened my eyes a bit."

Statements like those are what made this trip worthwhile. Even if I had come to Berkeley just to have God open James' eyes a bit, it would all have been worth it. As we parted ways, I wrote down the title of *More Than A Carpenter* by Josh McDowell on a piece of paper, handed it to him, and encouraged him to read it.

*

I walked around the large campus some more in my persistent pursuit to find where most of the students hung out and, at last, I found it. Directly off of Telegraph Road, there were swarms of students walking, talking, sitting, eating, playing music, kissing and studying. Jackpot!

I sat down for a little bit to pray in order to gain some spiritual strength before I engaged the massive crowd. Once I felt ready, I walked up to an Asian guy who had the build of a football player. He was sitting by himself on a flight of concrete stairs as he slowly munched his snacks.

We quickly engaged in a friendly conversation where I learned that his name was Jim and he was originally from China, but had lived in the United States for most of his life. As we began talking about God he unashamedly told me that he was a Buddhist and that he strongly believed in his Buddhist heritage and religion. We then proceeded to have the greatest conversation I had ever had with a devout Buddhist.

Initially, when he told me about his strong belief in Buddhism I didn't know what to say because it was very rare that I ever encountered a true Buddhist. So out of a place of honest curiosity and lack of knowledge I began to ask him several questions about his faith in Buddha.

"Do you believe in God?" I began.

"Yeah. I definitely believe in God," Tom replied.

I was somewhat surprised by his simple answer because I knew that some Buddhists don't believe in God. So I asked him, "Who or what is God to you? Is the man Buddha god?

"Yeah," he genuinely answered, "The man Buddha is god and I worship him, pray to him, and try to emulate him."

In response I inquired, "Do you believe there is any God who created Buddha and created us all?"

"No," he said, "I don't believe there is."

"So could I ask you a personal question then?" I asked.

"Sure," he replied.

I looked Jim straight in the eyes and sincerely asked him, "So do you have a personal, genuine, deep relationship with your god?"

He stared at me thoughtfully and then looked away in deep contemplation. Then he simply responded, "No. I don't. I don't have any sort of personal relationship with Buddha. I mean…I believe in him and I pray to him, but I only seek to emulate him. I don't seek to have a relationship with him."

Jim's honest answer both struck me and surprised him. I couldn't imagine how someone could love, believe in, and follow someone who they didn't even know. If a god could not be known, understood, and experienced then how could anyone genuinely follow that god? Why would anyone live for and even die for a god who was not personally real to them in their own lives and only existed in a philosophy or theory? And yet simultaneously I could see a question mark forming on Jim's face as he came to these honest realizations. This was his reality and he probably had never questioned it. Above all, it was his Chinese heritage, so in his eyes questioning Buddha's teachings may have been equivalent to questioning his Chinese identity. However, perhaps my question and his vocalized answer provoked him to realize the lack of sense in his reality because after that point in our conversation he completely opened up his heart and mind. He was suddenly hungry to hear what I had to say about my God who I actually knew personally and had a real relationship with.

"Jim," I asked, "Could I share with you how I have a personal relationship with Jesus and why I follow Him?"

"Sure," he nodded.

I passionately described to Jim my relationship with God and how gloriously real He was in my life. I expounded upon the intimacy I felt with God in prayer, times that God had miraculously answered my prayers, times where I had heard His voice, and powerful experiences I had lived through with Him. I told him about my mission trip and how God had guided me and provided for me every step of the way.

I could see in his eyes that he was both genuinely fascinated by the relationship I had with my God and deeply perplexed with the fact that he had never experienced any kind of real relationship with Buddha. He had never thought of having a personal relationship with Buddha, but now that he was clearly seeing someone who had an intimate relationship with God he seemed to be a little envious. How come he had never experienced any of the realities that I was describing to him through his devotion to Buddha?

All of this naturally led to the Gospel because I then explained why we were unable to have a relationship with God due to our sins that separated us from Him. I then went on to tell him about the judgment, the cross, repentance, and the afterlife. He understood and he was seriously impacted.

After talking about judgment and the afterlife, I asked him, "So what do you believe about life after death, Jim?"

"I believe that we reincarnate," he answered.

"So you really believe in reincarnation?" I inquired with some cynicism in the tone of voice.

"Oh yeah man," he stated with conviction, "wholeheartedly."

I had rarely ever met someone who genuinely believed in reincarnation, so I was a little skeptical at Jim's initial statement. I had known lots of hippies and new agers who were wannabe Buddhists and Hindus. They would say they believed in reincarnation, but as soon as they were seriously confronted about their convictions they would admit that they had no clue about what was really going to happen in the afterlife.

I was excited to finally talk to someone who devoutly believed in reincarnation. I wanted to pick Jim's brain a little to figure out why someone would ever seriously hold to such a belief because I myself had always considered it to be such a silly idea.

So we began talking about reincarnation. I asked him several questions such as, "Why do we reincarnate? Is it a good thing or a bad thing? How can someone reach Nirvana?"

Basically, he admitted that reincarnation was more of a bad thing than a good thing and that we reach Nirvana by our own efforts and conscience. As people sought to emulate Buddha and become more and more pure in their consciousness they would eventually attain Nirvana. Once they reached Nirvana they wouldn't enter into a "heaven" with Buddha or some other god. They would just become a part of the universe forever.

I respectfully listened to his explanations about reincarnation and Nirvana. I then asked him, "Would it be okay if I gave you my honest thoughts about reincarnation?"

"Sure," Jim said, "No problem."

So I elaborated on my thoughts by saying, "I believe that any philosophy that says that the answer is within our own selves is completely false because man is flawed and sinful and no man can earn his way to Heaven or Nirvana. The only way for a man to be transformed and go to Heaven is if he looks to, loves, and finds God because we all come from God and the essence of all things is in God. So then, all answers, purpose, and identity are found only when we find God."

"Have you ever read the Bible?" I inquired with a smile on my face.

"Honestly, I never have," he replied.

"Well," I began, "I encourage you to get one and read it. When you get one you should read through the Gospels. That's the section of the Bible that talks all about Jesus, His life, and teachings."

"Okay," he answered, smiling back at me, "I will."

"Seriously?" I asked. I wanted to make sure he wasn't just saying that to make me happy.

"Yeah," he stated matter-of-factly, "I'll read it for sure."

"Awesome," I concluded, "So could I ask you one more question?"

"Go for it," he replied.

"Do you want to follow Jesus?" I joyfully asked with a big smile on my face.

"No thanks man," he responded, "I'm always going to be a Buddhist. I'm not gonna change that. But thanks for sharing all this with me. Honestly man, some people have told me about Jesus and God and everything, but no one has ever explained it to me with such passion, conviction, and intelligence as you have. So I respect that man. Thanks, really."

"Thanks Jim," I humbly replied, amazed by his gratitude, "It's my joy! Hey, before you go could I just say a quick prayer for you?"

"Yeah, sure," he agreed.

We prayed together, he thanked me again, and we parted ways. I was blown away that I had approached Jim with no clue or experience on how to effectively share the Gospel with a Buddhist, yet the Holy Spirit was faithful to guide me and give me wisdom through the entire conversation.

*

I was so pumped from my conversation with Jim that I exploded with excitement as I introduced myself to another Asian young man. He responded back with almost equal excitement and asked me where I was from and what I was doing. I explained my mission trip to him and he was so blown away.

I quickly assumed that he was a Christian because of his exuberance towards my mission trip, so I asked him if he was a Christian. Surprisingly, he said that he wasn't. So I began to encourage him to follow Jesus. He was very attentive, but then a friend approached him and reminded him that they had a Student Government meeting that was about to start. He apologized to me for having to cut short our great conversation. But as he walked off with his friend I quickly encouraged him to seek God and read the Bible and he nodded his head at me with excitement.

I had no idea what had taken place in those few minutes, but I knew that a great seed had been planted in that young man's heart. Even short encounters such as these were never in vain.

I became so excited by the positive responses I was receiving from Asians that I went to talk to another Asian student about Christ. The guy looked at me coldly and said, "I don't want to talk about this," immediately standing up and walking away. Ouch.

*

As I paced the area in prayer, I noticed another Asian student sitting by himself on a concrete slab as he ate a sandwich. There were crowds of people eating in large roundtables with groups of friends and he was one of the only students eating by himself. It was somewhat intimidating for me to speak to an entire table of students while they were eating lunch, so I naturally approached people who were sitting by themselves.

When I first approached Nick he was pretty cold towards me, but he quietly listened for a little while since he was still in the process of eating his sandwich. He quickly told me that he was an atheist and I quickly responded by encouraging him to seek God because He was real. I began to explain why I believed that God was real, yet I could tell that he was getting bored and somewhat annoyed by me. He began to excuse himself and was about to get up and leave when I asked him a question, "So why don't you believe in God?"

All of a sudden, Nick became fully engaged in the conversation. We ended up having a two-and-a-half hour long conversation about the existence of God. It was definitely one of the most enriching metaphysical conversations I had ever had in my life. To record our entire conversation would take up at least sixty pages in writing, so I could merely sum up the gist of what we discussed.

Nick was an extremely intelligent young man and I could tell that he was most likely majoring in some tough science because he constantly spoke about new scientific theories, a few of which I had never heard of. It was such an enjoyable discussion because Nick sincerely believed that having faith in God was the most ignorant, foolish idea a person could ever have and I honestly thought that not believing in God was the most idiotic, arrogant assumption a human could ever conjure up. And the greatest part of it all was that we were kindly, yet brutally honest in communicating such opinions to each other.

I would make his atheism look foolish and ridiculous, but then he would respond with some philosophical theory that would neutralize my argument, at least in his own eyes. Then he would attempt to make Christianity appear absurd and I would reply with a wise answer from Scripture that would stump him, yet he still refused to doubt his atheistic beliefs. I would tell him about miracles I have personally witnessed, lives that have been supernaturally changed through Jesus, and the fact of Christ's resurrection. In response, he would come up with some totally obnoxious new scientific theory that, at least in his mind, explained away all the glorious phenomenons that regularly occur through the power of the Holy Spirit. Although Nick seemed not to flinch one bit from his faith in atheism, he became insanely frustrated that all of his arguments were being nullified by a Christian, supposedly the dumbest breed of humans on earth. Not only that, but he was incapable of reasonably disproving anything that I presented to him. After nearly two hours of intense discussion, he finally let down his guard and made some honest remarks that left me astonished and filled with joy.

He began by sincerely stating, "I don't believe in God at all, but I am absolutely amazed by how religion spreads. It's absolutely genius! You help people in times of need. You pray for the sick and do miracles. You have spiritual answers to all of life's questions. You have profound stories that teach life lessons and characters that people can relate with.

You help the poor, the rejected, and the weak, and I know that you don't do it out of any evil intention. You truly do this out of good intent, but it ends up bringing converts into your religion. It's absolutely genius! I wish we had things like that in our world to attract people to do other things."

I laughed with joy as he vented his frustrations concerning Christianity. His simultaneous amazement and aggravation were so intense that he began turning bright red and breaking out in a sweat as he protested against it all.

"It's not fair," he cried out in frustration, "Like you for example. You've been on this trip for six months having several conversations a day, yet I can only fend for myself in this one conversation."

I started telling him about how God speaks to me and gave him a few specific examples. I explained to him that these occasions were too miraculous to be disregarded as mere coincidences.

"Of course it's coincidence," he shot back, "Do you know that you are the fourth person this week with a Bible who has come up to talk to me? But I didn't talk much with the other three. You're the only one I've really talked to. And it always seems to happen when I'm sitting by myself too. That's not a sign from God! It's just coincidence!"

Utterly amazed by what I was hearing I replied, "Really? I have never in my life heard of someone being preached to four separate times by four different people within the same week. It sounds like God is trying to speak to you dude."

"Yeah right man. It's all coincidence," he emphatically declared.

"Well let me ask you this," I inquired, "Has anyone with a Bible ever come up to talk to you at any other time in your life?"

He stopped to think for a second and with a surprised face he answered, "No. No one ever has."

"See!" I laughed loudly, "God is really trying to speak to you man!" I was so full of joy to see God's sovereign hand working in Nick's life and honored to know that He was using me as part of the sovereign plan that he had for Nick's salvation.

Nick tried to shrug it off, but I'm sure that realization messed with him.

Later on, he asked me a hypothetical question proposing the following, "What if science in the next century develops a way to literally heal every disease and disability just as fast as faith healers do? Would that convince you that miracles are scientific?"

I responded, "That wouldn't surprise me at all because the Bible says that in the last days false prophets will arise and do great miracles, signs, and wonders in order to deceive the masses. That might be the way in which they do it."

"See," Nick exclaimed, "that's genius! How does religion come up with this stuff?!"

"No," I said, "It's not genius. It's supernatural. That was prophesied two thousand years ago and God knew that it would all happen one day."

"This sucks man!" he complained, "See, I don't believe in religion, but someday when I get depressed I am going to remember what you said to me today! Ahh!"

I just continued to laugh with joy because I could see that his cold heart was being touched by God.

"I challenge you to read the Bible Nick," I began stating, "After all, how could you ever truly call yourself a scholar if you haven't studied the most widely read and most significant book of all time?"

"AHH! See, that's what I mean," he protested, "that's so not fair! The Bible is so entrenched in all of Western Civilization that one day I'm going to have to read it just so that I could have a deeper understanding of history, literature, and art!"

I wrote down the titles and authors of *Mere Christianity* and *More Than A Carpenter* on a sheet of paper and gave it to Nick. I encouraged him to read those books and he said that he might check them out.

I asked him if I could pray for him and he responded, "Sure. If it makes you feel better."

So I prayed for Nick and it did make me feel a lot better because I knew that God was not only touching Him through my words, but through my prayers as well.

"This really was a great conversation man," Nick said in an attitude of somber reflection, "Thanks. I really enjoyed it."

"Man, if I lived here I would really love to hang out with you," I told Nick.

"Yeah," he said quietly.

This was truly one of the richest conversations I had ever had with a human being. It lasted a few hours, but I wish it could have become a friendship that ended in salvation. However, I know that God is sovereign and He will be faithful in guiding Nick to Himself.

In the cities I traveled to I would sometimes say to myself, "Man, I wish I lived here." This feeling made me all the more excited to return to Miami to preach the Gospel there.

*

I took a half-hour break upon finishing my discussion with Nick. After having such a long, intense conversation like that one I had to take a breather.

I eventually spotted a very intellectual individual named Isaac who seemed to be idly standing around as he waited for someone. I approached him, introduced myself, and began by asking him, "So do you follow God? Do you follow Jesus?"

"Well, do you believe that everyone who follows God must follow Jesus?" he inquired, taken aback by my questions.

"Eventually," I stated.

"What do you mean, eventually?" he asked as his eyebrows furrowed up with an air of curiosity.

"Well, if someone is honestly seeking God they will eventually see that Jesus is the only way to God and they will follow Him," I said very frankly.

"That is where I can't agree," he decidedly replied.

"Are you Jewish?" I asked him. I made this inquiry because I have many Jewish friends in Miami who would commonly make such statements.

"Yes, I am," he answered with a bit of surprise that I had correctly guessed his background after only talking to him for less than five minutes, "but I do not hold onto Judaism as my religion."

"Do you seek God?" I kindly asked.

"Of course I seek God," he politely replied, "doesn't everybody?" He spoke with the air of a Shakespearean actor. I tried to suppress my laughter, but failed miserably in doing so.

"No," I burst out laughing, "Unfortunately, not everybody does."

And from there our exchange flowed.

During our conversation, I learned that Jacob fluently read, wrote, and spoke Hebrew and was very knowledgeable about the Scriptures. I was really impressed when he told me that he had read the entire Hebrew Bible and the Gospels because most of my Jewish friends had never read any scriptures beyond the Torah. They often only knew about other Hebrew characters through hearsay and not through their own personal study. Also, he was only the second Jewish person I had personally met who had actually read through the Gospels.

I discussed the Messianic prophecies with him and I was amazed that he actually knew a few of the prophecies, though not most of them. I explained some of them to him as he respectfully listened. He tried to refute my interpretation concerning some of the prophecies, but I would logically prove his re-interpretations to be wrong and he would eventually concede that I might be right.

I soon shared the Gospel with Isaac, but he couldn't accept the fact that another man would pay for the actions that he was justly responsible for. He insisted that we should take responsibility for our own actions.

"I agree with you wholeheartedly," I answered to his declaration, "We all should take responsibility for our own actions, but if we did then we would all be guilty of sin and we would all be justly condemned. But God is merciful and He doesn't want to condemn us. That is why He was moved with such a powerful love for us that He chose to send His Son to take our place of judgment and pay the penalty for the sins that we justly deserve to suffer for."

Isaac had no response to my answer. He was speechless.

I challenged him to read the Gospels again.

"I read them several years ago," he honestly stated. He stared down at the ground in silence for a brief moment as if in deep thought. Then he finished his statement, "But I guess it's time for me to read them again. I will read them again."

I was overjoyed by his response because no seed is greater than the direct Word of God itself. I wrote down the titles for *More Than a Carpenter* and *The Case for Christ* and he promised to read them both.

Isaac seemed to be a truly honest man who genuinely wanted to find the truth and nothing but the truth. I was convinced that he would find it because God is a rewarder of those who diligently seek Him.

THE LAST DAY OF MY TRIP

I spent the last day of my mission trip in deep prayer and reflection concerning all that God had done in and through me in the last six months; what He had revealed to me about His Kingdom, His ways, and His Word; and everything He had shown me about the state of the Church and of America. Furthermore, throughout the entire day, I was filled with joyful anticipation to be reunited with Brooke, my family, my disciples, and my friends. I was especially excited to see Brooke because I was planning to propose to her as soon as I was able to acquire a ring upon my return.

After six months of plowing in other cities other than my own, I was overwhelmed with excitement to plow in my hometown. Miami was precious to me and I knew that as soon as I returned to Miami I would continue preaching the Gospel every day and see an incredible harvest of souls. During the last two months of my mission trip, the Lord had begun to clearly tell me that I was going to plant a church upon my arrival in Miami. This made no sense to me since I was a committed member of my church in Miami, my parents were assistant pastors at the church, and I was only twenty-years-old. Also, the Lord had told me that I needed to eventually move to Southern California because it was where the movement of itinerant preachers was going to be birthed. I had no idea how long it would take for me to one day move to California, but I knew that it was the Lord's clear direction.

Thus, I surrendered all of these words before the Lord as I meditated upon the last six months and as I prayed with vision and faith concerning the future.

*

After much prayer and discussion, Alex decided that he wanted to complete a full six month journey himself. The Lord had directed me to sow the first month of my trip in my hometown, Miami, and the two-and-a-half weeks that I had spent in Orlando I had spent on my own. Thus, Alex had only been on the road with me for nearly four-and-a-half months and he felt that he needed to complete a full six months just as I had. Although I felt total peace to bless Alex in his desire to complete his mission trip, we both agreed that he could not complete it alone. Therefore, he decided to join Howard, Sunshine, and their family as they traveled back from Stockton, California to Kansas City, Missouri. Alex had formed a special bond with their family as we had traveled together during God's Summer of Love Tour and had spent a few days with them in Stockton on our way up to San Francisco. We both felt total peace in Alex joining them for the final stage of his journey across America.

Thus, as I prepared to fly back to Miami on September 29, 2007, Alex was preparing to join Howard and Sunshine to preach the Gospel for

another two months across America. He eventually ended his trip in Kansas City and returned home to Miami in early December.
I bid farewell to Adam Hood and all the new friends I had made in San Francisco, I prayed together with Alex, and then I boarded the plane to Miami.

God had been faithful throughout the entire journey to provide me with an incredible partner, amazing host families to stay with, delicious food to enjoy, all the transportation we needed, and abundant finances to cover all of our expenses. He had used us to reach countless souls with the Gospel and to awaken countless believers to His heart for the lost. But above all, He had drawn us closer to Himself and had transformed us to become more like Jesus.

CHAPTER EIGHT

THE STATE OF THE CHURCH

I asked a few main Christian leaders in San Francisco if there were any churches, regardless of size, that were bringing about transformation in sections of the city and saving souls. All of these people who I asked were born and raised in the Bay Area and most of them had been working in full-time ministry there for several decades. If anyone knew the state of the church in San Francisco, they knew. Every one of them told me that there weren't any churches in the city that they were aware of that were seeing a significant amount of unbelievers come to Christ. In fact, not many churches even evangelized. One man who had been preaching the Gospel on the streets of San Francisco and Berkeley for more than thirty years told me that the only churches that he knew who were actively preaching the Gospel were the Latino churches in the Mission District, but they mostly ministered to other Latinos and not to the rest of the population. Another leader mentioned that the only church that she saw that was somewhat thriving was a Chinese church led by a Chinese woman. Why do so few churches vibrantly preach the

Gospel not only in San Francisco, but throughout the nation? This is a modern day tragedy the church has allowed to take place by becoming occupied with countless church programs and neglecting the preaching of the Gospel.

As we preached the Gospel six days a week for these six months, we only met someone else preaching the Gospel a handful of times. The only places where it seemed like there were some churches actively preaching on the streets were in Atlanta and Southern California and even in those places there was still a desperate need for more laborers.

Many times I looked around at the crowds we were preaching to and thought to myself, "95% of these people have gone to church sometime or another in their lives, yet the vast majority of them are still not saved. How could it be that so many people could go to church for one, three, five, or twenty years and still not be saved? Is it really their fault?"

In the end, it is each individual's responsibility to repent and give their lives to Jesus. However, I believe that the church is to blame for America's fallen state. For years, Americans have gone to church to find God, but they haven't found Him there. Instead, they have found that churches have become non-profit organizations that perform various activities for the community, play inspirational live music, and have a motivational speaker who provides a refreshing word for the week. Even worse, they have encountered hypocrisy, judgment, gossip, competition, authoritarian abuse, and false doctrines, which are often done in the name of God. Non-Christians could find all of these benefits at a local YMCA, university, or Boy Scout group, so why would they commit so much time to a church if it were not feeding their spirit?

What I found as I spoke to Christians across the country was that many Christians in America think that the Gospel is the most basic, elementary message of the Bible and if someone had heard it once and repeated the sinner's prayer then they never needed to hear it again. It would be more spiritually edifying to speak about more mature subjects such as social justice, the gifts of the Spirit, prosperity, the attributes of God, family values and other 'relevant' messages.

For six months, I asked thousands of people this exact question as I looked them straight in the eyes: "Jesus came and died on the cross. But what does that mean? What the heck does some guy you never met dying on a random cross two thousand years ago have to do with you today? What does Jesus dying on the cross personally mean to you?" About 80% of the people I spoke to would look me dead in the eyes and honestly tell me, "I don't know." Another 15% would respond by saying, "He died for us" or "He died for my sins." I would then follow up on their statement by asking, "Okay, but what does that mean? Everyone knows the cliché phrases 'Jesus loves you' or 'Jesus died for you', but what does that mean? What if Martin Luther King Jr. died for you or Gandhi? Would that mean anything? What makes Jesus death on the cross so special?" Those 15% percent would then say, "I don't know." Only about 5% actually knew the answer to the question I was asking them and not all of the people who knew the answer were Christians, some were agnostics or atheists. This is not a statistic; it is a living experience that Alex and I encountered for six months from the east coast to the west coast as we spoke to several thousand people face-to-face.

This is purely the church's fault. The church has wrongfully assumed that everyone learned the Gospel in Sunday school and it is now a boring and unnecessary message to preach on a Sunday morning service. In evangelistic outreaches it is most likely to be heard, but once someone becomes a church member it would be a miracle if they heard the full Gospel preached on a Sunday morning service even twice a year. I am aware and encouraged that in recent years more and more Gospel centered churches and movements have been growing both in Charismatic and Reformed circles. Nevertheless, the majority of churches and ministries in America have yet to make the Gospel the central message of their community.

The horrific result of the Gospel being sidelined as elementary and boring in Christian communities is that many churchgoers have no clue what the Gospel actually is. For millions of churchgoers, the Gospel is no more than a bunch of cliché phrases that their Sunday school teacher taught them to memorize or that some great preacher told them to repeat after being pushed to the altar by their friends and relatives.

The Gospel message is not the most basic, easy-to-understand message in the Bible. It is the deepest, most powerful, life-changing message the Bible contains and it is the principal message that Jesus commanded us to preach. During my trip, I discovered that every time I preached the Gospel to someone it would be revealed to me in a more profound, personal, and real way. I sometimes get tired of hearing messages on the end times, loving your neighbor, the gifts of the Spirit, and several other popular topics we hear being taught in church, but the one message I never have nor ever will get tired of hearing is the Gospel message because it is the power of God unto salvation for those who are being saved. It is the news that needs to be proclaimed to every person on this earth.

However, what grieved my spirit the most on this trip was meeting Christians who were against the very act of preaching the Gospel on the streets, whether it was one-on-one or open air evangelism. Some Christians told us that America had already heard the Gospel message too many times to count and that the only way that they would come to Christ was if they had a revelation of God's love. They would tell us, "Don't preach to people. Just love on them. Show them God's love and they'll come to Jesus." My response to that statement is that the greatest act of love that I can possibly demonstrate as a Christian is to preach the Gospel to someone because I believe it is far more important to satisfy someone's eternal and spiritual needs than to feed their temporal and physical needs. If I give someone water to drink and food to eat they will be hungry the next day, but if I give them living water and the Bread of life they will never thirst nor hunger again.

I am not against ministering to the felt needs of our communities. In fact, I burn with love for the poor and long to minister to them holistically as the Word of God commands us to do. However, when ministering to people's felt needs quenches the verbal declaration of the Gospel then we are sinning against God by being ashamed of Christ's death and resurrection and arrogantly thinking that showing God's love through our actions is more powerful than spreading the news of the greatest act of love that has ever been demonstrated, God's death on a cross for fallen humanity. Sadly, one of this generation's most quoted "scriptures" is St. Francis of Assisi's alleged statement, "Preach the Gospel always, and if necessary, use words." I fully believe in demonstrating the Gospel through our actions and lifestyle as St. Francis and many others have done, but our righteous actions were never meant to cancel out the verbal preaching of the Gospel. They were meant to complement each other, not fight against each other until one of them dies. There should be no false dichotomy between loving actions and verbal proclamation, but rather both of these must be working together in unity to establish the Kingdom of God on earth and bring salvation to every lost person.

Furthermore, many Christians have told me, "I admire you for preaching the Gospel, but that's not my calling." Many people believe that they are incapable of preaching the Gospel because they are shy, not very articulate, don't know the Scriptures well, and many other reasons. However, let me ask you a really serious question. When you die and stand before the judgment seat of Christ and He asks you, "Why did you not preach the Gospel to the lost?" What will you say to Him? "I was too shy?" or "I didn't know how?" And after responding to His question He shows you the faces of all the people that could have been saved if you had preached to them, but they are now in Hell because you chose not to preach. Then what will you say? There is no excuse. Preaching the Gospel is not a calling, a gift, nor a nice suggestion. It is the GREAT COMMAND that Jesus gave us and if we love Him then we have no option but to preach the Gospel. In fact, Paul passionately declares in 1 Corinthians 9:16, "For if I preach the Gospel I have nothing to boast about for necessity is laid upon me. But woe is me if I do not preach the Gospel!" If we were to apply this scripture to our lives and to the church in more down to earth terms it would basically be saying this, "I must preach the Gospel. You must preach the Gospel. Every single Christian must preach the Gospel. It is absolutely necessary. Woe is any believer who does not preach the Gospel!"

Let me tell you how I began preaching the Gospel. I was thirteen-years-old and I had been on fire for Jesus for more than a year. God had completely changed my life and I was in love with Him. I would often spend three or four hours a day in His presence, but I never once preached the Gospel to one human soul, partly because I was in homeschooling at the time, but more so because I had never felt a need or burden to preach the Gospel. Then one day, after spending over two hours in God's presence, I came out of my prayer room and overheard my brother talking with my dad about Hell.

He was saying, "I don't understand dad, is this place really real? Where in the Bible does it clearly say that Hell is real and who goes to Hell?"

My dad showed him several Scriptures about Hell and answered many questions that he was confused about.

My brother continued saying, "But dad, if this place is real then what the heck are we doing? What are all the churches doing? Why aren't we going out constantly and telling people about God so that they don't go to this horrible place? How could we just sit in church and let the world go to Hell?"

These statements pierced my heart and convicted me deeply. What was I doing to save souls? Nothing. Absolutely nothing. The next day I began praying, but after a while I heard the Lord say to me, "Joshua, how can you be so selfish? Here you are enjoying my presence and receiving from Me. I've given you a great church, a great family, and countless blessings. I've given you all of this Joshua, and yet you haven't shared it with one person. You are so selfish."

Suddenly, I felt the weight of the world fall on my shoulders and for six hours I was glued to the floor of my room weeping and groaning that the world was going to Hell and I was doing nothing about it. All day I

cried out, "God have mercy on me! God use me! I have no idea what to do.
I'm only thirteen years old God. But please use me! Use me to save souls!"
God marked me that day. I could never forget that encounter with Him.
Until today, if I feel my heart becoming cold towards the lost I simply
enter into prayer and reconnect to that time when God encountered me
with His heart for the lost and my compassion is immediately reignited.

     I don't believe that God wants us to walk around with the weight
of the world on our shoulders. That is His burden to carry. His yoke for us
is easy and his burden is light. However, I do believe that their are times
when God allows us to feel what He feels for a brief moment. That is what
happened to me that day. God allowed me feel the unquenchable love
that He has for every lost soul. He gave me His heart for the lost.

     When my dad came home from work that day my mom said to
him, "Paul, your son has been whining all day long that the world is going
to Hell and he is not doing anything about it. Go and take him out to
preach the Gospel!"

     My dad complied and took me out to downtown Oxnard, CA
where we found a strip of Mexican bars. We witnessed that night until
about one in the morning and from that moment on I became an
evangelist. For several months, we went out every Friday night to preach
the Gospel at the bars. Moreover, throughout all my high school years I
preached the Gospel to at least one person nearly every single day. Little
did I know that God was preparing me to one day preach the Gospel on
the streets of America for six months and raise up other itinerant
preachers to do the same.

     After this encounter and after years of sharing the Gospel with
others I came to realize that being a messenger and ambassador of the
glorious news of Christ is not a calling or gifting, it is a part of our identity
as believers. We have the joy of re-presenting Jesus to everyone we meet.

     When people see me share the Gospel they often comment that
I am such a gifted and anointed evangelist, but I am only this way as a
result of years of obediently and compassionately preaching the Gospel
in my school, neighborhood, work and on the streets. I had to start

somewhere. We all have to start somewhere. I am not an exception because I had an encounter with God's heart for the lost when I was thirteen. If anything, having such an incredible encounter at the age of thirteen should be a sign and encouragement to believers that we could all encounter God's heart for the lost regardless of how young or old we are. God wants all of us to have His heart for every person we meet. He loves every person unconditionally. He wants us to be just like Him. He wants us to love every person unconditionally.

Furthermore, there have been countless times where I have been stumped by someone else's argument, not known what to say, or not known enough Scripture, but I never let any of those embarrassing mistakes stop me from sharing with more people. I am compelled to preach the Gospel no matter how hard it may seem. I am convinced that if I am willing to study Mathematics for countless hours throughout my life just so that I could get good grades in school how much more should I dedicate innumerous hours of my life to studying the Word of God, so that I could preach His Gospel effectively.

Throughout this trip, there were several times where both Alex and I were extremely exhausted. Many times, I wished I could just sit down, read a nice book, have some hot chocolate and rest for a week, but we couldn't do that because we were on a mission trip from God. Sometimes we even felt like quitting and going back home, but we persevered and continued until the end. Whenever a discipline becomes a part of our daily lives, whether it be work, school, football practice, exercise, cooking, or even devotions, there will be moments and seasons when weariness may overtake us, even if it is our greatest passion in life. However, if we desire to succeed we must persevere. The same principle applies to evangelism.

I had a sobering conversation with a great man of God named Larry Rosenbaum. Larry was raised Jewish and was a hippie as a youth in the Haight Ashbury district of San Francisco. He got saved during the Jesus Movement in the 1970's and in 1980 he founded his evangelistic ministry. Every single week for nearly thirty years now Larry, with a city permit, sets up a sound system in several different busy locations of the city for hours at a time and preaches the Gospel. He always has a worship team with him who sings worship songs and after about thirty or forty minutes of music he grabs the microphone to preach the Gospel to the hearers on the street. The day we were with him he was at the United Nations Plaza on Market St. in downtown San Francisco from noon to 5 p.m. While the worship team sang he, along with a few others, would pass out tracts and witness to people individually. I admire and respect Larry so deeply because he has faithfully done this every week for nearly thirty years. However, Larry Rosenbaum is one of the most ostracized Christians in San Francisco. What's shocking is that it's not really the world that criticizes him, although they definitely do, but it is the Church who disapproves of him because he publicly preaches the Gospel instead of preaching the Gospel merely through his lifestyle.

He explained to me how several ministries come to San Francisco and say that they are going to do great things there, but after a short time give up and leave. Then he voiced a deep concern of his to me. He told me how he was worried about the next generation of Christians. "I'm tired," he told me, "I'm in my late 50's. I'm old. I'm ready to retire and pass on the baton to the next generation, but I don't see any young people willing to take the baton. There are lots of young people in love with Jesus, but I don't see any of them preaching the Gospel. I don't see what these ministries are trying to accomplish if they don't want to preach the Gospel."

Where is the next generation of preachers? Where are the John the Baptist's preparing the way for the second coming of the Lord? When will the church stop riding on the newest church trend and just live out the Gospel? When will we get sick and tired of being bench warmers in church letting the world go to Hell while we complacently sit there and listen to the preacher? When will we get into the game and win? When will we fight in the war against Satan's kingdom? God is looking for men, women, and youth of all ages to live radically for God, but who will hear His call and actually do it?!

The real reason why the church in America is not preaching the Gospel is not because there is a greater way to communicate the Gospel. Frankly, we are not preaching the Gospel because we are cowards. We tried to preach the Gospel to a few people, but after being rejected or cussed out a few times we got scared and intimidated and concluded that there must be a better way. We have the mentality that if someone is offended and angry by what we are preaching it must be because we are saying it wrong, but Jesus had the mentality that if people were getting enraged and hostile it was because He was preaching the Gospel accurately. In fact, He went so far as to say that we are blessed if we are persecuted, insulted, and ridiculed for preaching the Gospel.

Many Christians in America think that persecution against Christianity has not yet arrived at our shores. However, Alex and I were often yelled at, insulted, cussed out, nearly arrested, kicked out of places, and even threatened to be killed throughout our mission trip. I believe that the main reason why Christians are not being persecuted in America is because we are too intimidated to preach the Gospel face-to-face to a lost and dying world. If the church as a whole was so genuinely moved with compassion and filled with boldness that we actually preached the Gospel at all times, including at our work, school, neighborhood, and the streets, then we would definitely experience both intense persecution and genuine revival.

We are in a state of emergency, not in a state of victory. Our nation is more lost than ever in its history and we're spending most of our time trying to get spiritually obese while the world starves for the Gospel. WAKE UP CHURCH!!! WAKE UP!!!

We think that our nation is lost because of divorce, abortion, drugs, homosexuality, suicide, and violence, but the truth is that our nation is lost because the church has stopped shining the light of the Gospel. The Gospel is the cure for the sinful nature of man. If the sinful nature of man is destroyed then sin ceases to prevail. If we spend our main efforts in cutting off branches of immorality instead of cutting the problem from its root, which is the sinful nature of man, then we are wasting our time because the branches will continue to grow if the root is still in place. It is no use to tell a sinner to stop sinning if his nature is to sin. We must partner with the Holy Spirit to see prodigal sons be born again as righteous sons of God and then sin will decrease immensely in America and in the world and righteousness will reign.

We are the light of the world. If our nation is dark then it is because the light of the Church is not shining. We have either put our light under a bowl or it has been extinguished, but if we want to see our nation saved then we must begin shining the light of the Gospel once again.

The church must return to the basics. We must return to the Gospel. If we do not return to preaching the Gospel then our candle will be removed, we will no longer shine in the midst of darkness, and we will become marginalized and irrelevant in our world. It has already happened in much of Europe. If the church of America does not change it will only be a matter of time before the same atrocity takes place here.

Time is ticking. What will you do about it? Will you wait another year, another five years, another twenty years? Or will you act now?

EPILOGUE

During the last two months of my mission trip, God began telling me three things that would radically shift the course of my life. First, He told me that I would marry Brooke in seven months instead of two years as we had planned. Second, He said that I had to move to Southern California because this was where the movement of itinerant preachers was going to be birthed. Third, He told me that when I returned to Miami I would plant a church.

All three of these words from the Lord made no sense to my natural mind. I was only twenty and my wife was only nineteen and although we were incredibly mature for our age we still wanted to finish college before we got married. Furthermore, California was the last place on earth that I ever wanted to live. I had been born and raised there and had no desire to ever live there again. I preferred to live in New York, Europe, or overseas on the mission field. Lastly, my parents were assistant pastors and I was a youth leader at our current church in Miami and we had no intentions of leaving. Nevertheless, I knew God had spoken and I knew He would have His way.

Three days after returning to Miami, our family was kicked out of our church because we wouldn't comply with the churches cultish rule of "cutting off" people who had left the church. Thus, I planted a house church called Church of Acts that grew to about 50 people in regular attendance. Seven months later, Brooke and I were joyously married and in the summer of 2008 we moved to Southern California.

In September 2009, we established BUILDERS (formerly Global Gospel Movement).

Since 2009 we have developed three main areas of focus:

1.   EQUIPPING THE CHURCH: We have held weekend evangelism training seminars in several churches, ministries, and Christian clubs on campuses. Some of these trainings have birthed weekly outreaches.

2.   TRAINING AND SENDING OUT BUILDERS (i.e. spirit-filled evangelists: Every summer we hold a six week evangelism boot camp where we train our students in all styles of evangelism, how to operate in the gifts of the Holy Spirit, how to share the Gospel with people of all different religions, and how to follow up, make disciples, and start small groups. Then we commission them to preach the Gospel across America for six months living by faith just like Alex and I did. As I write this, we have currently sent out 27 BUILDERS on six-month faith journeys.

3.   CITYWIDE PRAYER AND EVANGELISM: The Firebase Movement is a network of prayer and evangelism ministries that unites together hundreds of people from dozens of churches and ministries in one city to carry out 24/7 prayer, worship, and evangelism for 7 days with the vision of making this a permanent expression of the church in that city. In 2014, we helped birth the Firebase Movement by leading the first 7 day LOVE 24/7 outreach, LOVE LA

24/7. Since then there have been seven day LOVE
24/7 outreaches in New York, Detroit, San Francisco,
Dallas, and twice in the Twin Cities. We have
continued to help mobilize and lead most of these
24/7 outreaches and the Firebase Movement is
spreading like wildfire across America.

Ways that BUILDERS can serve you:

1. **TRAINING:**
    a. Church/Para-Church Training: We would love to visit
        your church or ministry for a weekend to train your
        group in how to effectively preach the Gospel, follow
        up, and make disciples with the goal of launching a
        weekly outreach out of your church or ministry.
    b. Weekend Warrior Trips: Shadow and be mentored by
        one of our BUILDERS for one day, one weekend, or one
        week. One day would be for a full day of evangelism.
        However, the weekend or week would be for full days of
        evangelism along with a short faith journey where you
        take nothing with you and trust God for provision.
    c. Firebase Movement: Jump into one of our upcoming
        24/7 prayer, worship, and evangelism experiences and
        you will never be the same. Be ignited for God in a life
        of intimacy and mission.
    d. BUILDERS Boot Camp & 6 Month Faith Journey:
        Attend one of our 6-week evangelism boot camps and
        be sent out in a team on a six month faith journey
        preaching the Gospel wherever the Lord leads you.
    e. School of Church Planters: In the near future we hope
        to offer a school of church planters to the graduates of
        our boot camp and six-month faith journey. Our goal is
        to send out church planting teams into cities all across

America and the world.

2. **RESOURCES:**
   A. This Book and future books we will publish
   B. Spiritual Journeys Podcast: A podcast of salvation testimonies. This is a great place to point pre-believers to for them to hear the Gospel.
   C. Our Website and Blog: We have blog posts and videos to encourage and equip you in evangelism
   D. Tracts: You could download and print out our Spiritual Journeys Podcast tracts to share the podcast with pre-believers.
   E. Youtube: Be encouraged and equipped by our teaching and testimonies on our channel. Search "Builders Evangelism" on Youtube and you'll find us.

Ways that you could serve BUILDERS:

1. GO CRAZY FOR JESUS: The most powerful way you could get involved with Builders is to be fully activated into a radical lifestyle of intimacy and mission wherever you are. Preach the Gospel, make disciples, and activate other believers everywhere you go.
2. MOBILIZE: Share this book and our vision with others and encourage people to get involved in local outreaches in their area, to jump into a Firebase outreach, to attend a BUILDERS Boot Camp, or to go out on a faith journey.
3. PRAY: Without prayer our work is powerless and full of spiritual warfare. Please pray for our team and especially for our teams who are currently preaching the Gospel across America by faith.
4. HOST: Open up your home to be a host home for our BUILDERS as they preach the Gospel by faith across the country. You could register as a host home on our website.

5. GIVE: If you believe that BUILDERS is fruitful soil we encourage you to joyfully invest your finances, time, and resources into this movement. You could also give directly to our BUILDERS who are currently on their faith journeys. Please visit our website to give.

To get involved, find out more, or donate to our ministry please visit our website at:

WEARE.BUILDERS

LIKE us on Facebook

Follow us on Instagram

Also, please feel free to contact us directly:

626-437-6296

info@weare.builders

Made in the USA
Coppell, TX
30 March 2022

75755148R00144